Number 12

The Mantle of Jesus Today

By

Mark F. Hobson, Ph.D.

Title: Number 12

Author: Mark F. Hobson, Ph.D.

Printed in the USA

DISCLAIMER

This novel's story and characters are fictitious. Certain long-standing institutions, agencies, and public offices are mentioned, but the characters involved are wholly imaginary. Some real historical or public figures appear in fictional contexts.

DEDICATION

To my son, Luke Anthony Hobson, and daughter-in-law, Karissa Woodward-Hobson, whose kindness, intelligence, humor, and relationship are the inspiration for this book.

ACKNOWLEDGMENT

My faith in God was forever changed for the better by a dear friend and mentor, Raymond A. Cote. At a time when my faith was still growing, Ray opened his heart and home to me. For more than 20 years, Ray, I, and other close friends had breakfast together every Friday morning, followed by prayer and Scripture reading in Ray's home. Mostly, Ray taught me how to trust in God's word, to believe in myself, and to pray with expectation. Unfortunately, Ray passed away in the year 2000. As I wrote this book, I often thought Ray would be proud of me for using my talents and ideas and for taking a chance that God would bless this work.

ABOUT THE AUTHOR

Mark F. Hobson holds advanced degrees in business, education, and theology, and a doctorate in business administration. He holds Certificates of Advanced Graduate Studies (CAGS) in Mind, Brain, and Teaching at Johns Hopkins University in Baltimore, MD, and in Higher Education Administration from Northeastern University in Boston, MA. He is a retired senior associate dean from Southern New Hampshire University, a faculty member of Great Bay Community College in Portsmouth, NH, and an ordained minister. His research interests are Scripture, history, and neuroeducation, particularly not only what adults learn but also how they learn.

Dr. Hobson is the author of *The Mantle: The Secret History of the Mantle of Jesus Christ,* and *Homilies of a Deacon, Year A.*

TABLE OF CONTENTS

INTRODUCTION 10
CHAPTER 1: A STRAIGHT PATH 13
CHAPTER 2: TRANSITIONING 21
CHAPTER 3: JOHN MEETS JESUS 26
CHAPTER 4: MISSION ONE–SAN MIGUEL 34
CHAPTER 5: LAS CRUCES 39
CHAPTER 6: HEARING AND LISTENING 45
CHAPTER 7: THE SEVEN CHURCHES 51
CHAPTER 8: PRESIDENT KOVAL 56
CHAPTER 9: RUSSIA AND UKRAINE 62
CHAPTER 10: SUKHOI 35 MOVEMENT 68
CHAPTER 11: THE SAINT LUKE MOTEL 74
CHAPTER 12: THE RUSSIAN PRESIDENT 86
CHAPTER 13: MOTEL ROOM ONE 96
CHAPTER 14: HAIL TO THE PEACE 99
CHAPTER 15: GOD AT THE CENTER 108
CHAPTER 16: THE BEAST 121
CHAPTER 17: PRESIDENT PETROVICH RETURNS 126
CHAPTER 18: WORK IN SUDAN 132
CHAPTER 19: JUSTICE IN SUDAN 143
CHAPTER 20: PRIME MINISTER ABDUL BAATIN 149
CHAPTER 21: THE HOLE WITHOUT A BOTTOM 161
CHAPTER 22: WATER OF LIFE 166
CHAPTER 23: BABYLON HAS FALLEN 174
CHAPTER 24: FUNDING FOR IRAQ 187
CHAPTER 25: REBUILDING IRAQ 195
CHAPTER 26: THE SEVENTH TRUMPET 198
CHAPTER 27: THE ARK IN HEAVEN 203
CHAPTER 28: THE ARK ON EARTH 212

CHAPTER 29: WORD OF GOD, SPEAK! 222
CHAPTER 30: TWINS 225
CHAPTER 31: JESUS AND THE RABBI 229
CHAPTER 32: THE MANTLE IN ISRAEL 237
CHAPTER 33: PRIME MINISTER ARIEL RABIN 247
CHAPTER 34: EDEN RESTORED 252
CHAPTER 35: SEVEN DAYS OF HEALING 259
CHAPTER 36: DAY ONE 262
CHAPTER 37: DAY TWO 266
CHAPTER 38: DAY THREE 268
CHAPTER 39: DAY FOUR 271
CHAPTER 40: DAY FIVE 274
CHAPTER 41: DAY SIX 281
CHAPTER 42: DAY SEVEN 287
CHAPTER 43: JOHN WARD AT THE WHITE HOUSE 294
CHAPTER 44: GOD'S PLAN UNFOLDS 301
CHAPTER 45: THE PRESS CONFERENCE 306
CHAPTER 46: THE BRIDE OF THE LAMB 311
CHAPTER 47: THE MOST IMPORTANT WORK 322
CHAPTER 48: JESUS AND JOHN LUKE MEET 326
CHAPTER 49: THE MIND OF CHRIST 332
CHAPTER 50: PEOPLE PROTECT WHAT THEY LOVE 338
CHAPTER 51: THE HEALING OF THE NATIONS 342
CHAPTER 52: THE JORDAN RIVER 351
CHAPTER 53: THE RABBI'S DREAM 357
CHAPTER 54: JOHN WARD IN JERUSALEM 363
CHAPTER 55: THE LITTLE CHURCH 367
CHAPTER 56: FINAL STAGES 374
CHAPTER 57: A NEW PENTECOST 378
EPILOGUE: WORD OF GOD 388
AUTHOR'S REFLECTION 390
COMING SOON: *THE TWINS* 392

Number 12

The Mantle of Jesus Today

Introduction

"Trust in the Lord with all your heart and lean not on your own understanding; in all your ways submit to him, and he will make your paths straight" (Proverbs 3:5-6).

Number 12 continues the story begun in *The Mantle*, which recounts the sacred cloth that covered Jesus's head during His death and resurrection and traces the lives of those who have borne it throughout history.

For two thousand years, the Mantle of Jesus Christ has passed through eleven hands.

I was the eleventh.

My son would become the twelfth—and the last.

The story begins in the Gospel of John. Only in his account do we read:

"*He saw the strips of linen lying there, as well as the cloth that had been wrapped around Jesus' head. The cloth was still lying in its place, separate from the linen"* (John 20:5–7).

According to this tradition, John, the beloved disciple, quietly took the cloth from the tomb as a keepsake of the Master. In time, he came to understand that the Mantle held extraordinary power—the very imprint of Christ's presence and the mystery of the Resurrection itself.

When John first wore the Mantle, he heard the voice of Jesus, instructing him to use its power only in God's name and for His glory. At times, Jesus appeared to him—and later to others who would bear the Mantle across the centuries.

After John's death, the Mantle was passed in secret from one faithful servant to another. A tradition emerged: twelve bearers in all—six before the Crusades and six after—each called in a particular moment of need.

The powers of the Mantle are remarkable: invisibility, flight, healing, strength, protection from harm, and even the ability to appear in more than one place at once. Yet these gifts were never given for personal gain. Each bearer was called to serve quietly, helping to shape the course of history for the good.

Throughout the centuries—from the early Church to the Crusades, through the Middle Ages and into the modern world, the Mantle remained hidden, safeguarded by those entrusted with its care, including the Freemasons in England before its journey to America.

Number 12 tells the story of the final bearer.

I am Dr. John Mark Hopkins, the historian of the Mantle, its eleventh bearer, and the author of this account. The Mantle was entrusted to me by my grandfather, Harrison, a Freemason and guardian of the relic. Through it, Jesus called me to serve those who have a substance use disorder and to record the history of the Mantle for the first time.

Now the Mantle has passed to my son.

Dr. John Luke Hopkins lives in a time that echoes the words of Jesus:

"At that time, they will see the Son of Man coming in a cloud with power and great glory... your redemption is drawing near" (Luke 21:27–28).

He has been called to confront the divisions of our age—those rooted in religion, politics, and the care of the Earth—and to seek reconciliation in a world that longs for healing.

The first book closed with my decision to lay down the Mantle and entrust it to him. Before I did, I asked Jesus one final question:

"Is the tradition of the twelve bearers true? And does the time of the final bearer coincide with Your return?"

Jesus smiled and replied:

"Recall the Scripture where I say, 'But about that day or hour no one knows… but only the Father' (Matthew 24:36). I cannot tell you, John Mark, for I do not know. What I can tell you is this: I follow the Father's will at all times. Remain a faithful servant. Care for the people of God. My words will never pass away."

Chapter 1:

A Straight Path

"The crooked roads shall become straight, the rough ways smooth. And all people will see God's salvation" (Luke 3:5-6).

In this passage from Saint Luke's Gospel, John the Baptist quotes the prophet Isaiah as he prepares the way for Jesus. This verse matters for our story because God will once again make a straight path, this time for the Mantle to be passed to the next generation.

A psychology professor once told me that all change, even positive change, involves loss because our sense of reality shifts.

Giving up the Mantle and retiring from my role as a college dean brought both renewal and loss. In moments like these, we must trust in Jesus. He smooths the rough ways and straightens crooked paths, leading us toward our destination.

I believe God calls each of us to leave a positive mark on our generation, as if it were a destiny to fulfill. By writing the history of the Mantle, I hope to leave a legacy of faith for God's people.

On Sunday, after deciding to retire from both the Mantle and my role as a university dean, my wife, Joan, and I attended services at Saint George Church in our hometown. Later that evening, we had dinner with our son and daughter-in-law, John and Kristin.

Over coffee, I recounted my final conversation with Jesus. I explained my decision to retire from both the Mantle and the university and asked whether they would consider accepting the Mantle. I told John that Jesus agreed he would be a wise choice as the twelfth bearer.

John looked at Kristin and said, "I would love to carry on this work, yet we need to talk before making a final decision."

I provided them with the historical manuscript of the Mantle and suggested that they read it before deciding. They accepted the book.

"Thank you, Dad, for considering me to carry on your work," John said.

Kristin added, "We will do as you ask and get back to you soon. I know John loved hearing your adventures with Jesus."

I was relieved by their response. After clearing the table and saying our goodbyes, Joan turned to me and said, "That went well."

I smiled and nodded. While I would miss my conversations with Jesus and my work with the Mantle, I knew this was the right decision for me, my family, and the world. That night, I slept soundly.

The next morning, I woke early and drove to my office at Southerton University in Hillsborough, New Hampshire. Hillsborough is a lovely town in the northeastern part of the state, with the university as its largest employer. That morning, the familiar commute felt newly pleasurable. I noticed details I usually took for granted, the sunlight filtering through the trees lining the road and hawks circling above quiet ponds.

As I neared the campus parking lot, my thoughts turned to Kristin's resurrection following the graduation-day car accident two years earlier. On that day, Kristin and John were struck by an impaired driver in the parking lot. John suffered a serious leg injury, and Kristin died, at least for a brief time. Her resurrection, made possible through the Mantle, became the unexpected pinnacle of my ministry.

After twenty-five years at the university, I knew I would miss campus life. With graduation only weeks away, the timing felt right to retire. I had quietly submitted my retirement paperwork to Human Resources the previous week, without informing my team yet.

Once settled in my office, I asked our administrator, Donna, to speak with me. We worked together for twelve years. I offered to buy coffee, and we walked to the cafeteria. After asking about her weekend, I shared the news of my retirement. Donna looked surprised, then a little sad. After a moment, she smiled and said she was happy for me.

I told her I had a meeting scheduled later that day with the University President, Dr. Joseph White, and that afterward I planned to email the business school team. Donna asked if she could organize a retirement gathering.

“Of course,” I said, “as long as there’s chocolate cake and coffee.”

“Consider it done,” she replied with a smile.

Back in my office, I answered emails and prepared to walk across the quad to Dr. White’s office. I placed my retirement letter in a portfolio and stepped out into the sunshine toward a handsome three-story brick building adjacent to the campus center courtyard. The president’s corner office on the third floor overlooked the quad through large windows.

Dr. Joseph White is a brilliant leader in higher education. Known internationally for his student-centered vision, he made a bold and prescient decision years earlier to establish a low-cost, open-enrollment online college that offered accredited degrees to non-traditional students.

While my primary work focused on traditional undergraduates, I occasionally taught in the online program. I greatly admired those students, many of whom balanced families and full-time work while pursuing their degrees. The online college mirrored our on-campus programs in both rigor and quality.

As I entered the president’s office suite, I was once again impressed by the competence and warmth of his staff. Dr. White surrounds himself with people from diverse professional backgrounds in higher education, business, and government and often includes a student intern. His office operates with both efficiency and genuine care, reflecting his values as a leader.

Dr. White is a tall, distinguished African American man with gray hair and a neatly trimmed beard. Raised in the Bronx, he earned academic scholarships at respected institutions and became a widely admired intellectual. He is a wise and kind leader, though his allegiance to the New York Yankees, while living in Red Sox territory, may be his only flaw.

He greeted me warmly and welcomed me into his well-appointed office, its walls lined with diplomas and photographs marking a successful career. We sat at a conference table.

"John Mark, you look relaxed and happy this Monday morning," he said. "What can I do for you?"

I handed him the retirement letter. He read it carefully, then looked up.

"Are you sure?" he asked. "The School of Business is doing very well."

"Yes," I replied. "Everything is going well, and that's precisely why this feels like the right time. I want to step down after graduation next month."

Dr. White nodded. "I'll miss you. You're the kind of leader who develops others. Do you have someone in mind to succeed you?"

"While I know a national search may be conducted," I said, "Dr. Lydia Barnes would be an excellent internal candidate."

Dr. Barnes had long served as chair of the MBA program. She earned her MBA from Dartmouth and holds a PhD in computer science. Forward-thinking and highly respected, she had led several key initiatives, including the redesign of our MBA program. “She’s a natural choice,” I added, “though of course the decision isn’t mine.”

Dr. White considered this, then said, “Yes, she’s well qualified. I’m sure your opinion will carry weight. Please send me suggested members for a search committee, faculty, staff, and students, working with Human Resources.”

I agreed and later sent the names. As our meeting ended, Dr. White stood and shook my hand.

“I’ll miss you,” he said. “As a colleague and as a friend.”

He pulled me into a warm hug, and I left his office.

Walking back across the quad, I felt a wave of relief. I had been nervous about disappointing him, given my deep respect for his leadership.

At my desk, I drafted an email announcing my retirement to the business school staff. I read it three times to ensure the tone was positive and clear. Before sending it, I asked Donna to review it.

As she read, her eyes filled with tears.

“It’s perfect,” she said. “I already miss you.”

I smiled and clicked Send.

Next, I called Joan to tell her about the meeting and the email. As always, she was supportive and asked how I was feeling. I told her I was at peace.

“I love and appreciate you,” I said.

"I love you too," she replied. "I'm making your favorite Mexican chicken dish. Don't be late."

I returned to work and left promptly at 4:30.

On the drive home, I called my son John. We spoke about his day and his exciting projects as a research science manager in artificial intelligence (AI) at the Massachusetts Institute of Technology in Cambridge. Then, I told him about my meeting with Dr. White and the retirement announcement.

He was happy for me, though he recognized the difficulty of the decision.

"This is a big transition for you," he said. "Retiring from the university and giving up the Mantle."

"Yes," I replied, "but it's the right time for both."

John told me that he and Kristin had discussed the Mantle on their drive home after dinner with us. He assured me they would let us know their decision soon. I told him there was no rush, as the responsibility would profoundly change their lives.

They were reading the history of the Mantle and wanted to finish it first. I thanked him for his thoughtfulness. By the time we finished our conversation, I found myself turning onto our street.

John is our only child and, next to Joan, my closest friend. As a young man, he excelled academically and athletically, particularly in baseball and golf. After earning an undergraduate degree in graphic arts, he completed a master's degree in marketing and later a doctorate in education at Southerton, intending to follow me into academia.

His doctorate led to a leadership role at the renowned MIT. We are immensely proud of him.

As I ended the call, I whispered, “Thank you, Lord, that John is focused, pragmatic, and kind, like his mother.”

I pulled into the driveway, entered through the garage door, and found Joan waiting. I kissed her and wrapped her in a warm hug. She held me tightly.

“I love you, John Mark,” she said.

“I am grateful for your love,” I replied.

I was home.

Chapter 2: Transitioning

"The Lord will watch over your coming and going both now and forevermore" (Psalm 121:8).

Coming and going are integral to life, particularly in our professional journeys. We leave jobs for many reasons, and sometimes we transition from one career to another. Eventually, if we are fortunate, we find work that aligns with who we are and fulfills our career goals.

Although I spent many years in business administration, I always knew my calling was higher education, helping young people discover their professions. Looking back, I can see how God was present throughout my career transitions, from business to teaching to academic leadership. God has a plan for our lives, and we are asked to trust that plan.

The remainder of the workweek at the university passed quickly as my thoughts turned toward going. I developed a transition plan and schedule and shared it with Donna. I also scheduled meetings with the various teams in the School of Business to address any concerns before my departure.

I scheduled my first meeting with the business science team, faculty in finance, accounting, and economics. Individually, they are thoughtful and dedicated professionals.

As a group, however, they tend to think quantitatively and dichotomously, seeing issues in black-and-white terms. Administrative decisions are often labeled as good or bad, right or wrong. They respectfully, but persistently, question university leadership on matters such as faculty contracts, budget size, academic freedom, classroom technology, and enrollment limits. I knew this meeting could be time-consuming, so I made it a priority.

The meeting began cordially, with kind words and well-wishes. Soon, however, the conversation shifted to the search committee for my replacement—specifically, who from their team should serve and how many representatives they should have.

I reiterated that Dr. White would determine the final committee composition and suggested they nominate one representative and an alternate whom they trusted to speak on their behalf.

As that discussion concluded, several faculty members raised concerns about provisions in the recently ratified faculty contract. I listened carefully and reminded them that the contract had been approved by both faculty and university leadership. I suggested they compile a list of outstanding concerns and send it to me so I could share it with the incoming dean. I also encouraged them to continue dialogue through the Faculty Senate.

After ninety minutes, we reached an agreement on their representation and addressed their primary concerns.

When the meeting ended, retirement looked especially appealing. The remaining meetings with academic teams were pleasant and uneventful. Everyone was gracious about my retirement, and we spoke fondly of students, shared successes, and the meaningful work we had done together.

Following my meeting with the Master of Business Administration (MBA) team, I spoke privately with Lydia and asked whether she intended to apply for the dean position. I explained that while a national search would be conducted, I believed she was an excellent fit. I encouraged her to apply and shared that I had endorsed her candidacy to Dr. White. "I'm flattered by your endorsement," Lydia said. "Thank you for speaking with Dr. White about me."

By Friday afternoon, I noticed on the calendar that graduation was only two weeks away, with two more weeks until my final day. I felt both excitement and apprehension about my decision. I recognized these feelings as normal and allowed myself to experience them without judgment.

Before my time with the Mantle, and before my renewed relationship with Jesus, I would have perseverated endlessly. Now, I felt at peace.

I had discussed the decision to retire at length with Joan and John and had prayed often before submitting the paperwork. I was ready, emotionally, mostly, and financially.

Spending more time with family was my highest priority. I also longed for time to research and write. Writing *The Mantle* and reflecting on my many conversations with Jesus deepened my faith and trust in God's plan for my life. Jesus cares about our needs and desires a meaningful, personal relationship with us. I do not understand how He keeps track of all humanity, yet I trust that He listens and cares for each of us.

True to their word, John and Kristin called Saturday morning to say they had finished reading the history book and wanted to come by to discuss their decision. Joan and I eagerly agreed. They arrived shortly with a tray of our favorite coffee, and we gathered around the dining room table.

With a broad smile, John said, "We agree to be the twelfth bearers of the Mantle, with a few concerns."

"I want to use the Mantle and connect with Jesus," John continued. "Kristin is happy to support me in this work, but she's not ready to fly anytime soon, unless there's an airplane involved."

We laughed and nodded in agreement.

John then asked, "Dad, do you think Jesus would agree to let you continue writing the history book? My schedule is packed. I have time for the Mantle's work, but not for writing. It might be easier for me to share my experiences with you so you can continue in the same style. That way, you stay involved—and perhaps Jesus would meet with both of us from time to time." "I think your ideas make sense," I said. "You should discuss them directly with Jesus."

John paused. “How should I proceed? How should I prepare to meet with Him?”

“Go to your office,” I told him. “Say a brief prayer. Gently place the Mantle on your head, and it will envelop you. Soon, you will hear Jesus’s voice in your mind.”

“Just like that?” John asked. “I put the Mantle on my head and wait?”

“Yes,” I said. “Just like that. Jesus will do the rest.”

I excused myself and went downstairs to retrieve the Mantle from its ornate box, crafted in the 1400’s to resemble a miniature Ark of the Covenant.

When I returned, I handed the box to John. We smiled and embraced.

In that moment, the Mantle passed to its twelfth bearer, just as the legend foretold.

Chapter 3:

John Meets Jesus

"I am the Alpha and the Omega," says the Lord God, "who is, and who was, and who is to come, the Almighty" (Revelation 1:8).

All creation is an organic system made in the image and likeness of God. Creation reflects the Creator. All organic matter is formed, grows, expires, and returns to the Earth, including you and me. The part of creation that is eternal returns to God, most clearly seen in the human soul. Scripture teaches that the One present at the beginning and the end of all life is Jesus. His life, death, and resurrection changed humanity.

I am not a doomsday thinker, nor do I claim to understand the intersection of science and Scripture fully. I believe in science, and I trust in God. The stories found in Scripture are shaped by their historical and cultural contexts. Yet at their core is an enduring truth.

That truth is the God revealed in Three Persons throughout salvation history, Father, Son, and Holy Spirit. They are eternal, and the words of Jesus are true. While we may not fully understand all His teachings now, we will in time.

Jesus spoke to people in His own time and place, yet He also said that His words are eternal. He was speaking to His disciples and to people of every age. For this reason, I believe creation will one day return to God in a form we cannot yet comprehend. Jesus will come again, and life on Earth will be shaped according to God's plan.

After their Saturday meeting, John and Kristin returned to their home. John placed the Mantle and the history book inside the desk in his home office.

On Sunday morning, Joan and I met them at Saint George Church for liturgy led by Joan's cousin, Reverend Mark Johnstone. The service and homily were inspiring. Reverend Mark spoke on the second reading from the Book of Revelation, chapter 12, an ancient canticle called *The Judgment of God*:

"Now have come the salvation and the power and the kingdom of our God, and the authority of his Messiah. For the accuser of our brothers and sisters...has been hurled down" (v. 10).

Reverend Mark explained that the sacred author described a war in heaven between good and evil and that evil lost. The devil was cast down to Earth. Heaven, he said, is pure, while evil is a pervasive reality in the world. Only God's goodness and love can overcome it. Our role as believers is to call upon God for protection and to confront evil in the name and love of Christ.

The message felt timely as I reflected on John's coming work with the Mantle. I noticed that John listened intently.

After the liturgy, we stayed for coffee in the community center. Margaret, a widowed church elder who serves on the vestry, had baked a coffee cake that deserved an award. We enjoyed a slice with her as she shared stories of the church's history, dating back to the 1800's. Margaret's knowledge, dedication, and quiet faith exemplified the spirit of the parish.

When the tables were cleared and the plastic chairs were folded and stacked, we walked to the parking lot. John said he planned to use the Mantle that afternoon.

He looked at me seriously. "Dad, do you think Jesus will show up? I mean, does He know I have the Mantle? Will He recognize me?"

I told John his questions were natural and assured him that Jesus would appear within moments of wearing the Mantle.

"Say a prayer," I reminded him. "Place the Mantle gently on your head, and it will enfold you. You do not need to speak out loud. Just think about what you want to say. Jesus will hear you and respond in your mind. He has done this for nearly two thousand years. All will be well."

John nodded, visibly reassured, and we all headed home.

After lunch, John told Kristin he was going up to his office. They live in a beautiful two-story home with a large yard, just seven miles from us. Both have spacious home offices that they hope will one day become children's bedrooms.

As John climbed the stairs, he turned back and said, "Wish me luck."

Kristin smiled with her usual dry humor. "Be yourself. You are meeting the Creator of the Universe. Jesus does not rely on luck, and neither should you."

John laughed and disappeared into his office.

He pulled the ornate box containing the Mantle from his desk drawer. According to its history, the oak box was crafted in the 1400s by John Ward of London. It measured twelve inches wide, six inches deep, and six inches high.

A red Cross of Saint George adorned the front. The lid bore a gold Jerusalem Cross, also known as the Crusader's Cross. Red and gold trim framed the box, which resembled a miniature Ark of the Covenant rendered in an English style. Inside, the luminous linen Mantle lay neatly folded.

John placed the box on his desk, removed the Mantle, whispered a prayer, and gently placed it upon his head. Instantly, he was enveloped and invisible.

He looked at his hands and could see through them to the hardwood floor below.

Forgetting my advice in his nervousness, John spoke aloud. "Hello, Jesus. It's me, John. I'm John Mark's son."

A voice answered in his mind, playful and warm. "Hello, John. It's Me, Jesus. I am God's Son."

Jesus laughed softly at His own remark, then said, "John, I would like to appear to you in person. Would you be comfortable speaking face to face?"

"That would be wonderful," John replied. "Thank you, Jesus."

Jesus appeared instantly.

He had shoulder-length brown hair, a neatly trimmed beard, and deep brown eyes. He stood about five feet ten inches tall, slender yet strong, wearing a white linen robe with a gold sash and bronze-colored sandals. To John, He looked like the image described in the Book of Revelation.

Jesus smiled. "You know I can hear your thoughts?"

John blushed. "I forgot."

John invited Jesus to sit, and He did. As Jesus rested His hands in His lap, John noticed the nail marks in His palms and faint scars on His wrists. There were also nail marks on His feet. The wounds were visible but not disturbing, present, yet redeemed.

John thought of all his years in Catholic school learning about Jesus, and now Jesus sat before him. His elementary school nuns would be proud.

Jesus smiled at the thought.

"Do you mind if I call you John Luke?" Jesus asked.

John hesitated briefly. "Of course not, Jesus. May I ask why?"

"I like your full name," Jesus said. "It reminds me of old friends. I have always called your father John Mark. You are an educator and a doctor, like the Gospel writers John and Luke, and like your father. Your parents named you well before you were born. More importantly, your work with the Mantle will help fulfill the prophecy of my servant Jeremiah."

Jesus recited the verse from memory:

"Before I formed you in the womb I knew you, before you were born I set you apart; I appointed you as a prophet to the nations" (1:5).

"John Luke," Jesus continued, "your acceptance of the Mantle makes you a very special person. Yet no one will know that you are the one who brings miracles or shapes world events. If you accept My will, you will do even greater works than Me."

John Luke sat quietly, absorbing the weight of Jesus's words.

Finally, he said, "Jesus, I accept Your will. I will do what You ask."

"Good," Jesus replied. "Please include Kristin in this work. Share everything with her, as your father did with your mother."

"I will," John Luke replied. "And I have a request. Is it acceptable for my father to continue writing the history of the Mantle? My schedule is full, and writing will be difficult. He has the time, and it would keep him connected to this work."

Jesus smiled. "And you believe that writing will keep your father close to the Mantle and Me?"

"Nothing escapes you, Jesus," John Luke said.

"I am pleased with that arrangement," Jesus replied. "We will meet with him from time to time. Now, let me explain the big picture of this work."

Jesus continued, "First, when you wear the Mantle, you will be invisible and protected from harm. Second, you will not lose time. When you return, time will be as it was when you left. God governs time, as you recall from Joshua *(10:12-14)*, when the sun stood still. Your time will be honored."

"Third, we will proceed one mission at a time, but with urgency. Some tasks must be completed according to the Father's timetable."

Jesus paused. "You are familiar with the Book of Revelation. The author, John of Patmos, wrote of Me as the beginning and the end. Revelation is not only about the end of time. It is about God shaping humanity."

Jesus continued His explanation of the big picture.

"Think of Revelation as an ancient play," Jesus said. "You will walk in the role of John the Elder. The history book is like the scroll. Your work will take you to seven 'churches,' or seven nations. You will help shape the events of the seven seals for good and assist the work of the seven angels."

Jesus then explained, "By agreeing to wear the Mantle, you will help carry out the vision of the Father. Your actions will shape events and people. The scroll in Revelation is like the history book of the Mantle. The history book will document your work and its purpose. You will be instrumental in shaping the events of the seven seals for the better. You will assist the seven angels in their work through the Mantle."

Jesus concluded, "These events will unfold over time. I am always with you and your family. You will be protected. Your father will document this work for humanity."

"Wow," John Luke said quietly. "I will do everything you ask."

Jesus smiled. "Good. Our work begins now. Are you ready?"

"I am," John Luke said.

Chapter 4:

Mission One–San Miguel

"Blessed is the one who reads aloud the words of this prophecy and blessed are those who hear it and take to heart what is written in it, because the time is near" (Revelation 1:3).

After Jesus explained to John Luke that the mission of the Mantle aligned with the Book of Revelation, I felt compelled to reread the text. One verse stood out to me, particularly its call to take the message to heart. The time was clearly near for John Luke to begin his work with Jesus.

While John Luke sat with Jesus in his office, Jesus asked him to call me and see if I was available to meet immediately. John Luke did, and I told him yes.

"I want you to imagine," Jesus said, "that while you sit here with Me, you go to your father, take his hand, and bring him back here. I will wait." And He did.

I was overjoyed to see Jesus. Jesus stood, gave me a warm hug, and said, "I am so glad to see you, John Mark."

In that moment, John Luke experienced his first mission with the Mantle. He appeared in two places at once and brought me to his office within seconds.

I said, "Lord, it is good to be here!" - intentionally echoing the words of the disciples at the Transfiguration. Jesus smiled. "We have important work to discuss. You will remember all that we say and record it in the history book."

He then explained how John Luke's work with the Mantle aligned with the structure of the Book of Revelation—a pattern that fit naturally with the tradition of the twelve bearers. Then Jesus said, "You know the Families in Transition Center we established in Saint Theresa, New Mexico, Saint Luke's Home. I would like the four of you, John Mark and Joan, John Luke and Kristin, to travel there and prepare for an expansion as we begin other work."

He continued, "This new section will function like a motel, with seven identical rooms attached to the center. I suggest using the same builders who constructed Saint Luke's Home."

Jesus described the vision clearly. "From the outside, the building will appear to be offices. Inside, each room will contain a bedroom, a sitting area, a small kitchen, and a bathroom. Guests will stay for forty days, a time set aside for reflection and conversion. No outside visitors will enter this area. Staff from Saint Luke's Home will care for the guests. In the future, the space may be repurposed for the center."

Jesus continued, "John Luke, you will explain the plan to the administrators. They will agree. You will not encounter resistance. The facility will be fully secure with advanced technology, as these guests are well known." Jesus then assigned roles.

"John Luke, you will oversee construction with Joan's assistance. Kristin will assist in selecting and implementing the necessary technology. John Mark, you will assist with administration."

Then Jesus turned to me and said, "John Mark, I ask that you accompany John Luke to San Miguel, El Salvador, to the former residence of the crime boss and the *pequeña casa*, the small house behind it."

He continued calmly, "Although the crime boss remains imprisoned, the cartel has fractured, and the property is abandoned. The small house contains millions of dollars in illicit funds hidden within its walls. You will take burlap sacks, collect all the funds, and leave nothing behind. This money will finance the motel and future missions."

Jesus then quoted Scripture: *"A sinner's wealth is stored up for the righteous"* (Proverbs 13:22).

He looked at John Luke. "Are you ready?"

I looked down and saw burlap sacks on the office floor. I looked back at Jesus. "You said, John Luke?" I asked.

Jesus laughed. "John will explain the name change on your flight to San Miguel."

Then Jesus told John Luke, "To fly while wearing the Mantle, just think of your destination. The Mantle will take you to your destination at a comfortable speed."

I smiled, once again struck by the marvel of the Mantle.

"Let's go, Dad," John Luke said.

We picked up the sacks. John Luke took my hand, and I focused on San Miguel, a city in eastern El Salvador. The Mantle guided us effortlessly.

We rose and moved swiftly across the sky—over Florida and the Gulf of Mexico—before descending gently in front of the small house behind the former cartel compound. The journey felt both rapid and peaceful. As we traveled, John Luke explained why Jesus preferred his full name.

I smiled. “It suits you,” I said. “Be sure to tell Kristin.”

We arrived at the compound. We passed through the locked doors of the small house. As Jesus had said, the guards were gone. I told John Luke that, in the past, I had retrieved funds from the front walls to support Saint Luke’s Home, and that we should now check the rear walls.

Holding hands, we walked directly into the wall.

“Holy cow,” John Luke exclaimed.

The walls were indeed lined with millions of U.S. dollars, profits of violence and suffering, now reclaimed for good. We gathered the funds and left nothing behind. Miraculously, the vast sum fit neatly into the burlap sacks.

When we emerged, our task complete, John Luke said, “Keep holding my hand, Dad.”

The entire mission took approximately forty-five minutes. We departed at 1:30 PM and returned at 1:30 PM. Time stood still while the Mantle was at work.

Surprisingly, Jesus was still in the office chair waiting for us.

"I hope you do not mind, John Luke, as I stayed and spoke with the Father about His plans."

John Luke said, "I am honored, Jesus. Stay here as long as You wish!"

John Luke stood quietly, absorbing all that had occurred, meeting Jesus in person, appearing in two places at once, flying across continents, passing through walls, and retrieving the resources for future missions. It was a rapid initiation into life with the Mantle.

"We will need a safe," John Luke said at last.

Jesus nodded. "A wise thought."

"For now," Jesus said, "store the money in the sacks and keep them in your closet. Your home is protected."

John Luke did as instructed.

Jesus then told us to brief Joan and Kristin, begin preparations for Saint Theresa, and contact the builders. He reminded John Luke of the urgency of the work.

"You are a good servant, John Luke," Jesus said.

Then He was gone.

The Mantle had begun its next chapter, and I was humbled to take part in the work.

Chapter 5:

Las Cruces

"Jesus answered him, 'Truly I tell you, today you will be with Me in paradise'" (Luke 23:43).

The Spanish term *Las Cruces* refers to the three crosses on Mount Calvary where Jesus was crucified. Saint Luke's Gospel states that Jesus was crucified with two thieves, one on His left and the other on His right. One of the thieves mocked Jesus for not saving them from death. The other believed in Him and asked for mercy. Jesus assured the repentant man that he would be with Him in paradise.

I did not find it coincidental that the construction company Jesus chose for our next project in New Mexico was named Las Cruces. Once again, Jesus was at work, carrying out the Father's plan. His hand continues throughout this story. The following week at the university, Dr. White called to tell me that he had met Dr. Lydia Barnes and appointed her interim Dean of the School of Business. He explained that her background and experience made her an excellent candidate and that she could work closely with me during the transition. He also noted that Lydia would need to apply and interview for the permanent position along with other candidates.

Dr. White asked what I thought of this plan.

"I think having Lydia as interim dean makes perfect sense," I replied. "I will gladly support her to ensure a smooth transition. Is there anything else you would like me to do?"

Dr. White laughed. "How about staying on for six months?"

I laughed as well. "You are too kind, Joe, yet I am ready to live the retirement dream!"

"Well, at least I tried," he said. "You are not much older than I am, and I will be ready to retire in a couple of years. Thanks for supporting Lydia."

"Of course," I replied, and we ended the call. I felt good about Lydia and confident in her leadership.

That evening, John Luke sent a group text titled *Team Mantle* to Joan, Kristin, and me. He asked us to prepare for a long weekend in New Mexico. We all responded yes.

We met at John Luke's house at 9:00 AM on Friday. Joan brought a portfolio of motel construction materials. Kristin carried a folder outlining high-technology security systems. John Luke discreetly placed $100,000 in cash into his pockets. I contacted the administrators at Saint Luke's Home to inform them of our plans, arranged for a rental car, and reserved hotel rooms through Sunday.

I also contacted Las Cruces Builders, owned by Lucas and Paula Sanchez, and asked them to meet us at Saint Luke's Home at 10:00 AM. I brought my laptop to take notes for the history book. We all packed lightly.

Number 12

In the privacy of John Luke's backyard, he asked us to join hands. We lifted effortlessly into the clear morning sky, ascending to about 10,000 feet. The horizon was breathtaking as we headed west toward New Mexico.

After a few moments, Kristin said, "Whoa, John, I mean John Luke, could we slow down a bit? I am not used to this kind of flying."

I reminded John that, to control his airspeed, Jesus explained that one should consider driving a car at 55 miles per hour (mph). A small plane travels about four times that speed at 10,000 feet, and a jet flies at about 550 mph, reaching about 35,000 feet. I told him John could travel at the speed of light, 186,000 miles per second. He needed to think about his airspeed, and the Mantle would follow his thoughts.

John understood and slowed our pace.

About thirty minutes later, we landed safely in the parking lot of Saint Luke's Home. Kristin said she felt much better and even joked that John Luke could fly faster on the way back.

We were greeted warmly upon arrival. John Luke spoke Spanish with the residents, and we met privately with the administrators to explain the expansion plans. Just as Jesus had said, they agreed without hesitation and granted full access to the grounds.

Joan led us to the area Jesus had described for the new construction.

As we walked around the site, my phone rang. Lucas said he and Paula had arrived. I asked them to meet us behind the building.

Joan immediately noticed that Paula was pregnant.

The last time we saw Lucas and Paula was at their wedding about a year ago.

Joan gave her a big hug and said, “Congratulations seem to be in order! I am so happy for you both.”

Paula beamed and shared that they were expecting a baby boy in four months. She assured us she felt well and planned to remain fully engaged in the project. John Luke explained the building’s purpose. Though Lucas and Paula did not question the mission, I sensed curiosity about the extensive security requirements.

“This area will serve as a retreat for high-profile guests,” John Luke explained. “That is why security is necessary.”

That seemed to satisfy them.

Joan reviewed the building layout, and Lucas confirmed that he could move quickly. Paula, as both administrator and interior designer, asked thoughtful questions and took careful notes. They were the perfect team for this work, as Jesus had known all along.

After about an hour, Lucas said they had sufficient information to develop plans and order materials. He estimated the project could be completed within ninety days, weather permitting, using the same local crew as the original building. Joan confirmed that permits were in process.

John Luke handed Paula $75,000 in cash as a down payment.

"We will pay the remainder upon invoice. As before, we will handle payments weekly."

Paula smiled. "That is what I call cash flow! I will be sure to send a receipt."

Kristin then provided the folder detailing the security systems and explained that vendors had been contacted for just-in-time delivery. She handled their deposits as well.

Lucas said he would begin work the next day by laying out the foundation. He praised Joan's choice of location and noted that the building would appear to be executive offices from the outside. After exchanging hugs and congratulations, we returned inside.

John Luke quietly made a $20,000 donation to the senior administrator, Consuelo, thanking her in Spanish for her faithful service and encouraging her to use the funds as she saw fit. She placed the money in the office safe, visibly moved.

"That was a nice touch," Joan said afterward.

"I want to honor her ministry," John Luke replied. "I also kept $5,000 as a contingency, just in case."

I smiled. He was pragmatic, just like his mother.

We bought lunch from a nearby Mexican restaurant for everyone at St. Luke's, and shared a long afternoon with the residents. John Luke and Kristin played with the children, while Joan and I talked quietly and reflected on the day.

Joan leaned over to me and said, "It will not be long. I saw Kristin's eyes light up when she hugged Paula. Those two will make excellent parents."

I smiled and nodded in agreement.

Later, at the hotel, Joan confirmed that permits would be ready for Lucas to break ground the following week. The rest of the evening was peaceful, swimming, conversation, note-taking, and an early dinner.

The next morning, Saint Luke's Home buzzed with excitement. Consuelo announced plans to take the families on a beach trip, using part of the donation.

"The sunshine will be good for everyone," she said, "especially the children."

At the construction site, Lucas showed us his soil tests and explained that a concrete slab would be sufficient, saving both time and money. John Luke handed him $500 to cover the cost of the testing device.

"Thank you for being a problem-solver," he said.

After breakfast at a local diner, John Luke suggested we return home and manage the rest remotely. We agreed. After checking out early and donating our unused hotel rooms, we returned the rental car.

In the parking lot, when no one was watching, we joined hands. John Luke carried us home in minutes.

As we said goodbye, I reflected on the weekend. With Jesus as our guide, everything had unfolded exactly as it was meant to.

Joan and I headed home, deeply content.

Chapter 6:

Hearing and Listening

"Whoever has ears, let them hear what the Spirit says to the churches. To the one who is victorious, I will give the right to eat from the tree of life, which is in the paradise of God" (Revelation 2:7).

Biologically, hearing begins as sound waves travel through the ear canal to the cochlea, a spiral-shaped structure in the inner ear. There, the waves are converted into electrical impulses that travel along the auditory nerve to the brainstem and into the temporal lobes on both sides of the brain.

As sound moves through the brain, it passes through the limbic system, the region responsible for emotion processing, before reaching the auditory cortex, where it is interpreted as words, music, or noise.

The limbic system acts as a kind of filter, helping us determine whether a sound is pleasant, meaningful, alarming, or merely background noise. From there, the mind decides whether we merely hear or truly listen.

The human brain is one of the most miraculous aspects of God's creation, second only to the gift of His Son. We are indeed *"fearfully and wonderfully made"* (Psalm 139:14). Yet, hearing is not the same as listening. We may hear the Word of God and still choose not to listen. To honor this gift, we must be attentive to which words we follow and believe.

Jesus understood the power of sound and speech. The Gospels record thirty-four occasions when Jesus "spoke to the crowds." Through His words, Jesus called disciples, challenged assumptions, and invited listeners to move from hearing to believing.

In the Book of Revelation, the message to the seven churches echoes this same call: to listen, to respond, and to grow in faithfulness. To those who truly hear, the promise of the tree of life—first seen in the Garden of Eden (Genesis 2:9) and fulfilled in Christ—awaits in paradise. As John Luke wore the Mantle, he began to understand this more deeply. He experienced a growing faith and a more intimate understanding of Jesus, not only His words but His presence. He saw that Jesus followed the Father's will in both word and action.

And so John Luke listened carefully to Jesus.

He began to discern what those words meant—for himself, for his family, and for the world. Slowly, the big picture Jesus had described came into focus. I noticed the change in him. He became more attentive to Kristin, to Joan, and me, and above all, to Jesus. I had experienced this myself: the more time I spent with Jesus, the more I desired to remain in His presence. John Luke was discovering the same truth.

Being with Jesus felt like a sense of purpose and destiny. No experience compares to following the will of God through His Son, Jesus Christ.

The day after we returned from New Mexico was Sunday. As usual, the four of us attended church, shared coffee with the pastor and parishioners, and then returned home. We felt more united as a family because of the work of the Mantle in our lives.

That afternoon, John Luke had lunch with Kristin, then asked if she minded him going to his office to finish some work and connect with Jesus.

"Of course," Kristin said. "Just make sure your office is clean for our Guest."

John Luke smiled and went upstairs. Kristin later heard the vacuum running and smiled to herself.

After finishing his work, John Luke retrieved the box from his desk, said a prayer, and placed the Mantle gently over his head. He stood quietly, waiting.

"Good afternoon, John Luke," Jesus said within his mind. "It is so good to be with you this Sunday."

John Luke smiled. *Dear Jesus, I am learning how good it is to be with You as well.*

"I would like to meet in person," Jesus replied. "After all, you went to the trouble of cleaning your office for Me."

John Luke laughed softly. "Jesus, I never appreciated Your sense of humor when I read the Scriptures. I am so blessed to have You in my life."

Jesus appeared at once, smiling, and embraced him.

"The Mantle is changing you, John Luke."

"You are changing me for the better," John Luke replied. "I feel calmer, more focused, even wiser."

Jesus nodded. "Do you remember the Scripture that says, *'You have returned to the Shepherd and Guardian of your soul'?"* (1 Peter 2:25). "Our closeness reminds Me of that verse. I was never distant from you, but there was a time when you were distant from Me."

John Luke blushed, recalling his teenage years when he resisted church and neglected prayer.

Jesus gently said, "I remind you of that time not to make you feel bad, but for you to consider how much better life is with Me. I like being close to you. You are the apple of My eye" (Psalm 17:8).

John Luke shared that a song had recently come to mind, one that captured how he felt now. He began to recite the lyrics, but Jesus stopped him.

"Sing it for Me."

John Luke picked up his guitar and smiled sheepishly. "I am a little rusty."

"Do not worry," Jesus said. "Make a joyful noise unto the Lord."

John Luke sang:

When I'm with You /

I feel the real me finally breaking through /

It's all because of You, Jesus /
Anytime, anywhere, any heartache /
I'm never too much for You to take /
There's only love /
There's only grace /
When I'm with You...
(Citizen Way, 2016)

Jesus clapped with delight, "Bravo, John Luke. Thank you for singing for Me."

"Thank You for listening," John Luke replied.

Jesus smiled warmly. "Your singing reminds Me of when you were a child, riding in the car as your father played hymns on the cassette player. You sang joyfully from your car seat, learning the words by heart. Your mother would whisper, 'He has such a sweet, deep voice.' You have always carried music in your soul. You are a cherished child of Mine."

Tears filled John Luke's eyes as he embraced Jesus. Jesus held him tightly, patting his back.

"I had not planned on this conversation," John Luke said softly. "I wanted to tell You about our trip to Saint Theresa."

"Sometimes friends need time to connect," Jesus replied. "Now tell Me about your trip."

John Luke described the meetings, the building plans, and the timeline. He explained that the slab would be poured on Monday and that the project would be completed within ninety days, weather permitting.

"The timing fits perfectly with the Father's plan," Jesus said.

"Do You have any work for us today with the Mantle?" John Luke asked.

Jesus smiled warmly. "No work today. It is the Sabbath. Spend time with Kristin and rest. Remember to tell your father about our conversation for the history book. Continue sharing everything with Kristin. And do not forget to order the safe."

He paused, then added. "You do not need to count the money, but there is more than $10 million. Next time we meet, there will be work overseas."

With that, Jesus disappeared.

John Luke removed the Mantle and went downstairs to join Kristin. They spent the evening quietly watching television, sharing popcorn, and resting peacefully.

Chapter 7:

The Seven Churches

"Surely, he will save you from the fowler's snare and from the deadly pestilence. He will cover you with his feathers, and under his wings you will find refuge; his faithfulness will be your shield and rampart" (Psalm 91:3-4).

When John Luke was young, he learned Scripture through Christian music. One of his favorite hymns was *On Eagle's Wings*, based on Psalm 91 and written by Reverend Michael Joncas in 1976. Father Joncas composed the song to honor his father's death. Years later, he wrote a book of the same name describing his battle with Guillain-Barré syndrome and how praying Psalm 91 sustained him through illness and recovery.

John Luke was seriously ill twice as a child, first at age two and again at age five, both times with pneumonia. As he struggled to sleep, I often sang *On Eagle's Wings* to comfort him. By God's grace, he recovered fully and never experienced pneumonia again.

Psalm 91 holds deep meaning for many Christians. The image of God as an eagle sheltering His children beneath protective wings offers comfort, strength, and renewal.

The week following our return from New Mexico, John Luke remained in close contact with Lucas and Paula. Progress on the building was steady and encouraging. The concrete slab had been poured, materials delivered, and framing had begun. Paula emailed the finalized interior designs for the motel rooms, which integrate the advanced security system Kristin recommended, along with an invoice.

John Luke formally established a 501(c)(3) nonprofit organization named *The Mantle LLC*, obtained a federal identification number, opened a bank account, and mailed Paula a check.

On Wednesday evening, after dinner with Kristin, John Luke went upstairs to his office to speak with Jesus. He said a prayer and gently placed the Mantle over his head.

As the Mantle enveloped him, Jesus spoke to his mind.

"Good evening, John Luke. I trust you had a good day, and good news about the project at Saint Luke's Home."

"Yes, Jesus," John Luke thought. "The project is moving forward and appears to be on schedule. Lucas and Paula are doing excellent work."

"I am pleased," Jesus replied, "and so is My Father. As we discussed, your work with the Mantle will require you to learn new skills. Remember, you will not lose any time while performing this work. Are you ready for an assignment?"

"Yes, Jesus. I am ready."

Jesus reminded John Luke of the seven churches described in the Book of Revelation and the seven missions they symbolized.

"Your first 'church,' or country, is Ukraine," Jesus said. "You will travel to Kyiv and meet with Archeparch Stanislaus Medwit, leader of the Ukrainian Greek Catholic Church. He will be instrumental in this mission."

Jesus then recalled the story of Emmaus from Saint Luke's Gospel, where He walked alongside disciples who did not recognize Him.

"This meeting will be similar," Jesus explained. "Your identity will be concealed."

"The Archeparch is expecting you," Jesus continued, "though he will not know your identity. Wearing the Mantle, you may speak any language fluently, like Ukrainian. It is currently two o'clock in the morning in Kyiv, yet he waits for you at the Cathedral of the Resurrection of Christ."

Jesus instructed John Luke to bring $1 million for the meeting. The safe in John Luke's office held the funds, and a briefcase, provided by Jesus, sat atop it to transport the money. The donation was intended to aid those suffering from the war between Ukraine and Russia.

"You will also ask the Archeparch," Jesus said, "to arrange a confidential meeting with the President of Ukraine. You will offer additional private resources to help bring this conflict to an end."

"I will guide your words and actions," Jesus assured him. "I will speak directly to your mind."

Jesus then told him to use the alias of John Ward, the name of the fifteenth-century craftsman who carved the Mantle's ornate box.

"Do not be afraid," Jesus said. "I am with you. Are you ready?"

John Luke took a deep breath. "I am ready."

With the power of the Mantle, John Luke flew across the Atlantic Ocean, over France and Germany, and toward Kyiv. He landed quietly before the Cathedral of the Resurrection of Christ and rang the night bell.

A priest answered the door. As Jesus promised, John Luke spoke fluent Ukrainian. The priest nodded, said he was expected, and escorted him to the Archeparch's office in the rectory.

John Luke introduced himself as John Ward of The Mantle LLC. Archeparch Medwit greeted him warmly and offered black tea with lemon and sugar, a Ukrainian custom.

Guided by Jesus, John Luke explained the purpose of his visit and placed the briefcase on the table.

Archeparch Medwit's eyes widened at the generous gift.

"This donation," John Luke said, "is from a private source for the care of your people affected by the war. Use it as you see fit. I do, however, have one request."

The Archeparch listened attentively.

"I respectfully ask that you arrange a private meeting with the President of Ukraine," John Luke continued. "I have further resources to offer that may help bring this conflict to an end.

The Archeparch paused thoughtfully. “I will do what I can. How may I contact you?”

John Luke handed him a business card bearing the name John Ward, The Mantle LLC, along with a secure phone number designated for mission work.

The men stood, exchanged warm handshakes, and the same priest escorted John Luke out.

Moments later, John Luke returned home. The clock still read 7:00 PM.

Before he removed the Mantle, Jesus spoke once more.

“Well done. Be prepared to meet with the President of Ukraine on Friday evening at 8 o’clock Kyiv time.”

“I will be ready,” John Luke replied.

Downstairs, John Luke recounted his journey to Kristin. She listened in amazement.

“I feel like I am married to a character from a Matt Damon movie,” she said with a smile. “But I trust Jesus will keep you safe, for both of us.”

“I trust Him like never before,” John Luke said. “He guides every step. To be with Him, to see Him, to hear Him, it is beyond words.”

Despite the magnitude of the evening’s events, they went to bed early and slept soundly.

Chapter 8: President Koval

"To him who loves us and has freed us from our sins by his blood and has made us to be a kingdom and priests to serve his God and Father, to him be glory and power forever! Amen" (Revelation 1:5-6).

This beautiful passage from John of Patmos calls all of us to serve God forever. John Luke is following Jesus and serving as a disciple and priest for God's kingdom with the Mantle.

After meeting with the Archeparch in Ukraine, John Luke realized that the scope of his mission with the Mantle was worldwide. He realized Jesus was bringing peace and salvation to the world. John Luke was, as Kristin said, "God's secret agent."

The realization was overwhelming at times.

The next morning, the dedicated phone for the Mantle rang. The voice on the other end of the call identified himself as Mykola Koval, President of Ukraine. He told John Luke that the Archeparch gave him this number.

John Luke stumbled a bit and then recovered, replying in perfect Ukrainian, "Thank you for calling me, Mr. President. I contacted you because I have access to confidential resources that could help resolve the conflict with Russia. I ask you to please meet with me in person to explain the details."

Just as Jesus said, President Koval agreed to meet with John Luke on Friday at 8:00 PM in the Mariinsky Palace in Kyiv. John Luke thanked the president and said he would be there.

John Luke performed his usual university work for the next two days. At 12:45 PM on Friday, he told Kristin that he would wear the Mantle, meet with Jesus, and leave for Kyiv. He asked her to say a special prayer for the meeting's success.

He felt a quiet confidence. Jesus would guide his thoughts and words.

After a brief prayer, John Luke gently placed the Mantle over his head. "John Luke," Jesus said within his mind, "you are doing great work. The Father deeply appreciates your obedience to my word. In your closet is a briefcase that will hold two million dollars. Take the funds from the safe. The amount will fit in the briefcase for your journey. As before, President Koval will meet you under your alias, John Ward, and no one will recognize you. All will be well."

John Luke took the funds and flew directly to Kyiv following the same route as before. He landed near the front entrance of the Palace. A guard waited for him and led him through a security check, then to President Koval's office.

As John Luke walked down a grand hallway, he saw several men and a woman sitting in a conference room.

Jesus spoke quietly to his mind, "These people are the most trusted members of the president's cabinet."

President Koval extended his hand, and John Luke warmly took it, introducing himself as John Ward. He led John Luke to a beautiful and elaborate conference table in the office.

John Luke gave the president his business card and asked if he could place the briefcase on the table.

The president looked at the card and then joked, "As you went through security, I assume the briefcase is safe. So please, go ahead."

John Luke opened the case, revealing the money.

"This is a humanitarian gift for your people." The president's eyes grew wide, and he thanked John Ward for the generous gift.

President Koval said, "I am grateful. But I must ask—why are you here, bearing such gifts?"

"I have come with a plan from God to help end the war," John Luke replied.

The words came clearly, guided in real time. This was new for him—speaking without preparation, trusting completely. John Luke said, "Mr. President, God's plan is for The Mantle LLC to hire and pay for private Australian security contractors that previously worked in the Afghanistan war effort. You can use these private contractors to help regain control of the territories annexed by Russia, including Donetsk, Kherson, Luhansk, and Zaporizhzhia. You could then utilize your military for other defense areas of the country."

The president listened carefully, though with understandable caution. John Luke then said, "These private companies would help conduct a covert operation in Russia to capture and deliver twenty-four Sukhoi 35 (Su-35S) aircraft and provide them to Ukraine for use in the war effort. As we know, Russia is using private forces against Ukraine."

John Luke then said to President Koval, "This new show of force will confound the president of Russia and his military leaders. We have nearly unlimited private resources to make this a reality. The goal is to bring Russia to the peace table. God wants to help you end this war. These ideas are just the beginning of the help we may provide. What do you think?"

"How do I know you are genuine?" he asked. "My team found almost nothing about you—only your name connected to a nonprofit in the United States. You appear to be American, yet you speak fluent Ukrainian. Who are you?"

He leaned back, studying him.

"And yet," he added slowly, "something tells me to believe you. If what you say is true, I will be deeply grateful. I may even become a Christian."

John Luke smiled gently. "I ask only that you take a step of faith. I will arrange what is needed on my end. I ask that you proceed carefully and keep this confidential. It is best that you remain at a distance from the source of this assistance." The president got up from his chair, excused himself, and left his office. A guard stood at the open door.

Jesus told him that the president would speak with his cabinet members. He told John Luke that the Holy Spirit was present in the room and that all would be well.

John Luke took a steady breath.

A few minutes later, the president returned.

"My cabinet agrees," he said. "We will proceed. What comes next?"

John Luke told President Koval, "I will return home and arrange for the Australian military contractors to contact you soon. Their leader will speak directly with you to coordinate the efforts."

Jesus then told John Luke to return home. His work was done for now.

John Luke stepped out of the palace and saw a large black car with two men in the front seats. John Luke turned a corner and placed the Mantle on his head. He was invisible.

Jesus told him that the men in the car are from the *Vagnera Group*, a private mercenary company working with Russia. They are spying on President Koval.

Jesus told John Luke Vagnera was funded by a wealthy Russian oligarch named Mikhail Andropov. Jesus said Andropov, who goes by the nickname of *Zver*, or beast, is the Antichrist from Scripture. He told John Luke not to worry about the men or the beast for now.

Jesus said, "We will take care of these men in time. *Zver* is the nemesis behind much of the world's pain and suffering. The battle with him is Mine. Keep doing the work with the Mantle. Over time, peace will reign."

John Luke accepted His words, even without fully understanding them. Within minutes, he returned home and informed Kristin about the meeting and the Father's plan for peace.

Kristin responded, "Wow, you really are God's secret agent!"

Chapter 9:

Russia and Ukraine

"And when I turned, I saw seven golden lampstands, and among the lampstands was someone like a son of man, dressed in a robe reaching down to his feet and with a golden sash around his chest" (Revelation 1:12-13).

The term "Son of Man" appears in the Hebrew Scriptures in the books of Ezekiel and Daniel. In these two books, the Son of Man is both a human and a divine figure who possesses authority and an everlasting kingdom.

Christians, like the author of Revelation, believe the term refers to Jesus, who used it to describe Himself in the Gospels.

The war in Ukraine clearly grieves Jesus. It was foisted on a people who did not seek conflict with neighboring Russia. Many innocent people were killed and injured, and survivors were driven from their homes. Jesus, as the Son of Man, seems to be saying "enough."

Jesus instructs John Luke about a strategic plan to end the war. This plan begins in Moscow, Russia.

The next morning, John Luke had breakfast with Kristin. They spent an hour talking and laughing, and he delighted in her sense of humor. She was everything he hoped for as a partner. The mood in their home was light and joyful, and he cherished her.

After breakfast, John Luke called me and shared the details for the history book. I congratulated him on his successful meetings. When the call ended, he sensed a strong urging to speak with Jesus. He told Kristin, then headed to the office.

Once there, John Luke removed the Mantle from his desk, said a prayer, and gently placed it on his head.

Jesus spoke immediately in his mind: “Good morning, My good and faithful servant. Thank you for listening to the Spirit's prompting. We have work to do before you begin your day. Are you willing?”

“Of course, Jesus,” John Luke replied. “Please tell me.”

Jesus laid out a plan for John Luke. “The funds for the Australian military contractors to support Ukraine are in the Russian treasury. Once the war is over, we will repay the treasury with interest. For now, I ask that you go with Me to the Russian Central Bank in Moscow. We will find billions in foreign currencies. The cost of the work for the contractors will be €150 billion. I will be with you in the bank, directing your steps. Once we have the funds, we will go to the Swiss National Bank in Zurich, Switzerland, and open an account for John Ward and The Mantle LLC.”

John Luke understood the purpose, even if he did not fully grasp every detail. What struck him most was the justice in it—the redirection of resources toward peace. Jesus smiled at John

Luke's thoughts and said, "I would like you to close the account in your local bank and only use this new account for work with the Mantle. Your appearance at the bank will be disguised, and all the necessary paperwork needed is waiting for you. The bank will secure John Ward's identity even from the Russians."

"You will deposit the funds and initiate a €75 billion wire transfer to the Australian contractors, representing half of the funds needed for the effort. Then, transfer the rest of the money within forty days as peace will be in process in Ukraine."

Jesus appeared in person and said, "Are you ready, John Luke?"

John Luke said, "I am now," relieved at seeing Him.

Jesus said, "Good. We will go together."

They traveled swiftly across the Atlantic and into Europe, arriving in Moscow at the Russian Central Bank.

John Luke was pleased to have Jesus by his side. As they were both invisible, they walked through the doors, past security, and down a flight of stairs to the basement. They walked through a massive vault door, passing billions in gold bullion bricks, and went to the currency section. John Luke was grateful he did not have to carry any bricks.

"Here," He said.

John Luke gathered what was needed, marveling at how the weight and volume seemed to yield to the power of the Mantle.

Within moments, they departed and arrived at the Swiss National Bank in Zurich. At the entrance, Jesus paused.

"Here, you will be seen as your alias, John Ward. Everything has been prepared." Jesus walked invisibly beside John Luke, and, miraculously, the burlap sack turned into two large black briefcases that neatly held the euros.

John Luke held a case in each hand and walked to the front office. He told the person in charge, in perfect *Swiss German*, or *Romansh*, that he was John Ward.

The woman in charge nodded. "We have been expecting you."

John Luke handed over both briefcases. The woman raised her eyebrows at the 150-billion-euro figure that fit into the two cases. She walked into a bulletproof glass office and counted the funds.

As he completed the final paperwork, John Luke noticed a Swiss passport bearing the name John Ward. Every detail had been arranged.

The final paper John Luke signed authorized an immediate wire transfer of €75 billion to the Australian military contractor Labyrinth, based in Melbourne. Once the transaction was complete, Jesus and John Luke left the bank.

When the process was complete, he stepped outside.

To his surprise, the street was completely still—no pedestrians, no traffic. In the quiet, he and Jesus departed and returned home.

Their work was conducted in less than an hour. True to Jesus's words, the time was the same as when they left.

Jesus asked John Luke to call the Australian military contractor, Labyrinth's founder, General Oliver Williams. Jesus said the General would be expecting his call.

General Williams answered his private line. After exchanging pleasantries, the General said, "We just received your wire transfer for €75 billion, and we are ready to dispatch 50,000 private contractor troops to Ukraine. The Vagnera Group has about 50,000 personnel there now. If we need more troops, we will send them. I will lead the team personally. We will arrive at 0600 in Kyiv tomorrow."

John Luke then provided President Koval's contact information and asked that coordination begin immediately.

When the call ended, he contacted the president.

"The Australian contractors called Labyrinth will arrive tomorrow morning in Kyiv. Their leader, General Williams, will call you soon. Here is his information."

Before they ended the call, President Koval said, "I don't really know who you are, John Ward, but I believe God sent you. How did you make this happen so quickly?"

John Luke responded with a smile in his voice, "God provides, Mr. President. His plan for peace is in motion. I will be in contact soon regarding the Russian Sukhoi 35 aircraft delivery."

The call ended, and Jesus said to John Luke, "Good work, my friend. Enjoy the rest of your day. We will meet again tomorrow if you are willing."

John Luke said, "I always want to be with you, Jesus."

Jesus left, and John Luke told Kristin the latest news about the Mantle.

Kristin reminded John Luke, “Make sure you call your dad. This news is too juicy for you to keep to yourself.”

John Luke chuckled and said, “Honey, you are too funny.” He went back to his desk.

As Kristin said, John Luke called and told me about his latest adventure. I marveled at Jesus's mind and took copious notes.

Chapter 10: Sukhoi 35 Movement

"You have persevered and have endured hardships for My name and have not grown weary" (Revelation 2:3).

Ukraine's population is about 31 million, and more than 30 million are Christian. Ukraine has one of the largest Christian communities in Europe. The church in Ukraine is rooted in its Byzantine heritage and Orthodox tradition. God's people have suffered greatly under the Russian invasion, yet they remain faithful, praying for the war to end.

The next day after returning from Russia, John Luke and Kristin finished lunch when he felt the need to speak with Jesus. John Luke told Kristin about the urging and went to his office. He said a prayer and gently placed the Mantle on his head.

Instantly, Jesus spoke to John Luke. "Hello, my friend. I trust you and Kristin are well?"

John Luke said, "Yes, and we just finished a great lunch."

John Luke then said, "I told my office that I would like to work from home this week, as I felt the need to be close to the Mantle."

"Good decision," said Jesus. "We have work to do, if you are ready."

John Luke answered, "I am, Lord."

Jesus then explained His plan for moving Russian aircraft. "Right now, the Russians are aware of the movements of the Australian military contractors across Ukraine, headed to the territories annexed by Russia. The Russian president was told of the sacking of the treasury. He is disturbed and distracted by both events. Now is the time to move the aircraft because of this distraction. Russia currently has two dozen Su-35 aircraft at Besovets Air Base near the Finnish border."

Jesus continued, "While the task I will describe sounds arduous, you must have faith that you can do this work with the Mantle. I ask that you go to Besovets and take one aircraft at a time to the Ukrainian naval airfield of Vinnytsia. The final aircraft will have a pilot on board. He will notice the missing aircraft and try to secure his airship. You will take him and the aircraft to Vinnytsia. This pilot has family in Ukraine, and he is sympathetic to their plight. He will be convinced to help train Ukrainian pilots to fly the Su-35."

John Luke asked Jesus, "How long will it take for me to move one aircraft at a time? And I know you said so, yet will I have the strength to carry each aircraft?"

Jesus assured John Luke that the Mantle would do the heavy lifting.

Then Jesus said, "I suggest you carry the aircraft at the speed of light, as your father explained to you. The work to move all the aircraft will take less than an hour. Before you leave, please call President Koval and notify the commander in Vinnytsia that the aircraft will arrive soon. Please also tell him about the pilot passenger who will become the trainer."

John Luke understood the mission. He called President Koval on his private line.

"Mr. President, we are preparing to move twenty-four Sukhoi 35 (Su-35S) aircraft to Vinnytsia. The work should take less than an hour. Please tell your commander in Vinnytsia about their arrival. The last aircraft will carry a Russian pilot who is sympathetic to Ukraine. I suggest you use him as a flight instructor to train your pilots in how to fly the SU aircraft."

The president was both astounded and grateful for the work John Ward carried out.

President Koval said, "John Ward, this news is astounding. How can you move these aircraft in under an hour?"

John Luke responded, "You know the prophet's words that God's ways are far above our ways, Mr. President. Please make that call to Vinnytsia, and I am sure we will be in touch soon."

The call ended, and John Luke arrived in Besovets in seconds through the power of the Mantle.

John Luke looked at the first aircraft. He marveled at its sleek design, twin engines, and size. He remembered Jesus's words that the Mantle would do the heavy lifting. He walked under the belly of the aircraft near the landing gear and lifted it off the ground with ease. John Luke was ecstatic and grateful. The aircraft was now invisible, as was John Luke, through the Mantle. He flew at the speed of light, as Jesus directed.

The distance from Besovets to Vinnytsia was about 1,200 miles. John Luke flew with ease and gently set each aircraft down on the field, as several Ukrainian naval officers stood by in awe while each new aircraft appeared. John Luke repeated the same action twenty-two times, flying 1,200 miles in less than a second.

For the last aircraft, John Luke saw the pilot sitting in the cabin, about to start the aircraft. He moved swiftly under the belly and lifted the aircraft before the engines were engaged. The Su-35 was invisible, as was the stunned pilot. John Luke flew slightly more slowly to help the pilot adjust to the extraordinary events.

He landed in Vinnytsia, and Ukrainian naval officers surrounded the aircraft with guns drawn and ordered the pilot to exit the craft. John Luke flew to his home office in seconds. The work took less than an hour, as Jesus said.

When John Luke arrived at his office, Jesus was there in person waiting for him.

Jesus gave John Luke a warm hug and said, “Today, you were an instrument of peace for God’s people. The Russian president and military leadership are in turmoil over these events. Soon, the media will report the news. No one will know you are involved, and John Ward’s identity will remain a secret known only to a select few people. They will keep your identity secure. How do you feel, John Luke?” Jesus asked sincerely.

John Luke replied, “I feel great. Just as you said, Jesus, I feel like an instrument of peace in the world.”

Jesus then said, "Good. The balance of power has now shifted. The Russian president will be the last holdout for peace, yet his military leaders are fearful of the developments that have taken place. The Ukrainian navy will soon fly over the annexed territories to support ground operations by Australian military contractors. Donetsk and Kherson will be reclaimed and freed from Russian control. Luhansk and Zaporizhzhia will follow in due time. God's plan is unfolding, and you are His secret agent of peace."

John Luke smiled broadly.

Jesus then told John Luke, "President Koval will call you in a moment to thank you and congratulate you. I will guide your mind on what to say."

The phone rang, and President Koval's voice was higher than usual, excited. "John Ward, you are a man of your word. Thank you for all that you have done for Ukraine."

John Luke spoke the words Jesus placed in his mind. "All this work is for the glory of God and the cause of peace. As we agreed, Mr. President, please do not bring up my name to anyone except your most trusted advisors. This victory is for peace in Ukraine, according to God's plan. I suggest you publicly give the credit and glory to God for these actions."

The president responded, "Of course, John Ward. I will use those exact words that will cause great consternation for the Russians. You are humble and brilliant. Are you sure you are not Ukrainian?"

John Luke laughed out loud and said, "You are too kind, Mr. President. I am just a grateful servant of the God who loves us all. We will be in touch soon, as God has one more work to put the plan of peace in place for you and your people. Good night, Mr. President."

Jesus congratulated John Luke for handling the phone call so well.

Jesus told John Luke, "For the rest of this week, I want you to focus on your family, your work, and some rest. This weekend, we will have some work with the Mantle regarding the construction project in New Mexico. All is well, dear friend."

Jesus hugged John Luke goodbye and disappeared.

John Luke placed the Mantle back in the box in his desk and headed downstairs. He told Kristin about his adventure. She was astounded at the events and said, "This will surely be on the national news soon."

He told Kristin, "Yes, and our work will be kept secret per Jesus. I hope John Ward does not mind that I am using his identity."

They spent the rest of the day on their usual duties at work, had dinner together, and watched the evening news about the stunning shift of the aircraft into Ukrainian control. Then they went to bed.

Kristin was very proud of her husband, the secret agent of peace. John Luke was grateful for her affection and attention. They are a match made in heaven.

Chapter 11:

The Saint Luke Motel

"The first living creature was like a lion, the second was like an ox, the third had a face like a man, the 4th was like a flying eagle. Each of the four living creatures had six wings and were covered with eyes all around, even under its wings. Day and night they never stop saying: 'Holy, holy, holy is the Lord God Almighty, who was, and is, and is to come'" (Revelation 4:7-8).

The Book of Revelation depicts a heavenly image of the four Gospel writers of the New Testament. These images are based on a prophecy from Ezekiel 1:10, written around 568 BCE (Before the Common Era).

In Revelation, Matthew is represented by the face of a man. This image represents humanity and reason. A lion's face represents Mark. This image represents the voice of the wilderness, like John the Baptist's. Luke is depicted as an ox. The ox represents the physical and material aspects of Jesus's life. John is represented as a flying eagle. The eagle represents John's role as a firsthand witness of Jesus and a prophet.

These images are important to John of Patmos's writing, for the words and lives of the Evangelists give glory to God who sits on the throne. They also serve as a visual guide to each Evangelist's unique message. Their words point to the Son of God who is worthy of all praise and honor.

These images are important for us to appreciate as well. Each Evangelist had a unique personality who wrote to a particular people, in their place and time, to carry on the ministry of Jesus for all people, in all places, and for all time. Our calling as believers is to read, study, and believe the words of the Evangelists about the Savior of the world.

John Luke reads and believes the words of Jesus. As the twelfth bearer of the Mantle, he is one of the few people in salvation history who interacts with Jesus in person after the resurrection. Every disciple in history has had a similar experience: following the words of Jesus is both a sacred joy and a secret burden.

Loving Jesus is easy yet challenging because life is imperfect and Jesus is perfect. In the end, good conquers evil, life conquers death, and joy is eternal. God always wins.

That Saturday morning, John Luke and Kristin planned a hike and picnic on a scenic trail not far from their home. They drove to the spot, then walked about three miles on the trail and stopped at a pond. Kristin packed a lunch of sandwiches, fruit, and vegetables. They enjoyed their picnic and time in nature.

They arrived home in the early afternoon feeling refreshed and happy. Kristin then continued with a quilt project, and John Luke asked if she was comfortable with him connecting with Jesus about the construction project at Saint Luke's Motel.

“Of course,” said Kristin. “Please tell Him how much I love being married to an international spy.”

John Luke said with a laugh, “I will be sure to let Him know.”

“Oh,” said Kristin, “please let me know if you go off flying with Jesus.”

“Yes, good point. I will,” said John Luke.

John Luke went to his office, said a prayer, and gently placed the Mantle on his head. Jesus spoke directly to his mind and said, “Happy Saturday, John Luke. I admired the beautiful lunch Kristin packed for you both. More appealing than a few loaves of bread and some fish. You are blessed to have such a special spouse, and you make a great team.”

John Luke said, “I am blessed. And I am sure you heard her comments about being married to a spy?”

Jesus laughed and said, “Humor is a very important element for a happy home. She is right. You are My secret agent of peace. Are you ready for some work with the Mantle?”

John Luke said, “Absolutely.”

Jesus then described a change in the construction plan to discuss with Lucas. “I would like Lucas to finish the first motel room before he moves further into the construction. I want the room to be furnished for a guest soon. We can make a payment to accommodate this shift.”

John Luke said, “I think that makes sense, Jesus. Do You want me to call Lucas or see him in person?”

Jesus responded, "I would like you to see him in person. Allow me to explain some context for you in your conversation with Lucas."

Jesus explained, "We know the Russian president will impede peace. His mind is on the Soviet Union's past glory. He thinks Ukraine is a sovereign territory of Russia, which is why he started the war. We need to place him in that first room as soon as possible to move the peace plan forward. His military leaders fear him, yet they also fear how history will view them if they continue the conflict. They are losing the battle now, as two of the annexed regions, Donetsk and Kherson, were reclaimed by Ukraine."

Jesus continued, "The Russian president cannot tolerate losing face on the world stage. He is also under the control of the Antichrist, Zver. The beast convinced the president that taking Ukraine would be an easy and great victory. We must get the president away from Zver. Once he is in the motel, I will block the beast from contacting him. Zver knows the Mantle exists. Throughout history, I have blocked him from harming the bearers of the Mantle. Presently, Zver has no idea you are God's secret agent of peace."

John Luke said, "Thank You for protecting us, Jesus. The beast sounds rather ominous."

Jesus then appeared in person. "I will protect you and your family. When the Russian president is in the motel room, he will have time to reflect on his behavior. He has free will like everyone else. You will help broker a peace plan with the Archeparch, the

Pope, the Ukrainian president, and Russian military leaders. We will ensure the peace plan becomes public at the appropriate time, and the Russian president will hopefully agree to it once his forty days in the motel are complete. What do you think about the plan, John Luke, and your involvement?"

John Luke said, "I think the idea is great, and I am all in, Jesus."

"Good news!" said Jesus emphatically. "Please let Kristin know we are going to Saint Luke's Motel, and I will help guide the conversation with Lucas to make this change in the plan."

John Luke stepped out of the office and told Kristin he was leaving with Jesus. Kristin smiled and nodded approvingly.

Next, John Luke and Jesus flew to New Mexico and landed invisibly at Saint Luke's Motel near the construction site. Lucas and his crew were busy constructing the building's frame. The motel was securely connected to the main house, and the walls of the first motel room were intact.

He went inside the building and asked Lucas to speak privately. Lucas was surprised to see John Luke. "I did not know you were coming today."

John Luke apologized for the surprise visit and explained the request to finish the first motel room before the building was complete. Lucas was perplexed and hesitated for a while.

Finally, he said, "May I ask why, John Luke? The project is going well, but this change will slow it down. I will need sheet rockers, finish carpenters, an electrician and plumber, the furnishings, and security in place."

John Luke thought for a moment and then explained, "There is an urgent need for a motel guest to be booked in the room as soon as possible for forty days. We will pay you extra funds to complete the first room, while you have additional crew members, continue work on the rest of the building. If you and Paula can find the workers and materials, we will supply the funds to make it work."

Lucas laughed and said, "Why didn't you lead with that news? I have the crew members if you have the money."

On that positive note, Lucas called Paula and explained the request. He told Paula the change order would be covered with the necessary funds. Paula said she would get on the phone and order the supplies. Lucas then called another local crew who would help with the project. All was well.

With the change order in place, John Luke thanked Lucas and left discreetly with Jesus for his home office. When they arrived, Jesus said in person, "Well done. The motel project is now in accordance with the Father's plan. I have more work for you today in Ukraine. Are you up for another project?"

John Luke said, "Of course, Jesus. Just let me tell Kristin. As You promised, my time with the Mantle does not disrupt my time at home."

He then told Kristin about leaving with Jesus to go to Ukraine. This time, Kristin laughed out loud and said, "Have fun with Jesus and be safe!"

Jesus explained to John Luke a plan to advance peace while causing the Russian military to lose face on the world stage. This plan was the next surprise for President Koval.

Jesus said, "The Russians formed a blockade on the Azov seaports of Mariupol, Berdiansk, and Skadovsk, and at the Black Sea port of Kherson. This blockade is hindering the shipment of grain to people in need around the world. The grain is necessary for the daily bread of millions."

Jesus continued, "As I explained with the movement of the aircraft, this work may sound arduous, but you must trust that the Mantle will give you the necessary strength. I ask you to go to Mariupol and remove every Russian naval craft from that seaport and place those ships in the landlocked Caspian Sea. Russian military leaders will need to explain how and why their ships are now located there. The journey from Mariupol to the Caspian Sea is 122 nautical miles. Each round trip will take you less than two seconds at the speed of light."

Jesus paused, waiting for John Luke to digest this information. Then He asked, "Do you understand the mission so far?"

He responded, "Yes, Jesus. It sounds like the movement of the aircraft, except that I will go underwater."

Jesus responded, "Yes, again, know that the Mantle will protect you. The Ukrainian military will be able to recapture Mariupol, and the grain will flow again to countries in need of food. This action will cause turmoil for Russia. The Russian navy has twenty ships and ten submarines surrounding Mariupol. The Mantle will give you the power to lift those ships and place them in the Caspian Sea. The entire operation will take you less than thirty minutes. You will not be seen or harmed. I will be with you."

John Luke said, "I believe and trust in what You say, Jesus. I am ready." Then he added hesitantly, "Jesus, You know that I can't swim."

Jesus smiled and said, "Yes, I know, my dear friend. The Mantle will protect you and help you swim."

John Luke then flew immediately to Mariupol and saw the ships in the Sea of Azov. One by one, he dove into the water, swam under the belly of each warship, lifted it, and flew it to the Caspian Sea. The captains and sailors on the ships were astounded by the events and understandably had no idea what was taking place.

After John Luke moved the twenty warships, Jesus told him where to find the ten submarines. He dove into the water at the points where Jesus directed and lifted each submarine from beneath its hull. He flew each one to the Caspian Sea in seconds. Some of the submarine commanders shouted expletives. Some prayed.

All of them were placed safely in the waters of the Caspian Sea. As Jesus said, the entire operation took John Luke less than thirty minutes, and he arrived home safely to find Jesus waiting in his home office.

Jesus congratulated John Luke again for a job well done. "The Mantle protected you underwater and helped you swim, John Luke. Congratulations as you overcame your fear."

John Luke smiled broadly. “I am so relieved, Jesus. Thank You.”

Jesus said, “I would like you to call President Koval now. As in the past, I will speak to your mind and help guide the conversation.”

He called the president’s private number. The time was about 10:00 PM in Ukraine.

“Mr. President,” said John Luke, “the port of Mariupol is now free of Russian ships. I suggest you move all available forces to take over the port and move any available Ukrainian ships to the Sea of Azov. I also suggest that you call the press and have them send film crews both to Mariupol and the Caspian Sea. The Russian ships from Azov are now inexplicably in the landlocked Caspian Sea. The Russian navy has a lot of explaining to do.”

Jesus laughed at John Luke’s ad-lib. President Koval was taken aback by the news, which had not yet been reported to him or his cabinet. “John Ward, how were you able to accomplish such a maneuver? We had no idea. The port is now free?”

John Luke responded, this time speaking only the words Jesus gave him. “Yes, Mr. President, the port is free. As I said in our last conversation, God had one more work to accomplish to help bring peace to His people in Ukraine. Now that you have trained pilots for the Su-35, I suggest you fly those aircraft over Mariupol for the world to see. This news will hearten the people of Ukraine.”

President Koval responded, "John Ward, you must live right to be such close friends with God. This news is astounding, and again, I am so grateful."

John Luke responded, "Yes, Mr. President, God loves you and your people very much as well." The conversation ended, and the president carried out John Luke's suggestions afterward.

Jesus hugged John Luke, and said He was proud of him. Jesus said, "You have much news to share with Kristin and your dad. Perhaps you could spend time with them, and you might watch the evening news to see the fruits of your labor and experience the joy of the people of Ukraine."

Jesus then quoted Scripture. *"The salvation of the righteous comes from the Lord; he is their stronghold in time of trouble. The Lord helps them and delivers them; he delivers them from the wicked and saves them, because they take refuge in him"* (Psalm 37:39-40). "Remember, John Luke," said Jesus, *"the word of God is alive and active"* (Hebrews 4:12).

Jesus then looked at him and said, "Our work is finished for today. Tomorrow is Sunday, a day of rest and family time. Your work pleases the Father. Enjoy some time off."

John Luke responded, "The good news is I did not drown, and even my clothes are dry using the Mantle."

Jesus smiled and then disappeared.

The next morning, Sunday, John Luke and Kristin met Joan and me at church. We attended Mass, had a cup of coffee, spoke with parishioners, and enjoyed our time together. I excused myself, walked to the car, and retrieved my laptop. By this time, the news about Ukraine and Russia was a constant media headline.

I said to John Luke with a smile, “So you have been busy with the Mantle?”

He said, “Yes, Dad. I knew that I would see you today and have a chance to give you all the details.”

As I opened my laptop, John Luke recounted the amazing events with Jesus. He began with the trip to Saint Luke’s and the details about the first motel room. He explained that the Russian president will be a guest at the motel soon. Then he shared the information about moving the warships and submarines to the landlocked Caspian Sea. The level of detail in Jesus’s plan astounded all of us.

When he finished telling us the specifics, I said, “God’s ways are not our ways. The most stunning fact for me was how Jesus used Scripture to help explain the plan to you.”

John Luke said, “Dad, the most amazing fact for me was that I did not drown in the Sea of Azov.”

Joan and Kristin nearly spit out their coffee as they laughed heartily. Our young man has such a good nature.

That afternoon, as Kristin was catching up on work, John Luke went to his office, said a prayer, placed the Mantle gently on his head, and Jesus appeared in his mind.

“Hello, John Luke,” said Jesus. “I thought you would be relaxing today.”

He said, "Jesus, I did not want to trouble You. I want to tell You how much I love and appreciate You. I thought of You today at church, of course. Yet speaking with You and using the Mantle changed my life for the better. I am happier, and my confidence has increased greatly. You changed my life in the most positive ways. I want to thank You."

Jesus then appeared visibly to John Luke. He gave him a warm hug and said, "You are never any trouble. You are My brother and My friend. I am always here for you. Remember, you are the apple of My eye."

John Luke said, "And You are the apple of mine."

Jesus smiled and said, "Is there anything else you want to talk about?"

He said, "Not today, Jesus. I look forward to seeing You soon."

"And I, you, John Luke," said Jesus. Then He disappeared, for now.

Chapter 12:

The Russian President

"Before me was a great multitude that no one could count, from every nation, tribe, people and language, standing before the throne and before the Lamb. They were wearing white robes and were holding palm branches in their hands. And they cried out in a loud voice: 'Salvation belongs to our God, who sits on the throne, and to the Lamb'" (Revelation 7:9-10).

When Jesus appeared visibly before me in the first book of *The Mantle*, He wore a plain brown robe with brown sandals. I did not ask Jesus why He wore brown clothing, but I thought it might symbolize what He wore during His ministry on Earth. In Jesus' time, only rabbis who strictly interpreted the law wore white, such as the Essenes, who generally lived in monastic communities.

White robes in that period underwent an expensive bleaching process, making the wearer stand out as significant and wealthy. Jesus of Nazareth, a rabbi of humble means, most likely wore a brown or tan-colored robe made of wool or linen. His stately appearance and authoritative words made Jesus significant.

When Jesus appeared to John Luke wearing a white robe, gold sash, and bronze sandals, He resembled the image in the Book of Revelation *(1:13)*. I sensed that this obvious shift had meaning in

God's plan for the world. The other time in Scripture when Jesus wears white is at the Transfiguration, when He appears in white with Moses and Elijah *(Matthew 17:2)*.

The color white symbolizes sinlessness and heavenly purity. The 144,000 souls saved first at the end of days *(Revelation 7:9)* wear white robes as well. Jesus can obviously wear anything He wants. Yet in this story, He appears to deliver a message through a white robe and gold sash, perhaps symbolizing His glory and a time of purification for the world. Salvation is at hand.

This salvation is realized through God's plan, delivered by Jesus and carried out with assistance from John Luke, bearer number twelve of the Mantle.

Over the next few days, the Russians disseminated propaganda about recent events to the international press. Official statements from the Kremlin attributed the loss of treasury funds to the activities of Ukrainian mobsters and the incompetence of the Russian Central Bank's leaders, who suddenly "retired."

The loss of the Su-35 aircraft was blamed on Australian security management forces unlawfully hired by the Ukrainians and illegally fighting in sovereign Russian territory. Russia made no mention of the recapture of Donetsk, Kherson, or the port of Mariupol.

The most outrageous explanation concerned Russian Navy warships and submarines inexplicably appearing in the Caspian Sea, the world's largest landlocked lake, bordering Kazakhstan, Russia, Azerbaijan, Iran, and Turkmenistan. Without mentioning how the ships were transported to a landlocked lake, the Russians said the ships were placed there to thwart a secretly planned Ukrainian invasion of Kazakhstan.

Despite Russian propaganda, the press showed photos and videos of Su-35 aircraft flown by Ukrainian pilots, joyful celebrations of the people of Donetsk, Kherson, and Mariupol, the victorious Australian private military forces thwarting the Russian army and recapturing Ukrainian territory each day, and Russian warships appearing to float aimlessly in the Caspian Sea.

These events humiliated and infuriated the Russian president. At the command of the Russian oligarch Mikhail Andropov, the Antichrist, or Zver, dismissed the top Russian military leader and replaced him with executives from the Wagner Group, a paramilitary organization. Russia was in turmoil.

As Jesus expected, Zver was infuriated by God's plan to bring peace to Ukraine. He railed against God and took out his anger on the Russian president, calling him weak and useless and threatening to overthrow his presidency. Zver even plotted against Jesus and cursed the Mantle in a tirade aimed at heaven. He threatened to find Number Twelve and destroy him.

Jesus ignored the beast's threats and continued to carry out the Father's will. John Luke's identity was secure, and he was safe through the power of Jesus.

Meanwhile, at Saint Luke's Motel in Saint Theresa, the work in the first room was nearing completion. Lucas called John Luke and said the room would be ready by the weekend. That Friday,

John Luke returned home from Boston, had dinner with Kristin, and asked whether she agreed with his plan to use the Mantle that evening to speak with Jesus.

Kristin said, "Of course, and thank you for asking me, John Luke."

John Luke went to his office, said a prayer, and gently placed the Mantle on his head.

Jesus appeared in his mind instantly and said, "John Luke, you must be tired from your long day, including your commute on the train."

John Luke said, "I am tired, Jesus, yet I always look forward to being with You. Besides, I caught the early train and worked on my laptop. I am grateful for Wi-Fi. I want to tell You that Lucas called, and the motel room is ready."

Jesus said, "That is good news. After you get a good night's sleep, let's meet in the morning when you are ready, and we will carry out the next steps of God's plan."

John Luke said, "That sounds great, Jesus, and I will meet You shortly after breakfast."

Jesus said, "Sleep well, good and faithful servant." He removed the Mantle and went to bed early.

The next day, John Luke and Kristin had a leisurely breakfast on their deck in the glorious morning sun. Their deck was well constructed and located off the dining room, overlooking their spacious, tree-lined backyard. They were happy to be together and still acted like newlyweds.

They cleared the table and washed the dishes as John Luke told Kristin the plan to meet with Jesus. Kristin went to her office on the first floor to catch up on work, and John Luke went upstairs to his office.

As usual, he said a prayer and placed the Mantle gently on his head. Jesus appeared and sat in the office chair across from John Luke. Jesus appeared wearing His glorious resurrection clothes. John Luke was glad to see Him.

Jesus smiled.

"Good morning, John Luke. I would like you to go to Moscow and take the Russian president to the motel. His room is prepared for the next forty days. The room is secured with the technology that Kristin selected. In the room is a closet with clothing for him to wear. The refrigerator has been stocked with meals for him for seven days. Once a week, for one hour, we will remove him from the room. The president will not know where he is located. The staff at Saint Luke's will clean his room, replace his clothing, and provide an additional week of meals in the refrigerator. His room contains reading materials, including the Bible in Russian."

John Luke said, "Those details are ingenious, Jesus."

Jesus continued, "Thank you, my friend. I left the president a letter explaining why he is in the motel and encouraging him to repent and submit to God's plan for his life. The rest is up to him. He has free will. At the end of his stay, we will bring him back to Moscow, where the peace accord will be ready for his signature."

John Luke asked, "What if he does not repent, Jesus?"

Jesus responded, “That matter is in the hands of the Father. I am doing His will, and you are following that will. I also want you to know the Antichrist does not know what is to take place. He will be infuriated and seek revenge. Yet he will not know the president’s location or your identity. You are both safe. Zver will be unable to contact him.”

Jesus continued, “After you bring the president to the motel, I ask that you return to your office, as I will be waiting for you and give you more information about the plan for peace. Are you ready, John Luke?”

John Luke said, “Yes, Lord, I am ready.” With those words, John Luke flew to Moscow.

Russian President Ivan Petrovich, age 72, was born in Saint Petersburg and served as a longtime intelligence officer for the Soviet Union. He began his career in the Soviet Army. He rose to the rank of colonel and was stationed in East Berlin, where he earned the nickname “Ivan the Terrible” because of his inhumane treatment of perceived anti-communists.

He joined the *Komitet Gosudarstvennoy Bezopasnosti*, or the dreaded KGB, in 1988 before the fall of the Berlin Wall. He was promoted to Director of the Federal Security Service (FSB) and served in the cabinet of Russian President Boris Yeltsin.

When President Yeltsin died in 2007, Petrovich became prime minister. After serving as prime minister for six years, he became president. Four years later, he appointed himself president for life.

Shortly afterward, the Antichrist, Zver, invited Petrovich to a party at his mansion, where the beast influenced his mind with exorbitant gifts and promises of unlimited power, including the reunification of the Soviet Union. Petrovich became ruthless and seemingly devoid of conscience. He took directions from Zver in every decision of his presidency.

John Luke arrived at the Grand Kremlin Palace at 7:00 PM. Petrovich had just finished dinner and was back in his office, looking nervously out the window overlooking Red Square and the beautiful Russian Orthodox church, Saint Basil's Cathedral.

Petrovich is an avowed atheist and dismisses all religious teaching as "mythology." Recent events weighed heavily on his mind. Zver's words that he was "weak and useless" stung him to the core. If the beast no longer believed in him, nothing seemed left. The president felt empty and was at a breaking point.

Jesus had compassion on the president and asked John Luke to walk behind Petrovich, place his hand on his head, and offer a prayer for his salvation. John Luke did as Jesus asked.

The president was now invisible and sensed that a force of goodness was upon him. He tried to fight off whatever had hold of him, but to no avail. The president shuddered, his shoulders slumped, and an evil spirit left him.

John Luke took the president by the arm and immediately flew him to the motel room. He placed President Petrovich before the desk where Jesus had left the letter for him, with the Russian Bible. The envelope read, "For My son, Ivan Andrei Petrovich."

John Luke left and returned to his home office, where Jesus was waiting.

Jesus said, "Well done, John Luke. Ivan Andrei will soon read the note, and his journey toward redemption may begin. I ask that you and Kristin pray for his soul. He is desperate and needs prayer."

John Luke said, "Of course, Jesus. We will pray for him."

Jesus then told him the next steps in the Father's plan. He asked John Luke to call the Ukrainian Greek Catholic Church Archeparch, Stanislaus Medwit, on Sunday afternoon.

"I would like you to ask the Archeparch to contact Pope Paul VII in Rome. Ask him to establish a private meeting at the Vatican with you and the Archeparch. The Pope is expecting the call, as I appeared to him in a dream. I told him of God's plan for peace in Ukraine. I also told the Pope of the Antichrist's actions in the world and his grip on the Russian president. The Pope will gladly set up the meeting."

Jesus then said, "For the Antichrist to remain unaware of the meeting, I ask you to bring the Archeparch to the Vatican using the Mantle. The Archeparch will not understand at first, and I will guide you. Yet the Pope will understand and know you as John Ward, the twelfth bearer of the Mantle."

"When you arrive at the Vatican, I will open the Archeparch's mind to understand the power of the Mantle. Once that meeting takes place, the Pope will conduct a private meeting with

Ukrainian President Koval and provide details of the Father's plan that is unfolding."

Jesus continued, "Very soon, the Australian military contractor will join forces with the Ukrainian military and recapture the last 2 annexed territories, expelling the Russian army and the Vagner Group paramilitary soldiers. We will use the Mantle to free the captured seaport Kherson in the Black Sea during the same period. Ukraine will take control of the seaport, and that action will force the Russian military to consider a ceasefire."

"I will block the Antichrist from trying to control the outcome. God's plan is moving forward, and you are a trustworthy servant, John Luke. Our work is done for today."

Jesus added, "I would like to meet with you tomorrow, after church, so that we can discuss the call with the Archeparch. News will leak soon that President Petrovich is missing. The Russians will claim he is on vacation, yet rumors will spread about his absence, and some will claim he is dead. All this activity is in accordance with the Father's plan. The forty days will pass, and the president will reappear in the Kremlin. Time will tell of his disposition."

John Luke sensed the gravity of this plan for peace and his own role. This work seemed far bigger, on a world stage, than he ever thought possible.

John Luke smiled at Jesus and said, "Thank You for using me to bring peace to God's people. I will do as You ask."

Jesus responded to John Luke's thoughts and said lovingly, "I know this work seems daunting. I appreciate that you trust Me. I promise that all will be well."

When John Luke seemed more settled, Jesus hugged him goodbye and left. He went to Kristin's office and shared all this news. Then John Luke called me, and again I took careful notes of the latest work for the Mantle history book.

Chapter 13:

Motel Room One

"When he opened the seventh seal, there was silence in heaven for about half an hour" (Revelation 8:1).

In the Book of Revelation, the opening of the seventh seal brings a profound silence in heaven before the judgments of God unfold. These judgments, symbolized by the trumpets and bowls that follow, fall upon those who bring evil upon God's people. For many Christians, the seals represent the gradual unveiling of divine justice in human history.

Soon, the evil plans of Russia against Ukraine would encounter that justice. The Russian president would experience a different kind of silence, one meant not for destruction, but for repentance.

In motel room one, Ivan Andrei Petrovich was deeply perturbed to find himself in this locked room. He tried the door, and it was locked from the outside. The room had skylights and windows, yet none of them opened.

Petrovich felt a rising unease. Something was very wrong.

The president saw the envelope on the desk addressed to him. He sensed that whatever power had taken hold of him in the palace was responsible for the letter. The letter was written in Russian in cursive.

Number 12

Dear Ivan Andrei, I am writing this letter in the name given to you by your parents at your baptism long ago at the Church of the Savior in Saint Petersburg. You may recall that your mother named you after your two grandfathers, good men who worshiped Me. I am Jesus Christ, the Savior of the world, writing this letter in My own hand. Through this letter, I exhort you to bring peace to the people of Ukraine and Russia. The war will be lost while you are in this room for the next forty days. I chose this time of repentance for you purposefully to mirror My time in the desert at the beginning of My ministry on Earth. As you look around this room, you will find all that you need to experience new life.

During these forty days, you will have no visitors and time to reflect on your behavior and life. Not even the Antichrist, whom you know as Mikhail Andropov, will be able to contact you. However, I will be with you during this time. You may speak to Me anytime as a brother, a friend, and your salvation.

Somewhere along your life's journey, you denied your faith, and your life went out of control. You began to devalue human life. I am not angry with you, Ivan Andrei, yet I abhor sinful behavior and harmful decisions. I also know the Antichrist influenced you greatly. You now have a choice to live a life in Me. The Antichrist had hold of your mind, but not your soul, at least not yet.

When you leave this room, you will be taken to the palace. You will be asked to ratify a peace pact with Ukraine. That pact will soon be finished. You will again have a choice to do what is right and noble as a leader of God's people in Russia. Your legacy may be one of conversion and righteousness. We both know how you should choose.

Your friend,

Jesus of Nazareth

As Ivan Andrei finished reading the letter, tears welled in his eyes. He wiped them away and whispered, "This letter cannot be real."

He sank into a chair and sat in silence, thinking for a long time about his life- his choices, his actions, and his family.

Jesus saw his anguish and took pity on him.

At last, exhaustion overcame him. Ivan Andrei closed his eyes and drifted into a deep, peaceful sleep that lasted until morning.

Chapter 14:

Hail to the Peace

"Worthy is the Lamb, who was slain, to receive power and wealth and wisdom and strength and honor and glory and praise!" (Revelation 5:12).

The Old Testament records the sacred preparation of the Passover lamb, a ritual that commemorated the Israelites' deliverance from bondage in Egypt. It stood as a lasting reminder of God's power to free His people from slavery.

In the Gospel of John, John the Baptist reveals the deeper meaning of this symbol when he proclaims Jesus as *"the Lamb of God, who takes away the sins of the world"* (John 1:29). The Book of Revelation states that the angels of heaven declare that Jesus alone, through His sinless life and sacrificial death, has the authority to redeem humanity. All of heaven proclaims the glory of the Lamb of God.

Once again, God is moving to deliver His people. He is preparing to lead Ukraine out of the oppression of the Russian army and its president.

I do not believe there was merely a time of miracles. I believe there is a God of miracles, one who still acts, speaks, and intervenes, bringing salvation and hope to His people in every generation.

On Sunday afternoon, Ukraine time, John Luke did as Jesus instructed and called Archeparch Stanislaus Medwit. The Archeparch was not entirely surprised to hear from him.

He said, "John Ward, you have been a busy man. I may assume you are behind the joy of the people of Ukraine and the confusion of the Russians. To what do I owe the honor of this phone call?"

Speaking in flawless Ukrainian, John Luke replied, "Good afternoon, Your Eminence. I am calling to request a great favor. I ask that you arrange a meeting with His Holiness Pope Paul VII in Rome next week. This meeting must remain confidential, as powerful forces would seek to prevent it. For security reasons, I also ask that you travel with me to the Vatican. I will ensure swift and safe passage. The purpose of this meeting is to draft a peace pact between Russia and Ukraine to bring an end to the war."

There was a long pause.

At last, the Archeparch said, his voice measured, "I sense this request carries more than political weight. I will do as you ask and arrange the meeting. I will contact you with the date and time, allowing for the necessary travel time."

John Luke smiled at the thought of "travel time" and thanked the Archeparch for his willingness to arrange the meeting. The call ended, and John Luke thought of meeting with Jesus.

John Luke said a quiet prayer of thanksgiving, then gently placed the Mantle upon his head. At once, Jesus spoke to his mind.

"Congratulations on your call with Archeparch Medwit. You did well, John Luke."

"Thank You, Jesus," John Luke replied. "May I ask for Your guidance regarding the meeting with the Archeparch and the Pope? I do not want to presume anything. Please be with me in this work. I truly do not know where to begin with the peace pact."

"Of course," Jesus said. "I will be with you at every step. Pope Paul VII will be a great support in this process. Do not be anxious, John Luke. All will be well."

Jesus continued, "I would like you to complete one more task today. The Australian military contractors are advancing in the final two annexed regions, Luhansk and Zaporizhzhia. Your faith has strengthened President Koval, who has been praying to the Father for success in this mission. I intend to answer his prayers through the Mantle.

"I ask that you go to these areas in the Donbas region, near the Russian border and the city of Mariupol. It is nearly 11 PM in Ukraine. A miracle will take place, and you will learn a new power of the Mantle."

The thought of a new power stirred John Luke's wonder. Whatever was about to unfold would come not from his strength, but from his growing trust in Jesus.

"Of course, Jesus," he said. "What would You like me to do?"

"Fly to the seaport of Mariupol," Jesus said. "Once you arrive, I will give you further instructions. Thank you for doing this work."

John Luke flew to Mariupol and landed near the now-liberated seaport docks. Jesus instructed him to fly low over the Sea of Azov. John Luke felt Jesus's presence intensely, so close that His strong, steady hands seemed to guide his own.

Jesus instructed him to fly faster over the sea, first in tight circles, then in wider circles.

John Luke obeyed, flying in tight circles just above the water, then gradually widening his path. As he did, something extraordinary began to happen. A vast volume of water lifted from the sea behind him, drawn upward into the air and forming a powerful, flowing stream.

It became an atmospheric river, a long, narrow corridor of concentrated moisture transporting immense amounts of water vapor. When such a river makes landfall, it releases that moisture in life-giving rain.

John Luke watched in awe as the sea responded, rising to follow him and reshaped by a force not of nature alone but with a divine purpose.

Jesus spoke into John Luke's mind. "Fly higher, John Luke. Keep your circles tight, and the atmospheric river will follow you. Then move toward the battle area near Donetsk. You will see the Russian army there with dozens of tanks and combat utility vehicles."

John Luke rose, the sky opening before him as the vast river of moisture followed his path like a living force. When he reached the battlefield, Jesus spoke again.

"Now command the atmospheric river to descend. Let it fall upon the ground and flood the path of the vehicles. You are controlling the weather."

John Luke hovered above the scene, mesmerized by the words of Jesus, and said out loud, "Atmospheric River, I command you to fall to the ground now on top of these vehicles."

A great roar filled the air as the atmospheric river crashed down, flooding the terrain and washing out the paths beneath the vehicles. Mud and water surged forward, forcing the soldiers to leap from their tanks and vehicles and abandon them in panic to avoid being swept away.

Once the Russian soldiers had fled, Jesus instructed John Luke to fly over the immobilized tanks and vehicles, keeping his formation tight.

Then Jesus said, "Fly faster and higher. The water will rise again and follow you, forming another atmospheric river."

John Luke obeyed, lifting into the sky as the soaked Earth responded once more and the waters gathered and rose behind him. When he looked down again, the ground below was suddenly dry. Australian military contractors surged forward, capturing thousands of stunned Russian soldiers.

Right on cue, hundreds of Ukrainian troops rushed in from their positions and commandeered the abandoned Russian vehicles. The battle ended in a decisive victory for Ukraine and the Australian contractors.

Then Jesus spoke again. "Fly now to the battlefield at Luhansk, at the speed of light. The atmospheric river will follow you."

John Luke did as Jesus commanded. As he looked down, a fierce skirmish unfolded in the darkness. More than two thousand Vagnera contractors, wearing night-vision goggles, fired automatic weapons at the Australian positions. At the same time, two dozen Russian Kinzhal missiles streaked through the sky toward the contractors below.

Jesus directed John Luke. "Fly now to 35,000 feet. There, the atmospheric river will take on forms of ice and slush."

The river continued to trail behind him as he climbed. Then Jesus instructed him to turn back toward the battlefield and pass slowly over the Vagnera soldiers below.

"Now," Jesus said, "command the atmospheric river to release hail upon them."

John Luke spoke with steady authority. "Atmospheric River, drop hail upon these troops."

At once, the sky answered. Ice and slush crashed down in a violent cascade. The soldiers scrambled for cover as the hailstorm pinned them in place. As the hail struck their arms and hands, the Vagnera paramilitary fighters lost their grip and dropped their assault rifles, fleeing the field.

Then Jesus instructed John Luke to fly low over the Russian missiles and command the river once more to drench the soldiers with freezing rain and bury the missiles beneath heavy mounds of slush.

John Luke followed Jesus's instructions. Russian soldiers abandoned their positions and ran for cover as the missiles were silenced, jammed beneath heavy mounds of slush and ice.

Australian contractors surged forward, capturing the stunned Vagnera paramilitary fighters. Once again, Ukrainian soldiers advanced from their positions, taking custody of the frightened, near-frozen Russian troops and securing the missile equipment.

Then Jesus spoke with calm authority. "John Luke, one final work remains. Fly now to ten thousand feet, then move swiftly in tight circles. Command the wind to encircle the missiles."

John Luke commanded the wind. "Great wind, encircle the missiles and carry the ice and slush away behind me." The wind obeyed.

The ice and slush lifted gently into the air and streamed after him as he flew. The missiles were left intact, now valuable spoils of war for the Ukrainian army. Once again, the battle ended in a decisive and inexplicable victory for Ukraine's freedom.

As the storm dissolved beneath him, John Luke breathed slowly and deeply, amazed by the magnitude of what had been entrusted to him. Gratitude welled up quietly, gratitude for protection, for purpose, for the mercy woven through power.

Then Jesus spoke into his mind, calm and affirming. "Well done, good and faithful servant. Come home now at the speed of light, and we will speak in your office."

John Luke arrived home in seconds, where Jesus was already waiting for him.

Eyes wide and voice filled with excitement, John Luke said, "Jesus, that was incredible. I know our work has a serious purpose, but that was so exciting. Thank You for using me in this way."

Jesus laughed. "I am the original weatherman," He said, smiling. "And you are My disciple."

The next morning, international media outlets reported the "acts of God" that had unfolded overnight in the battles for the Donbas. One commentator compared the events to the account in the Hebrew Scriptures from Joshua *(10:11–15)*, where the Lord sent hail from heaven to defeat the Amorites and secure victory for Israel.

President Koval soon held a press conference declaring that God had answered his prayers and stood on the side of peace for the Ukrainian people. Nearly every major news channel aired interviews with Australian military contractors who gave firsthand accounts of the miraculous weather events that brought opposing forces to their knees. Reporters emphasized that the storms harmed neither Australian nor Ukrainian soldiers.

Russian military leaders were left stunned. From Moscow, there was no official response, only silence.

That morning, John Luke and Kristin sat on their couch with coffee, watching the news together. After moving into their new home, they adopted two older pets from the local shelter: a handsome tan dog named Tanner and a beautiful gray cat with a white mustache named Zoey. John Luke had nicknamed Tanner

"Dr. Dog" because he was clever, followed him everywhere, and seemed to enjoy watching him work.

As the news played, John Luke petted Dr. Dog while Kristin cradled Zoey in her lap. A deep sense of joy and relief for Ukraine settled over them.

Kristin turned toward John Luke, kissed him warmly, and said, "I am so proud to be married to God's superhero."

John Luke blushed. Even the animals seemed content, as if they too sensed that something good had happened in the world.

Chapter 15:

God at the Center

"Never again will they hunger; never again will they thirst. The sun will not beat down on them, nor any scorching heat. For the Lamb at the center of the throne will be their shepherd; he will lead them to springs of living water. And God will wipe away every tear from their eyes" (Revelation 7:16–17).

Like the promise revealed in the Book of Revelation, the people of Ukraine entered a season of joy and freedom they had not known for years. God wiped the tears from their eyes, and new life began.

Though minor skirmishes still flared in isolated areas, citizens who had long hidden in cellars and subway tunnels stepped once more into the light. Ukrainian soldiers and public workers began rebuilding war-torn communities. Food, water, and utilities returned, and with them a renewed sense of normal life.

Hope burned brightly across cities and countryside alike. In town squares once marked by fear, Ukrainian flags flew proudly again, signs not only of restored sovereignty, but of a people standing upright once more, shepherded toward peace.

Though Ukraine has long been a nation of believers, attendance at churches, temples, and mosques surged to historic levels. Worship moved to the center of public life. Religious leaders repaired damaged buildings and reopened sanctuaries with support from government funds and private donations, including contributions from The Mantle, LLC, resources given quietly, without recognition, and directed toward healing rather than acclaim.

Even President Koval attended services at the Great Choral Synagogue in Kyiv. In the aftermath of what many called the "victory of the weather," the Donbas battles won by wind, hail, snow, and slush, the nation embraced a shared conviction that God had been with them. Few understood how that help had come, or through whom, but the effects were unmistakable.

John Luke, the servant who carried out Jesus's work, watched with satisfaction, content to remain hidden. Faith had done what power could not. As Scripture says, *"Now faith is confidence in what we hope for and assurance about what we do not see"* (Hebrews 11:1).

The Ukrainian armed forces regained control of the 4 seaports previously seized by the Russians. Reinforced by captured Russian equipment, Ukrainian positions pushed the Russian army and the Vagnera paramilitary steadily back toward the Russian border. The navy and air force, now flying Su-35 warplanes, destroyed dozens of Russian naval vessels and aircraft. Thousands of Vagnera fighters and Russian troops were held in makeshift prisoner-of-war camps.

The captured Kinzhal hypersonic missiles were turned against Russian launch sites with success. The war was ending, and everyone knew it, including the Russian military.

Perhaps everyone except the Russian oligarch Mikhail Andropov, the Antichrist known as Zver. Despite his furious protests, Vagnera Group executives resigned their cabinet posts in the Russian government. They told Zver plainly that the war was over and that they were leaving.

Zver screamed in rage, "The war is not over until I say it is over!"

But his fury no longer carried power. The executives walked out of the Kremlin, leaving the beast alone with his denial.

Russia was now without a president for twenty days. Rumors flooded the international press. Some claimed the Ukrainians had captured President Petrovich. Others insisted he was dead. Few believed the Kremlin's claim that he was merely on vacation. Zver raged at this uncertainty, incensed that he did not know Petrovich's whereabouts.

On the twenty-first night of his confinement, near midnight, unable to sleep, President Petrovich rose from his bed and hesitantly opened the Russian Bible Jesus had left in the room. He turned to the beginning of the New Testament, the Gospel of Matthew, and began reading chapter two, the account of the Magi visiting the Messiah.

When he reached the passage describing Herod's order to kill the boys under the age of two in Bethlehem, his heart sank. A terrible clarity seized him. He saw himself in Herod, furious, threatened, and willing to destroy the innocent to preserve power.

Tears filled the president's eyes. His voice broke as he cried out into the silence, "What is happening to me? Jesus, what have You done to me? If You are real let me see You. Speak to me!"

Jesus appeared in person, seated across from Petrovich in the room's small office area. He wore a gleaming white robe, a golden sash at His waist, and bronze sandals that seemed to glow warmly rather than with fire.

Jesus spoke first. "Peace be with you, Ivan Andrei. You asked to see Me, and I am here."

Petrovich stared at Him, his voice unsteady. "I must be dreaming or losing my mind. This cannot be happening."

"I am real," Jesus replied gently. "And I am always with you."

Then Jesus quoted from the Gospel of John (20:26–27). Extending His hands toward Petrovich, He said, *"Put your finger here. See My hands. Reach out your hand and place it in My side. Stop doubting and believe*, Ivan Andrei. I am real."

The Russian president wanted to believe. Yet everything in his life, his training, his power, and his carefully constructed certainty, told him that God did not exist and that faith was nothing more than myth.

"This was a mistake," the president said, turning away. "I am not ready for this. Please leave me alone."

Jesus did not rebuke him. He answered quietly, "As you wish, Ivan Andrei. But you should know the war with Ukraine is nearing its end. God's plan for peace is unfolding. The Russian military is close to defeat. You have nineteen days remaining to decide whether you will believe in Me and become the leader your people want and need. When you are ready, call to Me, and I will answer."

Jesus disappeared, and the Russian president, exhausted and shaken, fell into a deep, peaceful sleep.

That Sunday, Jesus appeared on a battlefield near the Ukrainian city of Luhansk, one of the last Russian strongholds.

Soldiers later recounted that, at dawn, a glowing white figure walked calmly across the scarred field toward the Russian lines. Gunfire had been erupting between Russian forces, Ukrainian troops, and Australian military contractors.

Then, suddenly, the firing stopped.

Through the smoke and morning haze, the figure continued forward without fear. Jesus stood before hundreds of Russian soldiers, clothed in a radiant white robe, a golden sash across His chest, and bronze sandals that seemed to glow beneath Him.

He climbed atop a tank.

No one moved. No one spoke.

His presence alone commanded silence.

Speaking to them in Russian, He told them of the love of God, the power of forgiveness, and the call to choose peace over destruction. He urged the soldiers to return home to their families before more blood was shed.

The battlefield remained utterly still as His words settled over them.

One by one, the soldiers lowered their weapons.

Then, without another shot being fired, they turned and began the long journey back toward Russia.

When reports of Jesus appearing before soldiers reached the international press, Russian military leaders grew fearful. Intelligence confirmed that hundreds of Russian soldiers had abandoned their positions and were returning home. A grim realization took hold: they were losing the war because they were fighting against God.

Senior commanders in the Kremlin convened a secret meeting, without Zver, to discuss ending the conflict. They began drafting a peace framework when Zver, alerted by one of his spies, burst into the room in fury, shouting expletives.

For several minutes, Zver raged uncontrollably, pounding his fist on the conference table and demanding that all talk of peace cease. He ordered them to find more soldiers and continue the fight. Despite the Antichrist's blood-curdling threats, the commanders refused. Each one spoke openly of peace in Ukraine.

The chief strategist of the Russian military was Sergei Orlov, Chief of the General Staff, known among his peers as "General Armageddon." Zver turned his fury on Orlov, exhorting him to press on. Orlov had never disobeyed an order. He had never retreated from a fight.

This time, he rose from his chair.

Leaning forward across the table, he looked directly at the oligarch and said calmly, *"Нужно понимать, когда пора сдаваться."* You have to know when it is time to quit.

Then General Orlov turned to the assembled commanders and ordered them to prepare plans for a ceasefire to take effect within 48 hours.

The day after news broke of Jesus's appearance in Luhansk, churches across the city united to hold a prayer service in Dilyanka Tuspova Square. At the center of the square, honoring the faiths of all Ukrainians, the Archbishop of Luhansk erected a golden throne, its seat deliberately empty.

The empty chair spoke louder than words, proclaiming that no Earthly ruler, no army, and no ideology occupied the highest place. The throne belonged to God alone, sovereign over all. Standing before the gathered crowd, the archbishop exhorted the people to recognize that the God of all nations reigned as Ukraine's true protector and provider.

Thousands of believers, Christians, Jews, and Muslims lifted their voices together in prayer and thanksgiving. Around the empty throne, faith found a shared language, and a wounded nation remembered who truly sat at the center of its hope.

That same day, John Luke met with Archeparch Medwit in Kyiv. The Archeparch was astonished and jubilant at the miracles unfolding across Ukraine.

"John Ward," he said, "these wonders from the hand of God are truly of biblical proportion. I know you are involved in what has taken place. I am deeply grateful, and I am amazed by how God chooses to work through you."

John Ward replied quietly, "Your Excellency, I am only a grateful servant, just as you are. I ask you to trust me once more. We must go to the Vatican to meet the Pope, and you are about to witness another miracle."

John Luke reached into his attaché case and removed the ornate box that held the Mantle. He said a brief prayer in flawless Ukrainian, gently placed the Mantle on his head, took hold of Archeparch Medwit's hand, and instantly they stood in the office of Pope Paul VII, in the Apostolic Palace at the Vatican.

The Pope was alone, waiting for them.

When John Luke released the Archeparch's hand, he was stunned. "John Ward," he said, struggling to comprehend what had happened, "I do not understand. How did we get here?"

Then he looked up and saw the Pope. "Your Holiness, please forgive me," the Archeparch said, visibly shaken. "I am confused. One moment we were in my office, and now we stand before you."

Pope Paul VII did not appear surprised. He smiled gently, as if confirming something long discerned rather than newly discovered. Rising from his chair, he embraced the Archeparch and said quietly, "You are exactly where you are meant to be."

He then gestured toward the conference table. "Please," the Pope said, "let us sit. The work ahead of us is important, and heaven has been generous in bringing us together."

The Pope turned to Archeparch Medwit and said, "You have just witnessed the power behind the recent movements toward peace in the world. John Ward is the twelfth bearer of the Mantle of Jesus, a miraculous relic from the empty tomb of our Lord at the resurrection. Do not be afraid. God stands behind everything John Ward has done for Ukraine. Yet the existence of the Mantle, and John Ward's identity, must remain secret, just as Jesus instructed me in a recent dream."

Then, with gentle calm, the Pope added, "Please have a cup of tea and steady yourself. Time is short. I have reason to believe the Russians will soon call for a ceasefire."

He did not explain how he knew.

Pope Paul VII then presented them with a draft of a peace treaty to be delivered to President Koval. A small group of clergy and lay advisers from the Roman Curia prepared the document, working under the Pope's direct counsel. At the bottom were two signature lines, one for President Koval and one for President Petrovich.

The Pope looked at them calmly and said, "I am told that President Petrovich will be present soon to sign this document."

Once again, he offered no explanation for how he knew.

The Pope said, "The document calls for the peaceful withdrawal of all Russian troops from Ukraine immediately after the date of the signatures. The United Nations will coordinate the withdrawal with a security team. Further, the United States and Russia will coordinate the payment of reparations to Ukraine to rebuild from the war. The United States is aware that the Russian treasury is diminished." The Pope paused after this sentence and looked at John Luke.

He continued, "We know time is of the essence to rebuild Ukraine and provide food, water, electricity, and housing for the people. Several countries from the United Nations will help support the financial effort as well, including the Vatican."

When the men finished reviewing the document, Pope Paul VII handed a copy to John Luke. "I trust you will see that President Koval reviews this and suggests any necessary changes," he said. "I will ensure that the Russian president examines the document at the appropriate time."

Turning then to Archeparch Medwit, the Pope added, "I would like you to remain here at the Vatican for the next few days as my guest. The world needs to see our united effort for peace. If you agree, I will have your personal belongings brought from Kyiv at once. We might spend time together and strengthen the bonds between our churches."

Archeparch Medwit's face lit up. He accepted the invitation with gratitude and joy.

All was well at the Vatican.

John Luke returned to his home office, where Jesus was waiting for him in person. John Luke excitedly recounted everything that had taken place. Jesus smiled and listened, then said the time was right for John Luke to contact President Koval and arrange a meeting to present the draft peace treaty. He also told him that General Orlov had already called President Koval and established an immediate seven-day ceasefire to allow negotiations to begin.

Jesus then added, "Today is day thirty-three of President Petrovich's retreat. I want to meet with you once I hear from him."

"Of course, Jesus," John Luke replied. "I will wait to hear from You."

Jesus smiled. "I am with you always. I will leave the call with President Koval to you. And do not forget to release the remaining funds to the Australian military contractors. Their work has been invaluable."

Jesus disappeared, and John Luke called President Koval to arrange a meeting for the following day at 4:00 PM, over tea. He then contacted Melbourne and authorized the wire transfer of the remaining €75 billion from the Swiss National Bank. For John Luke, it was just another day at the office with the Mantle.

The next day, as John Ward, he met President Koval in his office and presented the draft peace treaty. The president said he would review the document with his cabinet and follow up with Pope Paul VII.

Rising from his chair, President Koval spoke with deep sincerity. "John Ward, you are always welcome in Ukraine. I wish we could honor you publicly, but I understand the need for your confidentiality. Please know this. Whatever history records, you are a hero in our eyes."

The men embraced warmly. Then John Luke departed the office and, unseen, returned home, his work once again complete and his name destined to remain unknown.

On the thirty-third night in the motel, President Petrovich finally called out to Jesus in prayer. Jesus found him on his knees, weeping. His presence entered the room as a soft white glow, filling the space with peace. Jesus walked to Ivan Andrei and held out His hand, lifting the president gently to his feet.

Before Ivan Andrei could speak, Jesus said, "I forgive you."

The president collapsed into Him, sobbing. Jesus held him close, resting a steady hand on his back as the tears came. Then Jesus spoke again, quietly and tenderly. "I desire a personal relationship with you, Ivan Andrei. Do you accept Me as your friend, your Lord, and your Savior?"

"I do," Ivan Andrei said through his tears. "I do not know how You can forgive me for all I have done."

Jesus replied simply, "I forgave those who crucified Me. I forgive you as well."

Jesus looked at Ivan Andrei and said, "You have lost weight, and you are not sleeping well. I want you to be strong for your people when you return to the palace next week. Use this time to rest, to eat properly, and to continue reading the Bible I gave you. In six days, you will return to the palace in the same way you came to this place."

Ivan Andrei said with quiet conviction, "I am ready to accept the terms of peace. I will restore Russia to a democracy by holding free elections next year, after which I will step down from office. I will order the release of all political prisoners and provide reparations for their time in prison. I will declare freedom of worship and guarantee a free press for the people of Russia."

Jesus nodded. "Well done, Ivan Andrei. You are becoming the leader your people need in this time of transition." Then He added, "I have left a copy of the peace treaty here for your review. If you wish to speak with Me at any time, call out, and I will come to you."

With that, Jesus disappeared.

Ivan Andrei went to the refrigerator and ate a proper meal. He reviewed the document, just as Jesus had advised, then lay down and slept deeply and peacefully.

Chapter 16:

The Beast

"Who is like the beast? Who can wage war against it?" (Revelation 13:4).

Revelation portrays the Antichrist as both a dragon and a beast, a force unleashed to ravage the Earth through deception, fear, and false power. John of Patmos assures his readers that this terror is not ultimate. The Lamb who was slain stands above the beast, possessing authority greater than all evil and power sufficient to overcome it. What appears invincible to the world is under heaven's command.

The next morning, after breakfast, John Luke sensed that Jesus wanted to speak with him. He shared the feeling with Kristin, then went to his office. After saying a prayer, he gently placed the Mantle upon his head, and Jesus spoke to his mind.

"Good morning, John Luke," Jesus said. "I trust you slept well."

"Yes, Jesus," John Luke replied. "I slept very well, and I am ready to work if You need me."

"Good," Jesus said. "First, President Petrovich is prepared to return home this Saturday, day forty. Please bring him from the motel to the presidential palace before 9 o'clock in the morning.

"Second," Jesus said, "I would like you to go to the Caspian Sea and relocate the warships and submarines to Nagayev Bay in the Sea of Okhotsk, near the Arctic. This move will benefit all parties involved. Are you willing?"

John Luke laughed. "Of course, Jesus, as long as You promise I will not drown."

Jesus smiled. "I promise, John Luke. The Mantle will protect you. When you are finished, return to your office. I will be waiting for you."

John Luke obeyed. One by one, he removed the warships and submarines from the landlocked Caspian Sea and delivered them safely to Nagayev Bay. The commanders were bewildered, yet relieved to find themselves once more in open, familiar waters.

John Luke returned to his office in less than thirty minutes. Jesus appeared in person and said, "Well done, John Luke. Thank you for this work."

Then His expression grew solemn, and His voice took on a graver tone.

"I do not want to alarm you, but you must know this. The Antichrist is greatly agitated. Zver has learned, through one of his spies, that you are the bearer of the Mantle. Tonight, shortly after darkness falls, he will come to your home."

Jesus paused, allowing the words to settle.

"He will attempt to provoke you," Jesus continued. "Do not act unless I tell you to act. You will not be harmed, but you will be tested. I have already prepared for this moment. As the psalmist wrote (34:7), *'The angel of the Lord encamps around those who fear Him, and He delivers them.*"

Jesus looked at him steadily. "Remain with Me in trust."

Then His tone softened. "Soon, the Antichrist will be bound for a thousand years through the work of the Mantle. You will witness these things, John Luke. But not tonight."

Jesus reminded John Luke once more not to be afraid, and then He departed.

John Luke returned to his work, steady yet thoughtful, holding fast to the words of Jesus.

After dinner, John Luke told Kristin about his conversation with Jesus and about the Antichrist. Kristin fell silent, stunned. At last, she said, "I trust Jesus. I truly do. I do not understand how something like this could happen."

John Luke took her hand. "One of the Antichrist's spies discovered my identity. But Jesus has already prepared for this. We will be all right."

Kristin nodded, drawing comfort from his calm, though the weight of the news lingered. John Luke wrapped his arms around her, holding her until her breathing slowed.

Later that night, shortly after darkness settled over the neighborhood, the air around their home began to shift. The wind died away. The trees stood motionless. Even the night seemed to hold its breath.

Then the Antichrist appeared.

He stood in the center of the backyard as if summoned from the ground itself, encased in armor the color of molten fire. The red metal shimmered, lit from within by his fury. In his left hand, a sword of searing crimson light burned. A black shield etched with ancient markings of defiance hung at his side. His presence pressed against the night, heavy and suffocating.

But he did not roar.

Instead, he spoke quietly.

"So," he said, his voice smooth as polished stone, "this is where you hide, Number Twelve."

Inside the house, Tanner's howl shattered the stillness. John Luke and Kristin rushed to the window. What they saw stole their breath.

The Antichrist lifted his gaze, not toward the sky, but toward the house.

Toward John Luke.

"You have the Mantle," he said calmly. "You know what it can do. One word from you, and this ends tonight. No more fear. No more watching over your shoulder. No more danger for her."

John Luke felt his chest tighten.

"You were told to wait," the Antichrist continued softly. "But waiting has a cost. Look at her. You would protect her with your life. Why not with your power?"

For the first time, John Luke felt the pull, not terror, but justification. He held the ornate box of the Mantle. He did not open it.

He remembered Jesus's words: "Do not act unless I tell you to act."

John Luke bowed his head and prayed, silently but fiercely, clinging to trust rather than certainty.

"I will not act apart from You, Jesus," he whispered. "The work is not mine."

The Antichrist's expression hardened. "Then you choose obedience over those you love."

Before John Luke could answer, the darkness broke.

Seven angels appeared in a flash of brilliant blue light, descending like lightning. Their armor gleamed with piercing purity, their swords and shields drawn. They moved in perfect unity, encircling the Antichrist before he could speak again.

A net of radiant blue light fell over him, tightening instantly. He thrashed and raged, his fury collapsing into impotence.

With a rumble of thunder swallowed by silence, the angels and their captive vanished.

The yard returned to stillness.

The night air softened. The stars shone again. Tanner settled and fell back asleep.

John Luke and Kristin stood quietly, then bowed their heads in prayer, hearts steady and unafraid.

"The Lord thwarts the plans of the wicked." (Job 5:12).

And peace rested over their home.

Chapter 17:

President Petrovich Returns

"Another angel, who had a golden censer, came and stood at the altar. He was given much incense to offer, with the prayers of all God's people, on the golden altar in front of the throne" (Revelation 8:3).

On Earth, the people of Ukraine remained faithful. In heaven, their prayers rose like incense, just as Scripture describes, carried by angels and placed before the throne of God. The Lord God, hearing those prayers, chose to act both in heaven and on Earth, using John Luke and the Mantle of Jesus as instruments of His will.

In Ukraine, the ceasefire held. Russia withdrew its warships from the seas surrounding Ukraine's ports. Russian soldiers began their evacuation.

The tide had turned.

On Saturday morning, day forty, at 8:30 AM, John Luke arrived at the motel, invisible through the power of the Mantle. He gently took President Petrovich by the hand and waited. The president sensed goodness and peace. Without a word, he returned the grip.

In an instant, they were airborne, crossing the distance to Moscow. John Luke set them down softly in the presidential suite at the Kremlin. Petrovich looked around at the familiar room, a faint smile crossing his face. He changed into a suit and tie, straightened himself, and then stepped into his executive office, returned, restored, and ready.

President Petrovich immediately summoned his military leaders and cabinet members to the Kremlin presidential office. News of his call spread quickly. The missing president had returned. He then contacted the press and requested their presence within the hour.

When the military leaders and cabinet members arrived, still visibly stunned, President Petrovich greeted them calmly and thanked them for their service during his time away, which he described simply as "a religious retreat."

President Petrovich spoke plainly. "I will sign the peace treaty with Ukraine. All troops are to return to Russia immediately and peacefully. Every soldier who served in this war will receive a financial bonus, and the families of those who died will receive the same amount."

He paused, letting the weight of his words settle.

"I also direct the immediate release of all political prisoners, along with full reparations for their time in prison."

The room was silent. Even for his inner circle, the announcements were staggering.

Then the president delivered his next declaration, stunning them all.

"I will resign from office in one year, after a free and fair election is held for the next president and prime minister. Russia will become a democracy with a peaceful transition of power. I also declare freedom of religious worship and a free, open press for our people."

He looked around the room, meeting each face in turn.

"Finally, I ask you, my closest comrades, to remain here for a press conference. I will make these same commitments publicly, before the world."

History, long frozen, began to move again.

As the press joined the meeting, President Petrovich welcomed them and publicly recognized each military leader and cabinet member for their work. The president then repeated the information he had shared with the military leaders and cabinet members.

President Petrovich then said, "I wish to offer a humble apology to the people of Ukraine for the suffering I alone inflicted upon their sovereign nation. To President Koval and the Ukrainian people, I ask for your forgiveness, though I am not worthy of it."

"I respectfully request that, if he will receive me, I travel to Kyiv immediately to meet President Koval, sign the peace treaty, and begin the process of reparations. I must face, directly, the harm I caused."

"I also ask that Pope Paul VII be present at the signing of the treaty, as he was instrumental in helping to forge this peace. Finally, I express my gratitude to the leaders of the United Nations for their steadfast support of Ukraine and for their assistance in addressing the reparations owed for the destruction of its homeland."

The room remained silent, no longer in shock, but in the presence of history being rewritten.

The president continued, "I will provide a written copy of my remarks to the press. However, I will not take questions at this time. There is much work ahead if I am to make amends, and I intend to begin immediately."

With that, the conference concluded. President Petrovich moved through the room, shaking hands with each military leader and cabinet member, as the astonished press captured the moment, aware they were witnessing the end of one era and the uncertain beginning of another.

When the president approached General Orlov, he clasped his hand warmly and said, "Thank you for your courage in calling the ceasefire. I am forever in your debt for your wisdom and resolve." The press captured the moment in a flurry of photographs.

After the room cleared, President Petrovich placed a private call to President Koval, who had been prepared for it by the Pope.

"President Koval," Petrovich began, "I offer my deepest apology for the harm I inflicted upon Ukraine. I intend to do everything within my power to make amends. If you will allow me the honor, I ask that you host the signing of the peace treaty in Kyiv tomorrow. I also respectfully request that Pope Paul VII be present, if he is willing."

President Koval responded with his customary grace. "Yes, Mr. President. I will make the arrangements immediately. Thank you for your call, and for your apology."

President Petrovich responded, "Please know that I just held a press conference announcing this information. It is I who am grateful to you."

The path to peace had begun.

The next day, at noon, President Petrovich and President Koval met at the Mariinskyi Palace. As requested, Pope Paul VII was present to witness the signing of the peace treaty. With the final signatures, the war was officially over. The international press aired the moment live around the world.

After the ceremony, President Petrovich approached President Koval and said quietly, "I want to humbly and sincerely apologize to you and to the people of Ukraine in person."

The two men met each other's gaze and shook hands.

The image of that apology appeared on front pages across the globe, a single photograph marking the end of a war and the beginning of peace.

President Petrovich departed immediately for the Kremlin to oversee the withdrawal of Russian troops from Ukraine and to authorize financial reparations from the Russian treasury. In an act of quiet providence, the funds taken to sustain Ukraine's defense were returned, with interest, now repurposed to rebuild what the war had destroyed. Jesus never lies.

After completing these orders, President Petrovich instructed his cabinet to issue reparations to all military personnel who served in the war, as well as to the families of those who died. He then secured the release of every political prisoner and provided fair compensation for their unjust imprisonment.

Next, he directed the immediate preparation of free and fair elections for both the president and the prime minister. Finally, he signed the official decrees guaranteeing freedom of religion and freedom of the press throughout Russia.

At the end of the long day, the president realized that Zver had not contacted him during the entire process. Alone at his desk, he knelt and gave thanks to God for his deliverance from the beast and for the grace to make amends to the people of Ukraine and Russia.

Though much work still lay ahead, including negotiations for a new nuclear arms agreement, President Petrovich felt *"a peace that surpasses all understanding"* (Philippians 4:7).

He ate a simple meal and went to bed, sleeping deeply and without fear.

At last, all was well in Ukraine and Russia. The people rejoiced and gave thanks to God.

Chapter 18:

Work in Sudan

"When he opened the seventh seal, there was silence in heaven for about half an hour... The smoke of the incense, together with the prayers of God's people, went up before God from the angel's hand" (Revelation 8:1, 4).

Just as the prayers of Ukraine rose to the throne of heaven, so did the prayers of the people of Sudan, rising like incense from northeastern Africa. God heard them, and heaven grew silent once more. This chapter tells the story of His response.

Incense, made from frankincense resin harvested from *Boswellia* trees in Africa and the Middle East, has long symbolized purification and prayer. Across faith traditions, Jewish, Christian, and Muslim, its rising smoke represents humanity's longing toward heaven. Scripture affirms this image clearly in Revelation, where angels offer incense mingled with the prayers of God's people before His throne.

Frankincense was given to Christ at His birth, and incense accompanies prayer at the end of days. It marks sacred moments where heaven and Earth draw near.

Incense matters to God.

The Mantle stands as a sign of that nearness, a reminder that life is eternal, that what happens on Earth matters beyond death, and that God still hears the prayers of His people.

John Luke is called to play a pivotal role in another conflict, the third and final civil war in Sudan. Jesus asks him to travel to the Republic of Sudan, Africa's largest country by land area.

Since gaining independence from the United Kingdom and Egypt in 1956, Sudan has endured decades of instability and unrest. Its population comprises many ethnic and religious groups, with Arab Muslims predominating in the north and African Christians concentrated in the south and west. Sudan is now engulfed in its third civil war in forty years.

The latest conflict erupted when two rival generals fought for control of the capital city, Khartoum. General Mustafa Hemedti leads a powerful paramilitary force rooted in tribal loyalties. His surname, meaning Mohammed, reflects his belief that he is carrying forward the prophet's tradition through armed struggle. He seeks to impose strict Islamic rule and religious law nationwide.

Opposing him is General Ahmed Al-Hussain, who supports an established government marked by a limited democracy and an open economy. Though resistant to Western influence and foreign intervention, he envisions a unified Sudan governed by civil authority rather than religious militancy.

Their power struggle has devastated the country. Hundreds have been killed, villages around the capital have been burned, and thousands have been forced to flee their homes. Once again, Sudan's people cry out for peace.

Caught in this struggle is Sudan's civilian prime minister, Abdul Baatin, a devout Muslim whose name means "servant of Allah." He longs desperately for peace and prays earnestly for an end to the bloodshed. God heard the prayers of the Sudanese people and of Abdul Baatin. Jesus is about to carry out the Father's will for peace in Sudan.

One week after the signing of the peace treaty in Ukraine, John Luke was working quietly in his home office when he sensed that Jesus wished to speak with him. As he had many times before, John Luke paused, said a prayer, opened the ornate box, and gently placed the Mantle on his head. He was ready to listen.

Jesus appeared immediately, in person. "Thank you for listening to the urging of the Spirit, John Luke. It is good to see you. If you have time, I would like to speak with you about another mission."

"Of course, Jesus," John Luke replied with a smile. "I appreciate the way You nudge me to speak with You. It is good to see You, too."

Jesus asked gently, "Are you familiar with the civil war in Sudan?"

"Only vaguely," John Luke answered. "Mostly from the news."

Jesus explained, "Innocent people are losing their homes and their lives. The Father has heard the prayers of the Sudanese people, especially the prayers of their civil leader, a good and faithful man named Abdul Baatin. He longs for peace for his people, and the Father will answer that prayer."

"This work will follow a similar path to Ukraine. Yet the difference is that Sudanese tribes are fighting one another, brother against brother. We must approach the Father's plan with great care. There can be no winners and no losers. The purpose is not victory, but reconciliation. The goal is peace and the unity of the people."

John Luke felt the weight of Jesus's words. Ukraine was a struggle against aggression. Sudan was a wound within a family, torn by fear, history, and mistrust. He realized this work would require more restraint and careful listening to Jesus. Quietly and quickly, he prayed for wisdom, asking Jesus to please explain more.

Jesus then explained further. "For this mission, I want you to appear openly, using your alias of John Ward. Your identity will remain hidden, and little will be known about John Ward. Peace will come through negotiation, persuading the warring tribes to find shared ground for coexistence in culture, faith, and daily life.

"The people of Sudan are largely farmers and herders, and much of their conflict centers on access to land and resources. These disputes have hardened over time into fear and resentment. Sudan is also home to two major religious traditions, Christianity and Islam. Any lasting peace must honor both. There can be no domination of one over the other, only mutual respect."

Jesus continued, "Sudan's divisions and differences were exploited by two generals who preyed upon fear and grievance, tearing the country apart. Both generals and their senior military leaders must be removed for God's plan of peace to take root. Each seeks supremacy, not reconciliation."

"Our first action with the Mantle will be to place these generals and their leaders in separate motel rooms for forty days. During that time, they will be removed from power while we work out the Father's plan for peace."

John Luke nodded. Then he smiled slightly and said, "Ah, now the number of rooms in the motel finally makes sense."

Jesus nodded and said, "General Mustafa Hemedti is currently in Darfur, west of the capital city, Khartoum. He is recruiting fighters for his paramilitary forces. Hemedti and 4 of his senior leaders have committed grave atrocities against the Sudanese people, including murder, rape, and the violent displacement of families. This general has aligned himself with evil."

"The Antichrist has also appeared in Sudan, this time under the guise of a wealthy South African diamond magnate named Crocosmia Kumalo, a name meaning greatest king. He calls himself Corn. The Antichrist can conceal his identity and manifest in multiple places at once. While sowing chaos in Ukraine, he was at work in Sudan, deepening the suffering of the people."

Jesus continued, "The other general, Ahmed Al-Hussain, remains in Khartoum, living in comfort while his people suffer. Though he is not as brutal as Hemedti, he, too, is under Corn's influence. Corn has financed this entire conflict, using wealth drawn from diamond mines to arm both sides in a war designed to destroy them and collapse the Sudanese government."

"Corn deceived each general into believing he would emerge victorious. In truth, he intends to discard them both and install his own proxy as ruler, removing Prime Minister Abdul Baatin. His chosen replacement is a military figure named Colonel Garang Hassan. For peace to take hold, he too must be removed from power and placed in the motel during this period of reconciliation."

Jesus paused, giving John Luke time to absorb the weight of what had been revealed.

John Luke responded, "Jesus, I had no idea the situation was this complex. I trust that You will guide me in what I do and say."

Jesus answered gently, "Of course, John Luke. The Mantle will protect you, and My words will guide you. Once the generals and their senior advisers are off the battlefield, I will block Corn from influencing them while they are at the motel. He will not know where they are or how to reach them. In this way, peace can be negotiated, and Corn will be sidelined from shaping the outcome."

Jesus looked at him steadily. "Are you willing to carry out this work with Me, John Luke?"

John Luke smiled. Quiet confidence settled over him. "Of course, Jesus. I am ready to do Your will."

Jesus said, "Good. Thank you, John Luke. Our first step is to contact Lucas at Saint Luke's Home to confirm the motel's completion date. Once we have that, we will move the guests into place."

John Luke nodded. "The timeline is coming up. I will call Lucas today to get an update and let You know."

"Yes," Jesus replied. "Thank you. I will wait to hear from you. And remember, I am always with you. You are never alone."

Jesus embraced John Luke, then disappeared.

John Luke picked up the phone and called Lucas. Thankfully, Lucas was in a good place with the work when he saw John Luke's name on his phone.

"Hello, John Luke," he said. "You have great timing."

"That is good to hear," John Luke replied with a laugh. "I was calling to hear how the motel completion is coming along."

"We are on track," Lucas said. "The motel will be ready no later than Wednesday of next week, day 88 of our timeline. Does that work for you?"

"Yes, Lucas, that is excellent news. Thank you," John Luke said, catching himself just short of adding that Jesus would be pleased.

Then he added, "Kristin, my parents, and I can come out Thursday morning. Would it be possible to do a walk-through and inspection with you and Paula then?"

Lucas agreed, and the plan was set. Lucas added, "The baby is due soon. I will make sure Paula feels well enough to attend the inspection."

John Luke added, “I hope and pray that Paula is feeling well. I am truly happy for you both. I will also have the final payment for the work, paid in full, in cash.”

Lucas laughed. “We both know Paula has a special fondness for cash payments. We will, of course, provide a receipt.”

On that cheerful note, the men ended the call. John Luke set down the phone, already eager to share the good news with Jesus.

On Sunday morning, after breakfast, John Luke said a prayer, gently placed the Mantle upon his head, and shared the good news with Jesus about the completion of Saint Luke’s Motel, including plans to travel to New Mexico on Thursday.

Jesus said, “That is good news. I want to meet with you after your visit.”

“Of course, Jesus,” he replied. “I will arrange my work schedule so we can meet.”

The plan was set.

Later that Sunday morning, John Luke and Kristin met Joan and me at Saint George Church for worship. The church follows the Lectionary calendar of Scripture readings, arranged in Years A, B, and C, and that day marked the Fifth Sunday after the Feast of Pentecost, commemorating the birth of the Church.

The pastor, Reverend Mark, Joan’s cousin, preached on the Gospel of Mark, chapter 4:35–41, the account of Jesus calming the storm as He and the disciples crossed the Sea of Galilee. The passage tells of a violent windstorm that threatened to swamp the boat while Jesus slept, until He rose, rebuked the wind, and said to the sea, “Peace! Be still!” At once, the storm ceased, and there was a great calm.

Reverend Mark reflected on the disciples’ fear. “After all they had seen, healings, exorcisms, and the feeding of thousands, they still panicked and thought they would drown,” he said. “Jesus asks them, ' Why are you afraid? Have you still no faith? Do you not yet trust Me? Do you not understand that I command even the weather?”

He continued, “Two thousand years later, storms still rise in our lives. The winds blow, and the seas feel deep and dangerous. But it is not the water around the ship that sinks it; it is the water that gets inside. We must trust Jesus and not let fear flood our hearts. In calm and in chaos, in joy and in suffering, God remains in control. God is still on the throne. We place our faith, our hope, and our love in the One who commands the storms.”

When Reverend Mark finished, I wanted to stand and applaud, but settled instead for a broad smile and an enthusiastic thumbs-up. During the coffee hour, we thanked him for his message and told him how much it meant to us.

Even servants of God, perhaps especially so, need encouragement.

As we walked to our cars, John Luke summarized his recent meetings with Jesus and the upcoming trip to Saint Luke’s later that week. He also shared details of the mission in Sudan and the civil war unfolding there. Joan and I were stunned by the scope of what he described. We had not realized how dire conditions were in that vast nation. When he spoke of the Antichrist's efforts to influence the outcome, we were shaken again, sobering reminders of how real and active evil can be in world events.

Reverend Mark's sermon echoed in my mind as we parted. Trusting Jesus, not only in our personal lives but in the future of the world itself, felt more urgent than ever.

When we arrived home, I turned to Joan and asked, "Do you mind if I spend some time writing in the Mantle history book before lunch? I need to catch up on the extraordinary things John Luke and Jesus have been doing."

Joan laughed. "Of course. Our son is a busy bee with Jesus!"

I wrote for nearly two hours, trying to capture the wonder of it all. Then Joan and I shared a relaxed lunch on our deck, enjoying the warmth of the summer sun, grateful, reflective, and at peace.

On Thursday morning, Joan, Kristin, John Luke, and I traveled to Saint Luke's Motel through the power of the Mantle. We arrived within minutes and walked into the home as casually as if we had come by bus, not crossing 2,000 miles at nearly the speed of light. Life with the Mantle was extraordinary and strangely normal.

Out back, we admired the motel Lucas and his crew had completed, beautiful, thoughtfully designed, and naturally integrated into the grounds.

Paula, *"being great with child"* (Luke 2:5), greeted us with hugs and smiles, delighting Joan and Kristin, who promised to visit after the baby's arrival.

The rooms were comfortably furnished, secure, and clearly ready for long-term guests.

I asked John Luke, “What do you think?”

“It is perfect,” he said loudly. “Outstanding work, Lucas and Paula.”

We applauded. Lucas and Paula bowed. The crew joined in, and everyone laughed.

John Luke quietly requested the final invoice and paid in cash. Paula beamed. “Oh, how I love cash flow!” We laughed again and said our goodbyes as Paula handed John Luke a receipt.

Inside, we spoke discreetly with the administrators about the confidential care of upcoming guests. “Please expect seven visitors within the next two days,” John Luke said. “The procedures will be the same as before. I will be in touch.”

They understood.

Outside, we found privacy, joined hands, and John Luke said a prayer before gently placing the Mantle on his head. In an instant, we were home again.

By now, Kristin was quite comfortable traveling without an airplane.

Chapter 19:

Justice in Sudan

"They did not repent of their murders, their magic arts, their sexual immorality, or their thefts" (Revelation 9:21).

This passage in Revelation speaks of those at the end of days who ignore God's warnings and refuse to repent of their evil. The words echo the deeds of the two generals in Sudan who act as though they are beyond accountability for the atrocities committed against their own people. Justice, long delayed, would soon be placed in God's hands.

On Sunday evening, after dinner, John Luke went alone into his office. He said a prayer, wore the Mantle, and Jesus spoke to his mind.

"Congratulations on the work well done in New Mexico, John Luke," Jesus said.

John Luke replied with his usual humility, "Lucas and Paula deserve the credit, Jesus. I am only following Your will."

Jesus then said, "You are a faithful disciple. If you are available for a quick mission tonight, I ask that you fly to Darfur and bring General Hemedti and his four senior military leaders to rooms one through five in the motel. After that, please go to Khartoum and bring General Al-Hussain and Colonel Hassan to rooms six and seven."

"I have placed copies of the *Qur'an* in each of their rooms for reading and reflection. They have free will. No one will compel them to change their beliefs. If they call out to God, I will come to them. The rest lies in the Father's will. The Father desires repentance and peace, but love is never forced."

Jesus asked, "Are you ready, John Luke? This work should take less than an hour."

"Yes, Jesus," John Luke replied. "Let me tell Kristin that I have a quick mission."

He did so, returned to his office, and said quietly, "I am ready, Lord."

Then, with the power of the Mantle, he flew at once toward Darfur.

John Luke arrived at General Hemedti's compound shortly after midnight, local time in Darfur. Jesus guided him to a specific tent. Inside were five young women who were held there against their will, forced to serve the general and his advisers.

Jesus asked John Luke to appear to the women in person to reassure them, protect them, and return them quietly to their homes in the northern region of Shamal Darfur.

John Luke stepped into the tent and spoke softly in Sudanese Arabic. "Please do not be afraid," he whispered. "I am a friend. God has heard your prayers. I am taking you home."

John Luke asked the women to hold hands. They gathered quietly around him in a small circle, hands clasped. In an instant, they became invisible and rose silently through the top of the tent, lifting above the compound without a sound.

Jesus guided John Luke in his thoughts, and he carried the women swiftly and safely to their homes. Each one was returned to her family, unharmed, unseen, and free.

After John Luke completed the rescue, Jesus directed him to another nearby tent, where the general and his military advisers were gathered. The men were drinking together. General Hemedti stood at the center, boasting loudly of his exploits.

"These people are fools," he declared. "They need a strong hand and strict discipline. Soon, the entire country will be under our control."

Invisible through the Mantle, John Luke stepped forward and took the general firmly by the arm. Hemedti let out a sharp, startled cry and vanished before the eyes of his stunned advisers.

Still shouting, the general was carried instantly to motel room one, unable to perceive where he had been taken. John Luke placed him before the desk where Jesus had left the *Qur'an*.

At Jesus's prompting, John Luke laid a hand upon the general's head and prayed. And he did.

Silence followed.

John Luke then returned to the compound and brought the four remaining advisers, one by one, to the motel rooms. Each was placed before the desk where a copy of the *Qur'an* awaited them. Over each man, John Luke prayed quietly, then departed.

With that task complete, he flew on to Khartoum.

Jesus guided him to the Governor-General's Palace, where General Al-Hussain and his leadership occupied the west wing on the third floor. The general sat with his chief adviser, Colonel Hassan, sharing cups of hot tea. Unknown to Al-Hussain, Hassan was an agent of Corn, the man Corn intended to install as Sudan's next ruler.

Invisible in the Mantle, John Luke stepped forward and took General Al-Hussain firmly by the arm. In an instant, the general vanished, leaving Colonel Hassan staring in stunned disbelief at the space where his commander had been.

John Luke brought the general to motel room six. At Jesus's prompting, he placed a hand on General Al-Hussain's head and prayed for the grip of the Antichrist to be broken. As the prayer ended, the general shuddered and drew in a sharp breath. John Luke sensed a change had taken hold. He positioned the general before the desk where the *Qur'an* lay waiting and departed.

He then returned to Khartoum and swiftly brought Colonel Hassan to motel room seven. As before, John Luke placed him before the desk, prayed quietly over him, and left without a word.

As he flew home, John Luke reflected on how completely the general had been deceived, never realizing that his closest adviser was a traitor and an agent of Corn.

The entire mission took less than an hour, just as Jesus had promised.

When John Luke arrived home, Jesus was waiting for him, in person, in the office.

John Luke asked, "Jesus, was General Al-Hussain freed from the evil spirit of the Antichrist? When I prayed over him, it felt like something broke loose."

Jesus answered gently, "Your prayer was effective. General Al-Hussain did not wish to remain under Corn's influence. There is hope that he may yet repent and, in time, serve the people of Sudan with integrity."

Jesus said nothing about General Hemedti, Colonel Hassan, or the other advisers.

After a moment, Jesus continued, "This part of the mission is complete. The balance has shifted. Tomorrow morning, I ask that you call Prime Minister Abdul Baatin." He then gave John Luke a private number. "He will receive your call gladly."

Jesus then said, "I ask that you meet the prime minister in person in Khartoum. He will agree to see you. I will guide your conversation. You will appear to him as John Ward. He will not know your identity. Tell him that God has heard his prayers and that the Father's plan is moving swiftly toward peace."

"In your office closet, you will find a briefcase. Take it with you to Sudan and place $1 million inside as a gesture of goodwill for the people. We will also confront the Antichrist to bring peace to this land. All of this will unfold in the coming days. Thank you, John Luke, for doing the will of the Father."

John Luke bowed his head slightly and said, "Jesus, I am deeply grateful to be used in this way, to help bring God's plan to fulfillment."

Jesus gave John Luke a warm embrace and said, "John Luke, you remind me of my disciple Nathanael. When I called him, I said, *'Here truly is an Israelite in whom there is no deceit'* (John 1:47). You are like that, without guile. You are genuine, and your heart is pure."

John Luke smiled, visibly moved. "Wow. Thank you, Jesus. That may be the kindest thing anyone has ever said to me."

Jesus smiled once more, and then He was gone.

John Luke hurried downstairs and found Kristin, telling her everything: the mission in Sudan, its weight, and the words Jesus had spoken about his heart.

Kristin listened, then smiled with quiet pride and said, "Well, Jesus obviously has excellent taste."

Chapter 20:

Prime Minister Abdul Baatin

"Then I saw another mighty angel coming down from heaven. He was robed in a cloud, with a rainbow above his head; his face was like the sun, and his legs were like fiery pillars" (Revelation 10:1).

The Book of Revelation often reveals heaven breaking into the world. In this vision, the mighty angel bears the unmistakable marks of God's authority. The cloud reflects divine mystery, the radiant face reveals heavenly glory, and the fiery pillars proclaim strength that cannot be shaken. Above all, the rainbow recalls God's ancient covenant, a promise of mercy, restraint, and renewed hope.

This image ultimately points to Jesus Christ, whose authority spans heaven and earth and whose mission is the salvation of humanity. Just as the rainbow once appeared over a world renewed after the flood, its promise now stretches toward Sudan. God has heard the prayers of His people, and the promise of peace is about to break into Sudan.

The next morning, John Luke called the prime minister on his private number, and, as Jesus said, the prime minister answered. John Luke introduced himself as John Ward and, as Jesus had said, agreed to meet in person the next day, Friday, at 10:00 AM Sudan time.

The prime minister remarked, "John Ward, how do you have such swift travel arrangements at your disposal? Do you have a private jet?"

John Luke responded with a smile, "In a manner of speaking, yes. I look forward to meeting you tomorrow, Mr. Prime Minister."

The prime minister's office was located on the first floor of the Governor-General's Palace in Khartoum, not far from where John Luke had previously encountered General Al-Hussain. After quietly telling Kristin of his plans with Jesus, John Luke left home while she was still sleeping and arrived five minutes early, a briefcase in hand.

He passed through security without delay, and a guard escorted him directly to the prime minister's office. Prime Minister Abdul Baatin was alone. He rose, warmly shook John Luke's hand, and listened as John Luke introduced himself as John Ward and thanked him for the meeting.

Educated at Harvard University, the prime minister spoke fluent English and quickly put John Luke at ease. "Please," he said with a gentle smile, "call me Abdul."

He invited John Luke to sit at a conference table, where they shared a quiet cup of tea as the conversation and Sudan's future began.

Abdul leaned forward and spoke plainly. "I have read reports that you and The Mantle LLC played a significant role in bringing peace to Ukraine. When I received your call, I felt encouraged. I desperately want, and pray for, peace in Sudan."

Jesus spoke quietly to John Luke's mind, guiding his reply.

John Luke said, "Please know that I deeply respect your Muslim faith and your reputation as a principled leader. The work of The Mantle LLC pledges allegiance to God alone. Jesus, whom your tradition honors as a prophet, sent me to tell you that God has heard your prayers and has set in motion a swift plan for peace in Sudan."

"At this moment, both warring generals, Hemedti and Al-Hussain, and their senior advisers are no longer in the country. They are being held in a secure, confidential location for forty days. During this time, God has asked me to support your efforts toward reconciliation and peace."

Prime Minister Baatin's eyes widened slightly. "This news is extraordinary. When did this happen, and where are they now?"

John Luke answered calmly, "They were removed earlier this week through the power of God. With respect, Abdul, I am not permitted to share their location. It is better, for you and for the peace process, that you remain at a distance from that action."

John Luke, still appearing as John Ward, continued, "In this briefcase, I have brought one million dollars as a gesture of good faith and immediate support for the relief of your people. Please use these funds as you see fit. The Mantle has the resources to help rebuild your country, without conditions and without political demands. As in Ukraine, our only purpose here is peace for God's people."

The prime minister studied John Luke for a long moment, then glanced at the briefcase. He was clearly moved, both surprised by the gift and steadied by the clarity of its intent.

"I am grateful," Abdul said quietly. "And I am humbled. This assistance is greatly needed. The generals would not listen to my appeals for peace, and I never trusted Colonel Hassan. There was always something hidden in his words. What you accomplished in Ukraine speaks to your credibility."

He leaned forward, his voice firm but hopeful. "Tell me then, what is God's plan for peace in Sudan? What must we do, precisely?"

John Luke, hearing Jesus's voice in his mind, spoke. "The top military leaders of General Hemedti are hesitant to negotiate. General Al-Hussain has some promise of listening to peace. Your feelings about Colonel Hassan are accurate.

"You must also know this. There is another force behind this war. A South African billionaire who calls himself Corn has deceived both factions. He has financed both generals, convincing each that victory was assured. His true intention was never peace. Once the war exhausted the country, he planned to discard both leaders and replace you with Colonel Hassan."

Abdul's face tightened, but he did not interrupt.

"With the generals and their advisers removed," John Luke continued, "the armed forces are now disoriented, leaderless, and uncertain. This creates a narrow window. We must act quickly. The message of peace must come directly from you before another voice fills the vacuum."

Abdul nodded slowly, absorbing every word.

"Thank you for trusting me with this," he said at last. "Tell me, what do you propose we do next?"

John Ward leaned forward slightly and spoke with calm conviction. "Respectfully, Mr. Prime Minister, you must become the voice of peace. The moment is fragile, but it is also ripe. I urge you to speak immediately and everywhere, to your people through television and radio, through social media and newspapers, and through local gatherings in towns and villages."

He continued, his tone steady but urgent. "Tell them that peace is not only possible, but it is also necessary. Remind them that Christians and Muslims, farmers and herders, have shared this land for generations. Sudan is vast and beautiful. There is room for all its people to live together in dignity, safety, and prosperity. The message must be clear. Before tribe, before faction, before grievance, we are all Sudanese."

Abdul listened intently, then nodded, a quiet tenacity settling over him.

"You are right, John Ward," he said. "This is the path forward. I will do as you advise."

John Ward continued, his voice measured and deliberate. "I also recommend that you engage the United States Institute of Peace and draw upon their established framework for negotiations. At the same time, seek the support of the United Nations Security Council to formalize a ceasefire and provide an international path toward lasting peace."

He paused, then added, "The Mantle LLC will support these efforts financially, as needed. With the military leadership in disarray, the people are searching for direction, and they will listen to you. As peace takes hold under the protection of a United Nations peacekeeping force, trust will begin to return, trust in safety, trust in governance, and trust in a shared future."

John Ward's voice softened slightly, but his words carried weight. "Those military leaders who refuse to stand down will be contained. And God Himself will remove Corn's influence from Sudan. This is not a victory of force, Prime Minister. It is a restoration of order, dignity, and peace."

Abdul nodded slowly. "I will do as you say, John Ward. I will trust your words and this plan."

While John Ward was still with him, the prime minister summoned his staff and called for a press conference in one hour, announcing a ceasefire and the start of peace negotiations.

Abdul turned back to John Ward. "Will you remain for the press conference?"

"I will," John Ward replied quietly, "but not before the cameras. I suggest you stand only with those government members whom you trust completely, those who will truly work for peace."

Abdul agreed. When the press conference began, he stood flanked by a small circle of trusted advisers and formally announced an immediate ceasefire and a national call for negotiations toward peace.

At the press conference, the prime minister announced, "The generals responsible for igniting this civil war, Hemedti and Al-Hussain, are no longer in power. I have assumed control of the Sudanese military. I now call upon all factions to lay down their arms and come together to forge a lasting peace. I will formally request the support of the United Nations to assist us in this effort."

The conference was received positively. Abdul's calm confidence, clear message, and commanding presence resonated with the press and the public alike.

Afterward, Abdul called the United States Secretary of State, a former Harvard colleague, and outlined the framework for peace. He then contacted the United Nations Secretary-General, shared the same details, and formally requested the deployment of an international security force to uphold the ceasefire.

Next, Abdul contacted the United States Institute of Peace and formally requested their assistance in facilitating negotiations among Sudan's tribes. John Ward remained with the prime minister as these initial calls were completed, offering quiet counsel but never drawing attention to himself.

Then Jesus spoke to John Luke's mind, guiding his words. John Ward turned to Abdul and said, "If you are willing to receive it, $2 billion will be transferred to the National Bank of Sudan by tomorrow. These funds are intended for humanitarian relief, peacekeeping efforts, and reconstruction."

He added gently, "This support can help stabilize the economy, rebuild Khartoum, and provide direct aid to farmers and herders whose lives have been disrupted by the fighting."

Abdul sat back in his chair, momentarily silent, absorbing the weight of what was being offered, not merely money, but tangible signs that peace was no longer an idea, but a future beginning to take shape.

John Ward added gently, "The people will respond to your message when they see that you can support their families and rebuild their city."

Abdul nodded, deeply grateful, and agreed to accept the extraordinary funds. John Luke emphasized once more that the money carried no conditions, only the hope of peace, stability, and shared prosperity.

By the time the meeting concluded, it was nearly 9:00 PM. John Luke left the Governor-General's Palace quietly and, unseen, flew home.

When he arrived in his home office, Jesus was waiting for him in person. Smiling warmly, He said, "Well done, John Luke. You are truly a secret agent of peace for God."

John Luke smiled and said, "Thank you, Jesus, for guiding me with Your words and direction. I do have one question, though. Where will we find two billion dollars?"

Jesus smiled back. "Ironically, Corn himself will supply it. The wealth he gathered from the diamond mines to fund the war will now be used to rebuild what the war destroyed. If you are willing, I would like to go with you tomorrow morning to the First National Bank of South Africa in Johannesburg. We will transfer $2 billion from Crocosmia Kumalo's account to The Mantle LLC's account at the Swiss National Bank. From there, the funds will be sent to the National Bank of Sudan."

Jesus continued calmly, "I will ensure that Corn learns of the transfer too late to prevent it. I want him to know that the Mantle is at work. He will be enraged and will seek vengeance, and when he does, we will be ready. I will ensure these funds will be restored, with interest, at the appointed time."

John Luke nodded, his expression steady. "That is a just plan, Jesus. The people of Sudan deserve peace."

Jesus said, "The words of prophecy from the Book of Revelation will unfold before your eyes in the Nubian Desert of Sudan. As I told you, the Father's plan moves swiftly. Take comfort in this. All the time you spent with Abdul, though momentous, has not disrupted your ordinary day. All is well. Enjoy your evening, and let us meet again tomorrow, after breakfast with Kristin."

John Luke nodded. Peace settled over him. Then Jesus disappeared.

The next morning, after breakfast, John Luke said a prayer as always, gently placing the Mantle on his head. Jesus appeared in person, even more radiant than before, clothed in a gleaming white robe, a golden sash at His waist, and bronze sandals that shone like fire.

Jesus said, "My appearance is radiant to fulfill what has been foretold. You will understand more in time. And speaking of time, it is now 2:00 PM in Johannesburg. The bankers are expecting us."

In an instant, Jesus and John Luke flew at the speed of light to the First National Bank in Johannesburg. They entered together, John Luke visible as John Ward, while Jesus walked beside him unseen.

At the front desk, the documents were already prepared. John Ward was escorted to a private office, where the paperwork awaited his signature. To John Luke's astonishment, Corn's signature was already affixed, authorizing the transfer of two billion dollars to The Mantle LLC account at the Swiss National Bank. Within minutes, the transaction was complete.

Without ceremony, Jesus and John Luke exited the bank, the work accomplished, the funds redirected from war to peace.

They went immediately to Zurich. The local time matched Johannesburg's, and once again, the bankers were ready for John Ward's arrival. He signed the wire authorization transferring the funds to the National Bank of Sudan. The transaction was completed swiftly, and moments later, Jesus and John Luke were back in John Luke's home office.

Then Jesus asked John Luke to call Prime Minister Abdul Baatin.

After exchanging greetings, John Luke told him, "The funds have been transferred to the Sudanese treasury account at the National Bank."

Abdul was silent for a moment, then spoke with deep emotion. "I do not understand how you accomplish these things with such speed, John Ward. I am in awe of how you are carrying out God's plan for peace. You are a man of your word, and I will be forever grateful."

The work of peace, once prayed for, was now unmistakably underway.

Jesus then spoke quietly to John Luke's mind, guiding his words. John Luke relayed the message. "Prime Minister, I will be in your country tomorrow. If you wish, I would be honored to stand with you at public gatherings as you speak to your people about the path to peace."

Abdul responded without hesitation. He thanked John Ward and asked him to call his private number upon arrival.

After the call ended, Jesus spoke again, His tone resolute. "Corn will soon learn of the transfer. He will be enraged and will demand a meeting in the Nubian Desert, a place he favors. We will go there together. There, we will confront him and fulfill what has been foretold. Afterward, we will return to Khartoum to meet with the prime minister."

Jesus looked at John Luke and asked, "Are you willing to go with Me?"

John Luke answered honestly, "Of course, Jesus. I do not know how useful I will be in confronting the Antichrist, but I will not be afraid with You at my side."

The path ahead was clear. What had begun in prayer was now moving inexorably toward its final reckoning in the desert.

Jesus said, "You will be useful, John Luke, and you will not be afraid. I am always with you. The Mantle will protect you from harm."

John Luke nodded, reassured.

After the call ended, Jesus spoke again, His tone resolute. "Corn will soon learn of the transfer. He will be enraged and will demand a meeting in the Nubian Desert at high noon, a place and time he favors. We will go there together. There, we will confront him and fulfill what has been foretold. Afterward, we will return to Khartoum to meet with the prime minister."

Now God is moving to the desert.

Chapter 21:

The Hole Without a Bottom

"Then I saw an angel coming down from heaven. He had in his hand a key to the hole without a bottom. He also had a strong chain. He took hold of the dragon, that old snake, who is the Devil, or Satan, and chained him for 1,000 years. The angel threw the devil into the hole without a bottom. He shut it and locked him in it. He could not fool the nations anymore until the 1,000 years were completed" (Revelation 20:1-3).

The Book of Revelation speaks of a moment when evil will no longer roam unchecked, when deception is restrained, and the nations are finally given rest. This chapter tells of that moment drawing near.

On the evening before the journey to the Nubian Desert, John Luke shared Jesus's plan with Kristin. At dawn, they would confront the Antichrist: 6:00 AM Eastern Time, noon in Sudan.

Kristin listened quietly and said only, "Stay beside Jesus, and you will be safe."

John Luke nodded, comforted by her calm faith.

He rose early, showered, ate a small breakfast, and prepared his heart and mind. Before stepping into his office, he sent me a text asking for prayer. I replied immediately, assuring him that my prayers were already with him.

Jesus appeared in person, radiant and steady, His presence filling the room with light.

"Good morning, John Luke," Jesus said. "You look rested and ready. Shall we go?"

John Luke met His gaze and answered, "Yes, Lord. I am ready."

The Nubian Desert is in northeastern Sudan, a vast expanse of the greater Sahara covering more than three million square miles in northern Africa. It is a place where travelers lose their bearings, where silence presses heavily, and where the horizon seems endless.

During the night, the Antichrist called out to Jesus, challenging Him to meet in the Red Sea Hills on the eastern edge of the Nubian Desert. At dawn, Jesus led John Luke there. They stood side by side near the rocky hills, the desert air still beneath the high sun.

Then the Antichrist appeared.

He was clad head to toe in crimson battle armor that burned against the sand. In his left hand, he held a glowing sword that gleamed in the light. In his right hand, he carried a blackened shield etched with ancient symbols of conquest. His presence warped the air around him. Jesus and John Luke were fully visible.

The Antichrist laughed, a sound like grinding stone, and called out in a voice that echoed across the hills.

"Jesus, I see you have brought your disciple, Number 12, the famous John Ward." His gaze locked onto John Luke. "I am Satan. You are my eternal enemy. Today, I will gladly destroy you both."

The desert waited.

When Satan finished speaking, the desert trembled. The ground groaned beneath their feet. Then the sky split with light.

A mighty blue angel descended from heaven and stood between Satan, Jesus, and John Luke. He was clad in radiant armor the color of the deepest sky, etched with symbols older than the desert itself. In his right hand, he carried a blazing sword. In his left hand, he bore an immense chain, links of shining blue iron heavy with divine authority, bound together by a great lock.

The angel turned and walked deliberately toward John Luke. Without a word, he placed the chain into John Luke's hands. Its weight was immense, yet steady, alive with power but obedient.

Jesus spoke calmly, His voice carrying over the wind. "John Ward, take the chain. Through the Mantle, you have been given authority to bind Satan. Do not hesitate. Bind him and witness the miracle the Father has prepared."

The desert fell silent. Creation seemed to hold its breath.

John Ward grasped the mighty chain. It pulsed with a living strength yet rested easily in his hands.

Satan towered over him, more than ten feet tall, his red armor blazing in the desert sun. He sneered and spat, "You? A puny boy sent to bind me?"

But fear did not rise in John Ward, only resolve.

A quiet fire kindled within him as he stepped forward, steady and unflinching. The weight of the chain vanished as if carried by another power altogether. With astonishing speed, John Luke moved around Satan, the links flashing blue as they wrapped tightly around the beast's massive form. The lock snapped shut with a thunderous crack.

Satan roared and cursed, struggling, but he could not move.

John Ward stepped back to Jesus's side.

At once, the Earth convulsed. A violent tremor split the desert floor, and a vast chasm tore open beneath Satan's feet, a hole without a bottom, black and endless.

Satan plunged downward, his screams echoing as he spiraled into the abyss. Rage and terror mixed in his voice as he bellowed, "Curse you, Jesus! I will have my revenge!"

John Ward watched as the darkness swallowed him, the cries fading into the depths until only silence remained.

A tremor rippled through the desert. The bottomless pit sealed itself as sand poured in, smoothing the ground until no trace of the chasm remained. It was as if the wound in the Earth had never existed.

The blue angel turned, bowed deeply before Jesus, and vanished in a flash of light.

Jesus and John Luke stood alone in the vast silence of the Nubian Desert, side by side.

Then Jesus spoke. "The prophecy is fulfilled. Satan is bound and vanquished for one thousand years. Well done, John Luke, my brave and faithful servant."

The desert grew still, as though creation itself exhaled. High above them, an eagle circled and released a clear, piercing cry that echoed across the sands.

Jesus looked upward and smiled.

"The Father is pleased."

Chapter 22:

Water of Life

"Then the angel showed me the river of the water of life, as clear as crystal, flowing from the throne of God and of the Lamb" (Revelation 22:1).

Biblical prophets often speak of water as a sign of life and salvation. The prophet Isaiah wrote that God promises peace that flows like a river, life poured out abundantly upon His people. Centuries later, the Book of Revelation, written by John of Patmos, echoes this promise in its fullest form: the river of the water of life, clear as crystal, flowing from the throne of God and of the Lamb.

This living water is a symbol of restoration, healing after judgment, and mercy following justice. With Satan bound and no longer able to deceive the nations, the water of life is free to flow once more. In Sudan, both figuratively and literally, God's renewal is about to begin.

The desert air was still, and the first light of morning spread across the sand. As Jesus and John Luke stood together, Jesus turned to him and said, "Thank you for being here, John Luke. I value having you at My side. Now there is still work to do for the people of Sudan."

John Luke answered, his voice steady with devotion. "Jesus, I love being with You. I am honored to be Your disciple, and I am ready to serve these people in whatever way You ask."

Jesus smiled and said, "That is good news. The work before us will echo the miracle you performed in the Donbas. We will bring the water of life to the people."

He gestured toward the horizon. "Fly now over Egypt to the Nile River, to the place where it meets the Mediterranean Sea. When you reach the Nile Delta, circle low over the water, tight at first, then faster and wider with each pass. An atmospheric river will rise and follow you."

Then Jesus added, His voice steady with promise, "Return to this place and command the waters to fall upon the desert. The river will spread across nearly 1,000 miles of the Nubian Desert, creating green pastures and pools of living water. Farmers and herders will share the land in peace. This miracle fulfills the prophecy of Revelation and advances the Father's plan. The people of Sudan need usable land, and they shall have it for generations."

Without hesitation, John Luke flew to the Nile Delta. As he circled the waters just as Jesus had instructed, a vast atmospheric river gathered behind him, shimmering and immense.

He turned back toward Jesus, the roar of rushing water filling the sky, and cried out with authority, "River of life, I command you, flow upon the desert!"

The river of life obeyed.

With a sound of rolling thunder, the water fell upon the desert, and the Earth drank deeply. Sand darkened, cracked, and gave way as living water spread across the land, filling vast basins where only dust had reigned.

At that same moment, a nomadic tribe of shepherds tended their fat-tailed sheep near the ancient city of Meroe, nearly 200 miles from the Red Sea. They felt the ground shudder beneath their feet, then heard a sound foreign to the desert, the rushing roar of water.

Astonished, they climbed a nearby dune. Beyond it, where barren wasteland had stretched for generations, lay a vast pool of shimmering water.

The shepherds ran back to the city, breathless, telling of a river that fell from the sky and flooded the desert. Word spread quickly. Hundreds of shepherds, farmers, merchants, and families, Muslims and Christians alike, made their way to see it with their own eyes.

Phones were raised. Images and videos flooded social media. Within hours, the miracle gripped Sudan, and then the world.

International news crews rushed to the Nubian Desert. The headline of *The Jerusalem Post* proclaimed what many were already whispering in awe: "Another Miracle of Biblical Proportions."

Jesus and John Luke then went on to Khartoum to meet with the prime minister. John Luke called Prime Minister Abdul Baatin on his private line. Abdul answered at once, his voice urgent.

"John Ward, did you have something to do with the miracle of water in the Nubian Desert?"

John Luke glanced at Jesus, seeking His guidance. Jesus smiled and gave a quiet nod.

"Yes, Abdul," John Luke replied. "God caused a miracle, an atmospheric river, a river of life, that flooded nearly 1.000 miles of the Nubian Desert. However, please tell the people that the waters came because of an Earthquake near the Red Sea that formed the atmospheric river."

Abdul agreed without hesitation.

Then he laughed softly, with wonder in his voice. "This is like what happened in Ukraine. John Ward, are you here in Khartoum now?"

"Yes," John Luke said. "I am just outside your office."

There was a brief pause, then Abdul said warmly, "Please come in, my friend."

Now the prime minister could share the good news: the ceasefire, the removal of the generals, the influx of relief funds, and the miracle of the river of life in the desert. The timing of Jesus was impeccable.

John Ward met with Abdul, who invited him to travel to Lower Nubia, to the region known as Wawat. There, the prime minister was greeted by thousands of jubilant Sudanese who welcomed his message of peace with cheers and open arms. The press captured every word, broadcasting hope across the nation, while John Ward remained carefully out of sight.

As Abdul spoke, John Ward felt quiet satisfaction, not pride, but gratitude. He noticed Jesus standing nearby, unseen by the crowds, watching with calm assurance as peace took root among the people.

Prime Minister Abdul Baatin shared his plan with the people.

"The warring generals have been removed from Sudan. Our nation now has the resources to rebuild our cities, villages, farms, and fields. Today, we witnessed a miracle as Allah brought forth an atmospheric river, a river of life, born from a great Earthquake that caused water to pour into the Nubian Desert, transforming barren land into fertile ground. This land is for all our people."

The crowd erupted with thunderous approval.

The prime minister continued, "We will use modern technology to capture this water in basins that will sustain livestock and nourish crops for years to come. Today marks the beginning of a new era, an era of peace, shared prosperity, and renewal for Sudan."

Government soldiers and former paramilitary fighters stood among the crowd, cheering side by side. Words of unity, coexistence, and hope drowned out the language of division and civil war. For the first time in years, the people of Sudan could imagine a future not defined by conflict, but by life.

Later that day, the United Nations Secretary-General informed Prime Minister Abdul Baatin that a peacekeeping force would arrive at Khartoum International Airport the following morning. Soon after, the United States Secretary of State called to say that a team of seasoned negotiators was already en route and would land that evening to establish peace talks in the capital. The prime minister immediately offered space in the Governor-General's Palace as their base of operations.

Abdul then summoned his most trusted advisers and instructed them to contact military leaders from both factions, calling for negotiations to begin the next day.

As expected, General Hemedti's advisers initially refused to attend. General Al-Hussain's military team, however, agreed to participate. In an unexpected turn, they offered to reach out directly to Hemedti's leadership and urge them to come to the table. Against all odds, the strategy worked.

The next day, the prime minister, his most trusted advisers, and negotiators from the United States Institute of Peace met with representatives from both warring factions for more than twelve hours. At dawn, they emerged to announce what few believed possible: a peace treaty had been signed. Sudan's third, and final, civil war was over. Peace flowed like a river through the nation.

Jesus and John Luke returned to his home office. There, Jesus appeared to him in person and explained that the binding of the Antichrist had lifted a heavy shadow from the Earth.

Jesus said, "There will still be wars and disputes among nations, and natural disasters will take place. But the absence of evil clears a path where goodness can rise and prevail. What you witnessed among the Sudanese is one of those opportunities where good won the day. You will see more of these opportunities with the Mantle before our work is finished."

John Luke smiled and said, "I am so grateful that You chose me for this work."

In His usual manner, Jesus hugged John Luke goodbye and said, "I love you like a brother."

And John Luke said, "I love You, Jesus." Then Jesus disappeared for the present time.

John Luke returned home and had much to tell Kristin. Then he kindly called me and shared the details of his latest adventure with the Mantle.

On the fortieth day at Saint Luke's Motel, Jesus asked John Luke to dismiss the remaining guests. General Hemedti and his four advisers had refused to repent. They neither prayed nor reflected, spending their days plotting revenge.

At Jesus's direction, John Luke delivered them to United Nations peacekeepers in Khartoum. They were arrested, tried before the International Criminal Court in The Hague, and convicted of crimes against humanity. Hemedti received a life sentence, while his advisers were each sentenced to twenty years in prison.

General Al-Hussain and Colonel Hassan chose a different path. Freed from the Antichrist's influence, they prayed, reflected on the Qur'an, and sought forgiveness. At Jesus's request, John Luke brought them before Prime Minister Abdul Baatin. The two men resigned their commissions and committed to five years of community service with the Ministry of Irrigation and Water Resources, helping restore the Nubian Desert.

Over time, they came to love the work of renewing the land and remained in that service until retirement. As Jesus foretold, repentance bore fruit, and heaven rejoiced at their conversion.

Both men grew to love the work of renewing the land and remained in that service until retirement. As Jesus foretold, repentance bore fruit, and heaven rejoiced at their conversion.

Chapter 23:

Babylon Has Fallen

"Then there came flashes of lightning, rumblings, peals of thunder and a severe Earthquake. No Earthquake like it has ever occurred since mankind has been on Earth, so tremendous was the quake" (Revelation 16:18).

The Book of Revelation foretells an earthquake of unprecedented magnitude, one that will surpass every seismic event recorded in human history. The Great Chilean Earthquake of 1960 measured 9.5 on the Richter scale, killing thousands and triggering tsunamis across the Pacific. Yet even that catastrophe pales beside the quake described in Revelation.

Iraq, historically linked to the land of ancient Babylon, sits above several active fault zones. Geological fractures such as the Abu Jir–Euphrates fault system stretch across the region, leaving the land vulnerable to powerful seismic activity. According to Scripture, this same land will again become the stage upon which prophecy unfolds.

The Earth's crust in this region, about 25 miles thick, rests upon the mantle, a vast layer of hot, slowly moving rock. The motion of this mantle drives the movement of tectonic plates that form the surface of the planet.

When these plates collide or shift along their boundaries, enormous pressure is released as seismic waves that ripple through the crust. The greater the movement of the plates, the more powerful the earthquake.

One late summer morning, as Dr. Dog was curled at John Luke's side, and Zoey settled contentedly beside Kristin, they turned on the news. They were met with staggering reports: a massive Earthquake had struck north-central Iraq shortly after midnight.

Seismologists estimated the quake at 9.9 on the moment magnitude scale, the most powerful Earthquake ever recorded. Nearly two-thirds of the country lies in ruins. Shock waves rippled far beyond Iraq's borders, felt in Turkey to the north, Syria to the west, and Iran to the east.

The epicenter was identified near the city of Tikrit, home to roughly 160,000 people. In Baghdad, more than 100 miles to the south, buildings collapsed across the capital of seven million. With the disaster only two hours old, the International Centre for Earth Simulation Foundation (ICES) projected a death toll approaching nine million, nearly twenty percent of Iraq's population. Continuous aftershocks threatened to push that number even higher.

Kristin turned to John Luke and said, "You need to speak with Jesus right now!" John Luke agreed, hurried to his office, said a prayer, and wore the Mantle.

Jesus appeared in person, His presence heavy with sorrow. His voice was low, measured, and filled with finality.

"John Luke, I grieve to tell you that the prophecy has come to pass."

He paused and then said, "Babylon has fallen."

Jesus explained to John Luke, "At one time, Babylon was the greatest city on Earth, now part of what you know as modern Iraq. The name Babylon means gate of the gods. It was once the heart of human civilization, rising along the banks of the ancient Euphrates River. This land was Mesopotamia, the fertile crescent, where the earliest cities, laws, and writings emerged more than 3 thousand years before My birth on Earth."

Though Jesus did not appear surprised, a deep sorrow rested upon Him. John Luke felt the weight settle in his own heart and asked the question that pressed most urgently on him. "What should we do?"

Jesus said, "We must help the survivors. And we must help rebuild the land. The aftershocks will continue. Remember what I told you. Natural disasters will still occur. Yet even in judgment, there is mercy. This moment is an invitation for the world to choose compassion and mercy."

He paused, then said, "If you are ready, we will go to the epicenter, Tikrit."

John Luke answered without hesitation, "Of course, Jesus."

He stepped out, told Kristin where he was going, kissed her goodbye, and returned, steady and resolved. "I am ready."

Jesus nodded. "Then we take our leave."

As John Luke and Jesus flew to Tikrit, Jesus reminded him of the "end times" He had spoken of in Scripture. *"There will be famines and Earthquakes in various places. All these are the beginning of birth pains"* (Matthew 24:8).

Jesus told John Luke, "These events are only the beginning of the end. Only the Father knows the day and hour when the end of the age shall come upon His creation. Babylon was the beginning of civilization, and the prophecy, unfortunately, also begins here."

Then Jesus added, "These events mark the threshold, not the conclusion. Only the Father knows the day and the hour when the age will finally close. Babylon was the cradle of civilization, and it is fitting, though tragic, that prophecy should also turn its page here."

He paused, then spoke gently but firmly. "John Luke, you must prepare your mind for what we are about to see. Many souls have already returned to the Father. Yet amid the ruins life remains, and some can still be saved."

John Luke swallowed and nodded. "Thank you, Jesus," he said quietly. "I have never experienced an Earthquake."

As John Luke and Jesus flew over Tikrit, they saw utter devastation. Entire neighborhoods had been reduced to rubble. Even with Jesus's warning, John Luke was stunned. He could scarcely comprehend how anyone survived such a cataclysm.

Jesus led John Luke to the remains of a high-rise apartment building. He said calmly, "Go to the bottom of the rubble, John Luke. The Mantle will protect you."

Beneath layers of shattered concrete, John Luke found a family, a mother, a father, and their infant, alive and nearly unharmed, sheltered by a fallen steel beam that had held back the collapse. With gentle care, John Luke gathered them and carried them into the open, placing them safely with a rescue crew.

A photographer captured the moment, and the headline soon followed: *"A Small Miracle in a Great Ruin."*

As they moved through the ruins, Jesus paused and said quietly, "Please go to that store. On the floor, beneath a fallen steel display case, you will find two survivors."

John Luke lifted the twisted metal and saw an older man and woman, broken, bleeding, yet alive. Still unseen, he gathered them gently and carried them to a waiting rescue crew. As he did, he prayed silently that God would restore what the Earth had taken.

When the rescuers examined the couple, their injuries were gone. What moments before had been fatal wounds were healed. The workers stood in stunned silence, unable to explain what they saw, only grateful that life had prevailed.

John Luke asked quietly, "Jesus, are there more we can save?"

Jesus paused, listening to what John Luke could not hear. "Yes," He said. "I hear the cries of children from a school nearby."

Though the ruins were silent to him, John Luke followed Jesus's guidance. Beneath collapsed walls and broken beams, he found five children, frightened and dust-covered. Most were bruised but alive. One child lay still, his leg badly broken.

Remaining unseen, John Luke carried them to a waiting ambulance. Before the door closed, he knelt briefly beside the injured child and prayed. The boy's leg straightened and healed at once.

The medics stared in disbelief, then moved quickly to help the children. John Luke stepped back into the ruins, grateful that the Lord heard the cries of His people.

John Luke returned to Jesus's side as they continued through the ruins. Jesus stopped, pointed toward a shattered structure, and said, "There is an orphanage in that building. Please go and find the survivors."

Inside, beneath fallen stone and twisted beams, John Luke found life where there should have been none: seven injured children and their teacher, badly hurt, blood matted in her hair from a deep head wound.

John Luke lifted them gently from the rubble and carried them to a rescue crew. When all were safe, he knelt briefly and prayed over the children and their teacher. Their injuries healed, quiet and complete, as God's mercy passed through them.

John Luke stepped back, his heart heavy yet grateful, aware that he could not undo the devastation, but thankful that in this place of sorrow, he had been allowed to carry life out of death.

Jesus then said, "John Luke, there are several men trapped in the stairwell of an office building. They are alive and need help."

Guided by Jesus speaking to his mind, John Luke descended into the ruins. He lifted shattered desks, bent railings, and slabs of concrete, uncovering eight men pinned beneath the wreckage. One by one, he carried them into the open air and handed them over to rescue crews.

Most were badly injured. John Luke knelt beside each man and prayed quietly. Their wounds closed, bones set, and breath steadied. John Luke stepped back, unseen, and gave thanks that God's mercy was moving through him.

Next, Jesus asked John Luke to go with Him to Al Sahra Airport in Tikrit.

"There is an aircraft in danger," Jesus said quietly. "There are about forty souls on board."

They arrived at chaos and fear. The twin-engine plane had landed safely moments before the quake struck, but the runway split apart beneath it. A vast fissure had opened in the concrete, swallowing the nose of the aircraft. The plane teetered at the edge, its tail lifted slightly, engines silent, the cabin filled with panicked voices.

Passengers pressed against the windows, the crew frozen between training and terror, all waiting and hoping for help.

Jesus turned to John Luke and said, "Go now, My friend."

As John Luke flew toward the aircraft, a violent aftershock rippled through the ground. The runway split wider, and the plane lurched forward, nearly vanishing into the Earth until only part of the tail remained visible above the debris.

Without hesitation, John Luke seized the tail and, with the strength of the Mantle, dragged the aircraft back from the collapsing fissure. He moved beneath the belly of the plane, lifting and guiding it toward the shattered terminal, settling it onto firmer ground.

He entered the cabin at once and evacuated the passengers, carrying them swiftly to safety. Most bore only bruises and shaken nerves. Returning inside, he found the four crew members at their stations. The pilot had a deep gash across his forehead, blood streaking his face. John Luke placed his hand on the wound and prayed. The cut closed instantly, leaving only stunned relief behind.

Jesus looked at him and said softly, "Well done, my friend."

After the miracle in Tikrit, Jesus told John Luke they must go to Baghdad. The city lay along the Tigris River, near the ancient ruins of Babylon, and now Babylon was truly no more. From above, they saw that the once-beautiful Haydar-Khana Mosque had collapsed into stone and dust. By mercy alone, no one had been inside at the late hour.

Museums, high-rises, tenements, and offices had been reduced to fields of rubble. Whole neighborhoods were flattened, their outlines erased. When they reached Rashīd Street, the heart of the financial district, banks and government buildings lay broken open like tombs. Bodies rested in the streets where life had moved only hours before. Along the Tigris, slabs of concrete had slid into the water, choking the river's banks.

The devastation was overwhelming. Jesus stood still and looked upon the city, and He wept.

Unsure what else to do, John Luke placed his hand gently on Jesus's shoulder.

Jesus said quietly, "My Father and I mourn for the dead, millions of souls lost. Thank you, my friend."

Another aftershock struck without warning. The ground convulsed, and chunks of concrete, brick, and masonry thundered down around them. Roofing collapsed in waves of dust and debris. From the shattered dome of the Assyrian Catholic Church of the Virgin Mary, the golden cross broke free and fell, clanging against the stone below.

Jesus stopped short. His voice was urgent. "We must go to the Baghdad Railway. There are survivors on the train. They need help now."

In an instant, Jesus and John Luke flew to the tracks. Before them lay a scene of chaos. Passenger cars were overturned and piled atop one another, twisted and derailed, scattered as a child's toy train flung across the Earth.

John Luke moved to the final car, stepping into a grim tangle of bodies, shattered seats, and scattered luggage. The air was thick with dust and silence. Jesus stood beside him, quietly directing his steps, showing him where life still lingered.

Together, they lifted twelve survivors from the wreckage and carried them to waiting rescuers. John Luke prayed over the injured as they were placed gently on the ground.

Then Jesus went to the engine. He knelt beside the engineer, placed His hands upon the man's chest, and spoke life into him. The engineer gasped and opened his eyes, restored from death itself.

Jesus returned to John Luke and said softly that the others were gone.

Finally, Jesus and John Luke came to the ruins of Al Karkh General Hospital. The building had collapsed entirely, leaving only a single hallway standing like a spine amid the rubble. They entered the corridor and, one by one, brought out more than twenty-five survivors. Jesus and John Luke moved among them, laying hands on each person, healing wounds, broken bones, and hidden illnesses.

When the last survivor was safe, John Luke felt a deep sorrow emanating from Jesus.

"They came here seeking healing," Jesus said quietly, "and instead they found death."

He lifted His hands toward heaven and cried out, His voice breaking with grief and obedience, "Father, Your will be done."

At once, the rubble trembled. Concrete and stone began to separate as if obeying a greater command. From beneath the ruins, more than one hundred people rose to their feet and walked toward Jesus, alive. Among them were three women, each carrying a newborn child.

Jesus exhaled and said, "Thank you, Father, for hearing Me."

John Luke recognized the words at once; the same words Jesus had spoken at the tomb of Lazarus. His heart trembled as understanding settled in.

Jesus embraced each person who had been raised, one by one, with the tenderness of a shepherd counting His sheep.

John Luke stood in awe, knowing he had just witnessed the greatest resurrection since the dawn of time.

Jesus turned to John Luke and said how grateful He was for his companionship.

"Just like the Scriptures," Jesus said, *"two by two"* (Matthew 10:7).

John Luke smiled and finished the verse, "*They anointed with oil many who were sick and healed them.*"

Jesus said sincerely, "Well done, good and faithful John Luke."

After this work, Jesus turned to John Luke and asked gently, "Are you willing to help with one more mission, to the refugee camps outside Erbil?"

John Luke did not hesitate. "Of course, Jesus. I will follow Your lead."

They arrived within seconds. What had once been rows of temporary shelters were now fields of shattered brick and broken stone. Thousands of refugees, many from Syria, had lived there. Silence hung over the camp.

Jesus surveyed the ruins and said, "Let us divide the work. I will take the rows to the left. You take those to the right. Bring out any who still live, pray for their healing, and then move on."

John Luke worked methodically, lifting rubble, listening for breath, watching for movement. After an hour, he searched nearly 100 ruined shelters and found only fifteen survivors. He brought each one to safety, prayed over them, and entrusted them to aid workers before returning to the wreckage.

When he rejoined Jesus, he learned that Jesus had found twenty more.

Jesus looked over the camp one last time and said, "Our work here is finished for now. Go home to Kristin. Tomorrow we will plan what comes next." Then He added quietly, "Before you sleep tonight, pray Psalm 86."

John Luke nodded and returned home to Kristin, drained and heavy-hearted, troubled by all he could not do. Kristin drew him into her arms as he said quietly, "I hope you do not mind. I want something light to eat and then to sleep."

She held him close and whispered, "I am just grateful you are safe and home."

Before turning out the light, John Luke prayed over *Psalm 86*:

"Hear me, Lord, and answer me, for I am poor and needy. Guard my life, for I am faithful to You. Save Your servant who trusts in You. You are my God. Have mercy on me, Lord, for I call to You all day long. Bring joy to Your servant, Lord, for I put my trust in You." (vv. 1–4).

As the psalm's words lingered in his mind, John Luke understood that Jesus was reminding him of a simple truth: I am with you. Trust the Father's plan.

Yet the images of death and devastation would not leave him. What he had witnessed shook him deeply, far more than anything he had seen in Ukraine or amid the wounds of war. This was mass loss on a scale he could not comprehend, and he struggled to see how such suffering fit within God's purposes.

Still, in the quiet of the night, he surrendered the question itself and whispered in his heart, *Jesus, I trust in You.*

Chapter 24: Funding for Iraq

"After this, I saw another angel coming down from heaven. He had great authority, and the Earth was illuminated by his splendor. With a mighty voice he shouted: Fallen! Fallen is Babylon the Great!" (Revelation 18:1–2).

The next morning, John Luke woke early. He had gone to bed at five o'clock the evening before and slept for more than twelve hours. His body had clearly needed the rest.

After sharing breakfast with Kristin, he spent the morning working in his home office. By noon, he felt a familiar stirring in his spirit, a gentle summons to speak with Jesus.

John Luke opened the ornate box on his desk, said a quiet prayer, and placed the Mantle upon his head.

Jesus appeared in person and said with a knowing smile, "You look better, John Luke. A good night's sleep makes all the difference in how we see and understand."

John Luke returned the smile. "Thank you, Lord. I do feel rested, though the tragedy still weighs heavily on my mind. Even with Your warning, I had never witnessed devastation like that. I grieve for the people of Iraq. Yet I am grateful that You are with me."

He paused, then continued more quietly. "I do not understand why such suffering happens. I want You to know that I prayed *Psalm 86* last night, just as You asked. Jesus, I trust in You."

Jesus said gently, "Thank you, my friend. I am glad the psalm steadied your spirit. Natural disasters are a painful part of creation. Their toll is great. Those souls are now with the Father."

He continued, "Yet the Father's work is not finished. Even now, the United Nations is mobilizing disaster relief, and the Red Cross is already on the ground. The Father's plan includes another stream of mercy through The Mantle LLC. We will provide funding for health care workers, housing, and reconstruction in Iraq."

Jesus looked at John Luke and said, "This work will be coordinated through you, as John Ward, and with the Prime Minister of Iraq, Mustafa Halam Sudinis. In this way, compassion will follow calamity, and hope will rise from the ruins."

John Luke said, "That sounds like a good plan, Jesus. May I ask, how will we raise the funds?"

Jesus smiled. "You will."

John Luke blinked. "Me?"

Jesus smiled again. "Last night, I appeared in the dreams of three generous, well-known Christian billionaires. In each dream, I told them you would be contacting them about The Mantle LLC's plan to help rebuild Iraq. Their hearts are prepared. They are expecting your call."

He added calmly, "I am confident they will donate the funds, and do so anonymously."

John Luke stood still, his mouth slightly open. Several thoughts rushed through his mind, but for a moment, no words came.

Jesus smiled and said, "No time like the present, John Luke. Please use the Mantle phone and call them now. Here are their names and numbers."

He continued matter-of-factly, "Ask the first to donate $3 billion and the next two to give $2 billion each. That will provide $7 billion to move the Father's plan forward quickly. Rebuilding Iraq is a most worthy cause."

John Luke glanced at the list, then back at Jesus, still astonished. "I will do as You ask," he said with a nervous smile. "I am stunned by this idea, but here we go."

He dialed the first number. The call was answered almost immediately.

"John Ward," the man said, "I have been expecting you. Jesus appeared to me in a dream last night and spoke of your work and the rebuilding of Iraq. Tell me, how much is needed?"

John Ward smiled, grateful and still amazed. "Thank you for taking my call, sir. It is an honor to speak with you. Would you be willing to donate $3 billion to this cause?"

The man paused, taken aback by the amount. Then he replied thoughtfully, "This is a worthy cause, and yes, I will donate the funds anonymously. I have followed your work around the world,

John Ward. Please call my office and give my assistant the wire-transfer details. He will be expecting your call."

John Luke thanked him profusely for his generosity, and the call ended.

Jesus smiled and said, "See? That was easy. You are becoming quite the fundraiser, John Luke. Go ahead and call the next two. They are expecting to hear from you as well."

John Luke laughed softly. "Jesus, You never stop surprising me."

He placed the next call. A woman answered and, without hesitation, agreed to donate the funds. The final call went to a man with an Australian accent, who also committed to the full amount. In just a few minutes, seven billion dollars was pledged.

Jesus said warmly, "Well done, John Luke. Please ensure each donor has the correct wire transfer details for The Mantle LLC. Now our focus turns to rebuilding Iraq and comforting those who remain."

John Luke shook his head in awe. "I do not even have words for what just happened. You truly are an amazing God."

Jesus smiled. "Thank you, my friend. Your identity will remain protected throughout this work. We will coordinate relief efforts in Iraq through Episcopal Relief & Development. I would like your pastor, Reverend Mark, to help connect us with the appropriate leaders."

He continued, "In this way, the funds will be used wisely and distributed discreetly. The involvement of the Episcopal Church will help strengthen trust between Christian and Muslim communities in Iraq. It is a win for relief, a win for unity, and a win for peace."

Jesus smiled at His own quietly Trinitarian remark.

Then Jesus said, "I will leave you now to take care of the details. Once the funds are successfully wired to The Mantle LLC, we will meet again to discuss the next steps with Episcopal Relief & Development."

John Luke handled the arrangements, and by the next day, the funds were transferred. He and Kristin worked from home, and shortly after lunch, he asked if she minded him connecting with Jesus.

"Of course not," she said with a smile. "Thank you for asking."

John Luke went to his office, said a prayer, and placed the Mantle upon his head. Jesus spoke directly to his mind. "Hello, my dear friend. Thank you for taking care of everything. The funds arrived today."

It was not a question. Jesus already knew.

"Yes, Jesus," John Luke replied silently. "The funds are in place. I believe the next step is reaching out to Reverend Mark to make the introductions to Episcopal Relief & Development."

Jesus answered, "Precisely. After that call, please set up a call with their New York City home office. They will, of course, be pleased to hear the news of the donation. I trust you will handle every detail with great attention."

With that confirmation, John Luke connected by phone with Reverend Mark to make introductions to the organization's headquarters in New York City. He explained his friendship with John Ward, who led the nonprofit organization The Mantle LLC. Reverend Mark was thrilled that John Luke was involved in supporting efforts to help people affected by the Iraqi Earthquake.

John Luke asked Reverend Mark to keep his family's involvement with The Mantle LLC confidential. Reverend Mark agreed, though his expression revealed clear disappointment at not being able to share such good news with the parish.

Sensing this, John Luke offered a compromise. "Perhaps you could simply announce that a parish family is working with a nonprofit agency and plans to make a generous contribution to the relief effort."

That answer seemed to satisfy Reverend Mark.

He promptly connected John Luke with the President and CEO of Episcopal Relief & Development, Dr. Robert Urban, and the Chair of the Board, Reverend Susan Duvall. Before making the call to arrange the donation and meeting, John Luke quietly asked Jesus to guide his words once again.

The following day, Friday, John Luke joined a conference call with Dr. Robert Urban and Reverend Susan Duvall. Jesus was present in John Luke's office, quietly guiding his words.

John Luke began, speaking with calm assurance.

"Thank you for taking my call, Dr. Urban and Reverend Duvall. Through the nonprofit organization, The Mantle LLC, we would like to donate $7 billion to support Episcopal Relief & Development's humanitarian work in Iraq.

"Our goals are threefold: to provide direct medical and reconstruction aid to the Iraqi people, to foster reconciliation and cooperation between Christian and Muslim communities, and to help rebuild both churches and mosques damaged in the Earthquake.

"We propose distributing the funds as follows: $3 billion directly to Iraqi Prime Minister Mustafa Halam Sudinis for national relief and rebuilding; $3 billion to Shia and Sunni community leaders for humanitarian and reconciliation efforts; $500 million to Saint George Episcopal Church in Baghdad; and $500 million to the Episcopal Relief & Development general fund.

"We respectfully ask for your assistance in making the appropriate introductions to the prime minister and to the religious leaders so that this aid can be delivered swiftly and transparently."

John Luke asked gently, "What do you think of the plan?"

Silence filled the line. After a moment, John Luke said, "Hello, are you still there?"

Dr. Urban finally spoke; his voice measured with disbelief. "Did I hear you correctly? Did you say seven billion, with a b?"

John Luke smiled. "Yes, capital B."

Reverend Duvall inhaled sharply. "This is truly extraordinary. Such generosity is almost beyond comprehension. We are deeply grateful that you would entrust this work to us."

John Luke replied calmly, “Please know this plan comes from God. We want our organization’s representative, John Ward, to meet with you in your New York office to arrange the donation and help coordinate its use. In addition to the funds designated for the prime minister, we want religious community leaders to have discretion to serve their people as they see fit.”

“We hope this gift will inspire other private donors to support the relief efforts as well. We ask that our family’s name remain private. Publicly, this work should be attributed solely to John Ward and The Mantle LLC.”

John Luke continued, “We want to emphasize the work of the Episcopal Church as God’s agent of peace and generosity. Dr. Urban, Reverend Duvall, does this approach feel right to you?”

Dr. Urban replied without hesitation, “Absolutely. I cannot adequately express my gratitude to your family. I am both thrilled and humbled by this extraordinary generosity.”

Reverend Duvall added warmly, “I am deeply grateful for this remarkable gift. We will arrange for John Ward to meet immediately with our teams so we can begin organizing the work.”

John Luke glanced at Jesus, who smiled and nodded in quiet approval.

“Wonderful,” John Luke said. “We look forward to hearing from you soon.”

The call ended.

Chapter 25: Rebuilding Iraq

"They fell down on their faces before the throne and worshiped God, saying: 'Amen! Praise and glory and wisdom and thanks and honor and power and strength be to our God forever. Amen!'" (Revelation 7:11-12).

The survivors of the tragic Earthquake in Iraq were emotionally torn, grateful to be alive yet mourning profound loss. These same tensions echo in the Book of Revelation, where the 144,000 survive the calamities of the end times. The passage reminds us that in desperate moments, perhaps especially then, we must cling to our faith and give thanks for our blessings.

The following week, John Luke, operating as John Ward, met with leaders from Episcopal Relief & Development to coordinate distribution efforts. Together, they arranged introductions to the Iraqi prime minister and key religious leaders. John Ward traveled to Iraq and met first with the prime minister, then with the religious leaders, to outline the donation and distribution plan.

Prime Minister Sudinis, though grateful, remained cautious about John Ward's motives.

Leaning back in his chair, the prime minister spoke thoughtfully. "Our government is aware that your organization played a role in recent events in Ukraine. You may know that Iraq maintains trade agreements with Russia for food and energy. We did not support Russia in the war, and since the conflict ended, we resumed relations with Ukraine. We do not want this donation to carry political overtones."

John Ward replied evenly, "We agree. The Mantle LLC was involved in negotiating peace in Ukraine. I encourage you to speak directly with leaders in both Ukraine and Russia regarding our intentions and actions. I believe you will find that each holds a favorable view of our organization."

The prime minister nodded. "We will do so. In the meantime, please sign the appropriate documents regarding your presence in Iraq. Once those matters are complete, we will contact you concerning the acceptance and distribution of the funds through our government."

John Ward inclined his head. "That sounds reasonable. We will await your word."

The meeting concluded without friction, and the framework was set. John Ward departed to meet with the religious communities, carrying the quiet weight of what had been agreed.

The Shia and Sunni community leaders welcomed John Ward and readily agreed to accept the funds. Their focus was fixed on the survivors, on shelter, sustenance, and rebuilding their mosques. They received John Ward with gratitude, untroubled by suspicion, and accepted his intentions as sincere.

The leaders of Saint George Episcopal Church were equally gracious. Their pastor, Canon Dunstan Taylor, a native of Liverpool, asked whether the funds might be distributed beyond their own congregation to assist other Christian churches throughout Iraq. John Ward considered the request and smiled; it was a splendid idea, wholly aligned with the mission.

Each meeting unfolded without resistance. Quietly, steadily, God's plan moved forward.

News of the donations, channeled through Episcopal Relief & Development, and of John Ward's meetings with Iraq's political and religious leaders spread quickly through the international press. Within days, multiple large contributions flowed in from private benefactors and philanthropists around the world. By the end of the first month, donations exceeded $1 billion. Within two months, they surpassed $4 billion.

The words of Jesus, that disaster presents humanity with the choice to do good, came to fruition. Though more than ten million lives were lost in the Earthquake, Iraq began rebuilding far sooner than anyone anticipated. Over time, the Father's plan to strengthen relations between Christians and Muslims took root. From tragedy, good emerged.

God cares for all His people.

Chapter 26:

The Seventh Trumpet

"The seventh angel sounded his trumpet, and there were loud voices in heaven, which said: 'The kingdom of the world has become the kingdom of our Lord and of his Messiah, and he will reign for ever and ever...Then God's temple in heaven was opened, and within his temple was seen the ark of his covenant" (Revelation 11:15, 19).

The Ark of the Covenant was an ornate, gold-plated chest of acacia wood, fashioned to hold the two stone tablets of the Ten Commandments given by God to Moses. The *Book of Exodus* recounts that the Lord instructed Moses to build the ark during his forty days on Mount Sinai, providing precise specifications for its design and furnishings. Constructed nearly 3,000 years ago, the ark endures as one of antiquity's most coveted and elusive artifacts. With all due respect to Indiana Jones, its location remains unknown.

Exodus describes the ark as measuring approximately three feet, eight inches in length and two feet, four inches in width and height, and weighing roughly 300 pounds.

"Overlay it with pure gold, both inside and out, and make a gold molding around it. Cast four gold rings for it and fasten them

to its four feet, with two rings on each side. Then make poles of acacia wood and overlay them with gold. Insert the poles into the rings on the sides of the ark to carry it. The poles are to remain in the rings of this ark; they are not to be removed. Then put in the ark the tablets of the covenant law, which I will give you" (Exodus 25:11-16).

Scripture tells us the ark journeyed with the Israelites through the wilderness, a visible sign of God's presence among His people. It rested in Shiloh, was later brought to Jerusalem by King David, and placed in the temple built by Solomon (1 Kings 8). Wherever it stood, the ark marked sacred ground, where heaven and Earth seemed to touch.

Though legends claim the ark was carried to Egypt or Ethiopia, history records only its disappearance after the Babylonian invasion. Revelation, however, resolves the mystery. At the sounding of the seventh trumpet, God's heavenly temple is opened, and the ark of His covenant is revealed, not lost but preserved. The trumpet announces not only judgment but fulfillment: the covenant secured and God's reign made manifest (Revelation 11:19).

The history of the Israelites and the ark is inseparable from the nation of Egypt. The prophecy of Revelation acknowledges how the stories of these two ancient peoples are intertwined. Jesus affirms the significance of this shared history as He prepares John Luke for their next mission.

Once the work in Iraq had concluded successfully and rebuilding was underway after the devastating Earthquake, Jesus met with John Luke to reveal the Father's next purpose, one that would draw Israel and Egypt together.

This mission, Jesus explained, was devoted to peace between those nations and the Palestinian peoples, and to the glorification of God and His plan for the world, in accordance with the prophecy of Revelation.

After a long Monday at the university, John Luke rode the train home. He was grateful that Kristin had traveled with him to Boston that day and that they returned together around 7:00 PM. They tended to Dr. Dog and Zoey the cat, shared a light dinner, and cleaned the kitchen.

When the dishes were done, John Luke felt that quiet sense that Jesus wished to speak with him. He turned to Kristin. "I have the feeling that Jesus wants to meet. Do you mind if I go to my office now?"

Kristin smiled. "As always, Jesus has perfect timing; the kitchen is clean. Thank you for asking, and please don't keep Him waiting."

John Luke smiled in return and went to his office. He said a prayer and wore the Mantle. Jesus appeared in person, greeted him warmly, embraced him, and said, "I have missed seeing you, My dear friend. Yet remember, I am always with you."

John Luke spoke with quiet enthusiasm. "It is so good to see You, Jesus. I have missed You. Work and home have kept me busy."

Jesus smiled. "I understand, and I honor your devotion to both your family and your work. Tonight, I want to explain our next mission, and I won't keep you long from Kristin. You have both had a long day."

Jesus offered a high-level view of the plan. "You may know that Israel and Egypt signed a peace accord in 1978, fostered by U.S. President Jimmy Carter. Since then, the two nations have maintained a measure of peace, though mistrust still lingers beneath the surface. A central tension remains over the State of Palestine and the land of Gaza. Now, a paramilitary group called Hamas is engaged in conflict with Israeli forces, and too many of the Father's children have lost their homes and their lives to skirmishes and bombardment. Cultural and religious divisions continue to deepen the strain."

Jesus paused as John Luke listened intently. Then He continued, "The Father plans to bring the leaders of these peoples together and cultivate a lasting peace. We will begin with acts of goodness, small at first but meaningful, so that trust may take root. The Father would like us to begin this work soon. Perhaps later this week?"

John Luke answered, "That works well with my schedule, and I look forward to being with You."

Jesus said, "John Luke, I have another Scripture for you to pray over tonight before you rest. This passage is for you, and especially for the people of this region. They are all God's children." Then Jesus recited Psalm 121 by heart:

"I lift my eyes to the mountains. Where does my help come from? My help comes from the Lord, the Maker of heaven and Earth. He will not let your foot slip. He who watches over you will not slumber; indeed, he who watches over Israel will neither slumber nor sleep. The Lord watches over you. The Lord is your shade at your right hand. The sun will not harm you by day, nor the moon by night. The Lord will keep you from all harm. He will watch over your life. The Lord will watch over your coming and going both now and forevermore" (v. 1–8).

John Luke said softly, "Jesus, this psalm is one of my favorites. It is so beautiful to hear You quote Scripture. I will read them again tonight."

Jesus replied, "I know this one is dear to you. Let Scripture guide your life. My words are everlasting, and they remain a living source of comfort."

John Luke said, "Thank You, Jesus. I love You."

"I love you, My dear friend," Jesus answered. And then He was gone, for now.

Chapter 27:

The Ark in Heaven

"The kingdom of the world has become the kingdom of our Lord and of his Messiah, and he will reign for ever and ever" (Revelation 11:15).

Jesus teaches in Scripture that, in time, the prophecy of Revelation will come to pass, and that heaven and Earth will be gathered into a single kingdom under His reign. This writing style is *apocalyptic* literature, rich in symbolism and vision, pointing beyond the present age. Some scholars believe the rebuilding of a third temple in Jerusalem will signal the end of days.

Our story aligns with the imagery and promise of Revelation, holding history and prophecy in deliberate tension.

On Friday, John Luke and Kristin planned to work from their home offices, grateful for the flexibility their positions allowed. They shared breakfast on the deck, lingering for a moment in the morning light before heading to their respective workspaces.

Kristin was a director at an e-commerce retail company, working both remotely and in Boston. Her days were spent in meetings with her team, shaping product lines, refining the website's presentation, and tracking sales. The work suited her, drawing on her background in technology, marketing, and advertising. She was respected as a leader and a careful decision-maker.

John Luke took quiet pride in her success. She was kind, precise, intelligent, and beautiful. He loved her deeply.

John Luke loved his work at the university, where he designed academic programs and applied artificial intelligence (AI) to support teaching and learning. An early authority on AI, he was often asked to speak about its role in educating students and employees.

He was intelligent, thoughtful, pragmatic, and quietly athletic. Together, they were a dynamic couple. Their lives were full, and the Mantle only added to their sense of purpose.

Before lunch, John Luke felt the familiar stirring, the sense that Jesus wished to meet with him. He paused at his work, said a prayer, and wore the Mantle.

Jesus spoke gently into his mind. "Good morning, John Luke. How is your work today?"

John Luke smiled. He loved that Jesus asked about the ordinary details of his life. "It is going really well," he said. "I just finished a project with a big customer, and my boss is happy."

Jesus laughed softly. "You are skilled in many ways, my friend. I am proud of you."

"Thank You, Jesus," John Luke replied. "You are always so encouraging. Are we ready to begin our work for Israel and Egypt?"

Jesus laughed again. "This time, you have read my mind. We could take about one hour of your day and travel somewhere you have never been."

John Luke smiled. "That sounds wonderful, Jesus, though there are not many places we have gone that I have seen."

Jesus used the moment to remind John Luke of the larger design. Their work would carry them to seven nations, part of the Father's plan for peace in the world. So far, John Luke had used the Mantle in Ukraine, Russia, Sudan, and Iraq. Soon, Israel and Egypt would follow.

When Jesus finished, John Luke asked, "Where to this time?"

Jesus looked at him for a moment, smiling as the silence lingered.

"Heaven."

John Luke rose from his chair. "Heaven?"

Jesus nodded gently. "Yes. You know from the Book of Revelation that the Ark of the Covenant is now kept safely in heaven. After Babylon raided Jerusalem, the Father sent His angels to the temple and carried the ark there for safekeeping. Now the Father intends to reunite Israel around His holy presence."

He continued, "As Scripture and history tell us, the first temple was destroyed by Babylon, and the second by the Romans. The Third Temple will rise again in the holy city, with the ark restored to its sacred place. We will use the Mantle to help prepare the way for that temple."

John Luke spoke quietly. “The plan sounds extraordinary, Jesus. But how will I travel to heaven?”

“I will take you,” Jesus replied.

In Jerusalem, the sun was sinking toward the horizon, and Shabbat was about to begin.

Jesus reached for John Luke’s hand. “Are you ready?”

He drew a steady breath. “Yes.”

In the next instant, Jesus lifted him upward, carrying him swiftly beyond the atmosphere of the earth. The stars flashed past, and ahead of them a radiant light grew brighter and brighter until it surrounded them completely.

They entered the light.

John Luke suddenly stood within an immense expanse of luminous blue, vast beyond imagining.

He had arrived in heaven.

At the center of the brilliant space stood a gleaming ark of gold. Four blue-robed angels stood watch at its corners like those he had once seen restraining Satan in his own backyard.

As John Luke’s eyes adjusted to the brilliance, he noticed the ground beneath his feet. It felt like a cloud, yet firm and radiant, its surface glowing with a soft white light.

When the angels recognized Jesus, they bowed deeply and declared in one voice,

“My Lord and my God.”

Jesus answered gently, “*Berachah,*” blessed be God.

Then He turned to John Luke.

"Before we depart with the ark," Jesus said, "there are two people I want you to meet."

John Luke blinked in surprise. "You want to introduce me to two people in heaven? I thought meeting angels was more than enough."

Jesus held his gaze and smiled.

"Yes, my friend."

The light around them deepened, and in the next moment, two figures appeared beside Jesus, calm and radiant.

The Blessed Mother Mary and Saint Joseph. They stood before John Luke with quiet grace.

Jesus spoke warmly. "Ema and Abba, I would like you to meet the young man I have spoken of with such fondness. John Luke, please meet My mother and My earthly father."

John Luke found himself completely speechless. Should I bow? May I touch their hands?

Even their presence carried a gentle warmth, like the fragrance of incense, familiar and yet entirely new.

Before he could move or speak, Mary and Joseph stepped forward and embraced him.

Mary smiled kindly.

"Yeshua speaks very highly of you. Shalom and Mazal Tov, dear John Luke."

At last, he found his voice.

"I am deeply honored to meet you both."

Then he turned to Jesus.

"Thank You for this beautiful moment I will never forget."

Slowly, Mary and Joseph faded from sight.

John Luke remained still, his hands lingering where they had touched him. The faint fragrance of incense seemed to hover in the air, as though the moment itself did not wish to pass.

Only when he drew a quiet breath did he realize he was smiling, overwhelmed and deeply grateful for the grace of what he had just experienced.

Then Jesus said softly,

"Now, my dear friend, take the ark with both hands and carry it back to Jerusalem with Me."

The four blue angels stepped away. John Luke approached the ark and lifted it carefully, cradling it in his arms. It was lighter than he expected, yet full of weight and meaning.

"Let us take our leave," Jesus said.

In an instant, they were borne back to Jerusalem to the court of the Western Wall, the last standing remnant of the Second Temple, at the edge of the Temple Mount. The courtyard lay empty in the hush of Sabbath, untouched by footsteps or prayer.

Jesus asked John Luke to set the ark upon the beveled stone floor. He did so with steady reverence, easing it gently into place.

Jesus stepped forward, raised His arms, and lifted His gaze toward heaven in prayer. At once, the ground began to tremble. A soft wind stirred the still air in the courtyard.

Then, before John Luke's eyes, great slabs of limestone and marble appeared, massive and luminous, assembling themselves one upon another. Walls rose and aligned, stone meeting stone, until the vast outline of the temple emerged, 1,600 feet wide and 900 feet long, rebuilding itself in silence and power.

Next, three pinnacles rose atop the Western Wall, climbing nine stories into the air, which was the height originally intended for the Second Temple before its destruction. The ark then lifted from the courtyard, moving with quiet grace, and came to rest upon a marble altar at the very heart of the temple.

Acacia wood appeared and assembled itself into an elegant amphitheater with broad, welcoming seating for worshippers. All lines of sight converged on the ark. Bronze pillars emerged and took their places around the structure, bearing cedar beams that now spanned the marble ceiling above.

At the eastern front of the temple, a slightly elevated space formed, simple, refined, and intentional. Two cedar lecterns stood there, creating a sanctuary for the Rabbi and the worship leaders facing the rising sun.

At the front of the sanctuary stood a beautifully carved cedar *aron kodesh*, an open ark, housing the Torah scrolls of the five books of Moses: *Genesis*, *Exodus*, *Leviticus*, *Numbers*, and *Deuteronomy*. Absent was the Holy of Holies, once believed to contain the dwelling of God. In this temple, the presence of God was not confined to a single room but shared and constant, made visible through the Ark of the Covenant itself.

Though vast in scale, the Third Temple felt intimate in spirit, designed for worship and praise. A single outer court welcomed all, men and women, Jew and Gentile alike. The complex embraced the present age with conference rooms, classrooms, a small theater, a library, and modern amenities: widescreen monitors along the walls and discreet surround-sound woven into the space.

When the work was complete, Jesus bowed His head in thanksgiving to the Father. Then He turned to John Luke and said, "Our work is done for now. Please return home, and may we meet again tomorrow?"

John Luke said, "Of course," and did as Jesus asked. He returned home and told Kristin about the extraordinary events and the astonishing design of the Third Temple. Almost breathless, he said, "Kristin, you will not believe this, but Jesus introduced me to the Blessed Mother and Saint Joseph when we were in heaven!"

Kristin stood for a moment, her mouth slightly open. Then she smiled. "John Luke, of course, I believe you. Jesus must be very proud of you to introduce you to His parents."

"And they smelled like incense," John Luke added.

Kristin laughed. "Of course they did."

Later, John Luke called me and recounted everything that took place. I struggled to take notes, as I was absorbed in the details of his story. I admit I felt a small trace of envy; my son traveled to heaven and met the Blessed Mother and Saint Joseph!

The next morning, Kristin and John Luke sat at the kitchen table, eating breakfast as the television carried breaking news from Jerusalem.

Reporters and commentators struggled to explain how a vast and magnificent temple had appeared overnight, rising from the ancient stones near the Western Wall, less than a mile from the Dome of the Rock and the Al-Aqsa Mosque. Images of the structure filled the screen, its gleaming walls catching the morning sun, its courts already crowded with astonished onlookers.

Soon, the Sephardi Chief Rabbi, Rabbi Cohen, appeared on the broadcast. His voice trembled with emotion as he tried to make sense of what the world was witnessing.

The Sephardic Jews traced their diaspora to Spain and Portugal, and Rabbi Cohen explained that his own grandfather had come from Spain to Israel, resettling his family in Jerusalem generations earlier.

Looking directly into the camera, he spoke slowly, choosing each word with care.

"Only *Elohim* could have caused this marvel to appear before our eyes. The Holy Temple stands again in Jerusalem, and the Ark of the Covenant rests within it."

He paused, visibly overwhelmed.

"I am astonished… and frightened at the same time. The Lord is marvelous." Lifting his hands toward heaven, he declared, *"Hallel!"*

Chapter 28:

The Ark on Earth

"Now have come the salvation and the power and the kingdom of our God, and the authority of his Messiah" (Revelation 12:10).

In Christian theology, the authority of the Messiah rests on the belief that Jesus possesses divine power over creation. Foretold in the Old Testament and affirmed in the New Testament, His authority extends over both the universe and the spiritual realm, culminating in His reign on the Day of Judgment. Christians believe that Jesus is the fulfillment of the messianic promise and that His authority is complete and divine. It was this power that rebuilt the Third Temple in Jerusalem.

The day after the temple was restored and the Ark returned to Earth, John Luke, and Kristin shared breakfast and cleaned the kitchen together. As they finished, he felt the familiar stirring in his spirit, a gentle sign that Jesus wished to meet with him.

He told Kristin, went to his office, said a quiet prayer, and gently placed the Mantle upon his head.

Jesus appeared in person. "Good morning, my friend," He said. "I trust you slept well."

John Luke said, "Good morning, Jesus. It is so good to see You. When I woke this morning, my thoughts went straight to our work in Jerusalem; it felt like a beautiful dream."

Jesus smiled. "Yes. The Father has also dreamt of this day for a long time. God does great work, and His plan continues to unfold." He paused, then added, "John Luke, how would you feel about appearing in Jerusalem, as John Ward, before the press, with Me at your side? I would remain invisible, supporting your words as you speak about the Temple. Of course, no one would know your identity."

John Luke said, "Of course, Jesus. If You are by my side, I can do it."

Jesus nodded. "Good. We will appear at sundown tonight, at the close of the Jewish Sabbath. I came to Rabbi Cohen in a dream last night and told him to expect you. He was deeply moved to learn that I am real, and I told him you would explain the rebuilding of the Temple to the world."

Jesus continued, "I also ask that you contact a reporter, Judith Schwartz of *The Jerusalem Post*, at this number. Please tell her you will grant an exclusive interview following the press conference. I arranged for international media to be present. You do not need to prepare remarks; the Holy Spirit will give you the words to speak. The press will ask many questions, and you will have the answers."

He paused, then added gently, "Please come alone with Me. I do not want your family to be recognized."

John Luke agreed to everything Jesus asked of him. Jesus said they would depart from his home office at 1:00 PM Eastern Time (8:00 PM in Jerusalem), at sundown. Then Jesus was gone, for the present.

John Luke went downstairs and told Kristin about his conversation with Jesus. Kristin listened carefully, then smiled. "I am so glad Jesus asked you to speak to the press about this miracle," she said. "I know you will do a wonderful job."

John Luke then called me and shared the details. I told him I wished we could be there to support him, though I understood Jesus's reasoning. Afterward, John Luke called reporter Judith Schwartz and left a voicemail, explaining the events in Jerusalem and offering an exclusive interview.

Precisely at 1:00 PM, Jesus appeared in the office of John Luke. In the next instant, they were on their way to Jerusalem.

Rabbi Cohen stood waiting in the newly formed courtyard, his posture revealing that he took Jesus's dream to heart. He prepared the Temple sanctuary for the arrival of John Luke.

John Luke introduced himself as John Ward, representing The Mantle LLC. He was dressed in deliberate respect: a black suit, white shirt, black tie, and a black *kippah*, a yarmulke, resting on his head in accordance with custom.

Rabbi Cohen addressed him in English. "I recognize your name from the news in Ukraine and Iraq. I am honored to meet you, John Ward. Your good works preceded you, and now, I presume, include this miracle of construction." He paused, his voice lowering. “Tell me, how did you bring the Ark of the Covenant back to our people?”

John Ward responded in perfect Hebrew, “I am honored to meet you, Rabbi Cohen. Thank you for allowing me to appear in the temple. I know you have many questions, and I am here to answer them. And yes, the Mantle is behind the return of the ark and the rebuilding of the temple, yet this mighty work is from God, as you said. The temple was not built by human hands but by the power of heaven.”

The Rabbi was honored and surprised that John Ward spoke flawless Hebrew. He thought that John Ward was no ordinary person. Clearly, God sent him, and he treated John Ward with great respect.

Within minutes, more than 100 reporters and dignitaries filled the courtyard. Rabbi Cohen invited them into the Temple, and they became the first public witnesses to its grandeur. Audible gasps rippled through the group as they took in the scale and beauty of the space.

Rabbi Cohen and John Luke took their seats in the sanctuary. Then, as John Ward, he rose and stepped to the *amud* (pulpit). The lights and cameras pressed in, and he felt a flicker of nerves. Present were the Prime Minister of Israel, Ariel Rabin, and the Mayor of Jerusalem, Shlomo Kariv. Rabbi Cohen also invited Imam Abdul Sadat and Episcopal Archbishop Andrew Sterling, signaling the breadth of the moment.

Jesus stood invisibly by his side and gently touched his arm, a quiet assurance. John Luke drew a steady breath. Calm settled over him. Guided by the Holy Spirit, as Jesus promised, he began the conference. He spoke first in Hebrew. The Mantle gifted him with the ability to speak any language.

"Dear friends, firstly, I want to thank Rabbi Cohen for hosting this press conference. Secondly, my gratitude to Prime Minister Ariel Rabin and Mayor Shlomo Kariv. *Shalom* to all Jewish people who hear these words."

Then he shifted seamlessly into Arabic. "I also welcome Imam Abdul Sadat, the esteemed leader of the Al-Aqsa Mosque in Jerusalem. *Salam* to our Muslim brothers and sisters listening today."

Reporter Judith Schwartz was present, having received John Ward's voicemail. Already, she found herself impressed.

John Luke continued, now in English. "I also extend a warm welcome to Archbishop Andrew Sterling. My name is John Ward, and I represent the non-profit organization The Mantle LLC. Our mission is to do the work of God, to bring peace and healing to all of God's people."

"You may know of our efforts toward peace in Ukraine, our work among the people of Sudan, and our mission of healing in Iraq through Episcopal Relief & Development Services."

At these words, the crowd erupted in sustained applause.

John Ward continued, "The rebuilding of this final and Third Temple in Jerusalem is indeed a miracle of God, and a gift from

God for the people of God, to Israel and the world. While The Mantle LLC played a role in returning the Ark of the Covenant, this Temple was not raised by human hands. No crews, no machines, no instruments of labor brought this structure into reality - only the Word of God."

At the Vatican City, Pope Paul VII watched the conference on television with his closest advisers, his attention unwavering. When he heard the words "the Word of God," he leaned forward and exclaimed, "I knew it. Jesus and John Ward are behind this miracle; they rebuilt the Temple overnight."

Then the Pope spoke from memory: *"For the word of God is alive and active, sharper than any double-edged sword*" (Hebrews 4:12).

John Ward spoke, "The Word of God designed this Temple as an inclusive and welcoming house of worship for the people of Israel and for the world. Its form honors the intent of the ancient builders, recognizing Israel's past, while its function serves the present. The structure includes contemporary spaces, conference rooms, classrooms, a community center, sound systems, kitchens and restrooms, an auditorium, and a library so that it may serve a living, modern congregation."

He paused, gathering himself. Speaking without notes did not come naturally to him. Then the Spirit stirred, and he continued.

"The three pinnacles represent the perfection of God and the three3 great faith traditions of this region: Judaism, Islam, and Christianity. The single courtyard stands as a symbol of unity and welcome, inviting all people to enter and worship in this House of God. We know that no place or symbol can contain God. Yet the Ark of the Covenant, safely kept in heaven for more than 2,000 years, is returned as an enduring sign of the love of God. Once given to a chosen people, it now stands as a gift to all people. The Ark is placed at the center of the congregation as we are called to live oriented toward the Word of God, and to follow it."

John Ward said, "This Temple contains no inner sanctuary, no Holy of Holies, because God is not confined to a single room. He surrounds us in this sacred space, and He dwells within each of us. We are called to holiness. We are all forgiven and redeemed by the Word of God. Israelites and Egyptians, Muslims and Palestinians, are part of God's creation. We are made in God's image."

At the mention of Palestine, Ariel Rabin shifted uneasily in his seat, the weight of the words settling heavily upon him.

John Luke paused and glanced to his right, where Jesus stood unseen. Jesus smiled and nodded.

John Ward continued, "As with the end of the war in Ukraine, the close of the civil conflict in Sudan, and the rebuilding of Iraq, the construction of this Temple stands as a sign of God's love and His desire for peace among His people. God abhors violence against any of His children. We know that good and evil exist, that there is heaven and there is hell. Yet the Word of God has restrained the enemy, Satan, and opened a season meant for peace on Earth."

He went on, “Natural disasters, like the tragedy in Iraq, will still occur. Such events do not mean that God is absent, nor that the end of time has arrived. The Earth and all who live upon it are finite and fragile; what is created is imperfect and will one day pass away. For this reason, we are called to cherish the Earth and one another now. Only heaven is eternal. These tragedies remind us to stand together, to do good, and to comfort one another with the love of God.”

John Ward concluded, “Let me affirm this: God is present, and His Word is among us. He loves us and forgives us. We are called to live rightly before God and in peace with one another. This Temple will stand until the end of days as a place of worship and reconciliation. It is a sign that God dwells among us, a living testimony that He remains a God of miracles.”

He paused, then added, “With the approval of Rabbi Cohen, I will now take any questions.”

Back in Vatican City, Pope Paul VII watched in silence, then nodded appreciatively. “Bravo, John Ward,” he said. “Dynamic, yet elegant.”

Applause filled the temple. Cameras flashed, video feeds rolled, and microphones pressed forward. For nearly one hour, John Luke, as John Ward, answered every question, guided by the Holy Spirit.

By nightfall, the name and image of John Ward spread across households and government agencies around the world. Reporters scoured the internet for any trace of his past, for details about the

Mantle and its work. That evening, John Ward did more than make headlines; he nearly broke the internet.

When the conference ended, John Luke, with Jesus invisibly by his side, went to reporter Judith Schwartz for an exclusive interview, as promised.

They walked to a nearby open coffee shop. Over coffee, John Ward shared what Jesus wanted him to reveal: the history of the Mantle, its work in Ukraine, Sudan, and Iraq, and now its role in Jerusalem. He spoke as well of prophecy fulfilled, that Satan had been bound in the bottomless pit for 1,000 years, in accordance with Scripture.

Everything he said was measured and deliberate, offered not for his own acclaim, but for the glory of God. After more than one hour, Ms. Schwartz concluded the interview with sincere gratitude and returned to her office to write the exclusive front-page story. She would remember the encounter and John Ward, always.

After she left, John Luke asked Jesus why He chose Judith Schwartz.

Jesus smiled. "Recall the headlines in *The Jerusalem Post* while we were at work in Iraq. She wrote with discernment and care. She is a woman of faith, laboring in a field still largely shaped by men. This story will reveal her gifts and advance the Father's plan for this region. Her words will help heal cultural and political divisions. She has become the agent of God for peace within the Fourth Estate. We may call upon her again."

Then Jesus added, smiling, “John Luke, you were excellent before the media and the dignitaries. I am very proud of you. It has been a long day, and I ask that you return home to Kristin. Share everything with her, and be sure to tell your father as well, for the sake of the history book. Tomorrow is Sunday. Rest. Enjoy time with your family. We will speak again soon. And one more item: watch the evening news tomorrow. I think you will be pleased with the coverage.”

With that, Jesus disappeared as Jesus does, without sound or trace. John Luke stepped out of the café and flew home, returning at last to the loving arms of Kristin.

Chapter 29:

Word of God, Speak!

"Then I looked, and there before me was the Lamb, standing on Mount Zion, and with him 144,000 who had his name and his Father's name written on their foreheads" (Revelation 14:1).

In Revelation, this passage describes a faithful remnant of 144,000 people redeemed from the earth and marked for their loyalty to God. Many theologians understand this number symbolically: twelve tribes of Israel multiplied by the twelve apostles, and then by 1,000, a number often used in Scripture to represent fullness or completeness. In this interpretation, they represent the faithful followers of Christ, set apart by their devotion and purity. They represent the faithful people of God whose witness continues through every generation of the church.

The morning after John Luke spoke at the Temple, Kristin, Joan, I, and he met for Sunday liturgy at Saint George Church.

After the service, Reverend Mark joined us for coffee and spoke glowingly about John Ward's work with Episcopal Relief & Development. He was astonished by The Mantle LLC's generosity and could not fathom how the organization had secured $7 billion for the relief effort. He shared that Dr. Urban and Reverend Duvall were deeply grateful.

Reverend Mark then spoke glowingly about John Ward's press conference, describing the appearance as "masterful." We smiled, nodded, and enjoyed his enthusiasm. Then, we headed home. John Luke told us that Jesus had said to watch the evening news.

After dinner, Joan and I watched, as did Kristin and John Luke. Just as Jesus had said, the news confirmed it, and we all received the message with quiet satisfaction.

The media reported that Jesus Christ appeared in Zion Square in Jerusalem around 10:00 AM Israeli time wearing a glowing white robe, a gold sash, and gleaming bronze sandals. He preached in both Hebrew and English, telling a large crowd that He is the Word of God, the Alpha and the Omega, and Savior of the world.

Jesus told the listeners, "God the Father loves you. You are created in His image and likeness. He eagerly forgives the sorrowful and penitent. He chose you to be a sign of love, light, and peace for the world. The Father wants you to believe in Me as His only begotten Son, and to believe in My words."

Jesus continued, "All people are the children of God, and We, as Father, Son, and Spirit, desire a plan for peace among the peoples of Israel, Egypt, and Palestine. The rebuilding of the Third Temple in Jerusalem is a sign of that peace. We desire peace in the whole world. Remember My words to My disciples: *Peace I leave with you; my peace I give you. I do not give to you as the world gives. Do not be afraid.* My friends, now is the time for love, peace, and courage to reign in the world."

Amazingly, at the same time in Zion Square, Jesus appeared in Tahrir Square in Cairo, Egypt, and in Palestine Square in Gaza City on the West Bank. Jesus spoke to the crowds in these city squares in Arabic and English, giving the same message in all three places simultaneously. God really does like "threes."

Phone cameras captured these miraculous appearances, and the message was broadcast on television news outlets and shared on social media. At the same time, the front-page story of *The Jerusalem Post* appeared in the Sunday edition, and the accolades for John Ward and the story by reporter Judith Schwartz caught the attention of international news outlets. Jesus, John Ward, and the Mantle were everything, everywhere, all at once.

In Jerusalem, Cairo, and Gaza City, Jesus closed His message with this passage:

"Do not let your hearts be troubled. You believe in God; believe also in me. My Father's house has many rooms; if that were not so, would I have told you that I am going there to prepare a place for you? And if I go and prepare a place for you, I will come back and take you to be with me, that you may be with me. (John 14:1-4).

When He finished speaking, Jesus disappeared.

The crowds broke into wild cheers and applause. The worldwide Church saw Jesus as He appears in the prophecy of Revelation.

Chapter 30:

Twins

"Two are better than one, because they have a good reward for their labor" (Ecclesiastes 4:9–12).

The Hebrew Book of Ecclesiastes, part of the Old Testament and attributed to an unknown author, is a collection of meditations on how to live rightly before God. This chapter begins with this passage for a reason that will soon become clear.

The morning after Jesus's surprising and miraculous appearances in the Middle East, John Luke and Kristin sat at their kitchen table eating breakfast. Without announcement, Jesus appeared before them in person, wearing a radiant white robe, a golden sash, and glowing bronze sandals. He took a seat at the table and said nothing.

Kristin looked up, saw Him, and blurted out, "Jesus!"

Both John Luke and Jesus burst into laughter.

Jesus said gently, "Forgive me if I startled you. I wanted to see my beautiful friends in person."

He turned to Kristin. "I want you to know how deeply I appreciate that you share John Luke with Me, and with the work of the Mantle. You are a woman of great integrity."

Then He looked to John Luke. "And you, your words in Jerusalem were extraordinary. The Father is pleased and proud of you. You are a man of character."

Kristin caught her breath. John Luke thanked Jesus quietly.

After a moment, John Luke asked, "Can I get You anything to eat or drink?" He hesitated, then smiled. "That is probably a foolish question. I have never seen You eat or drink."

Jesus laughed. "Actually, John Luke, I would love a cup of coffee, hot and black."

They laughed. John Luke poured a steaming cup and set it before the Lord of the universe. Jesus took a long sip and nodded. "Perfect," He said. "Just as God intended."

Once again, laughter filled the room.

Then Jesus became serious and said, "John Luke, we have two more missions, and our work with the Mantle will be complete for now. I will tell you more soon. Yet I came in person because I have a special gift for you both. I appreciate how you genuinely celebrated Lucas and Paula on the birth of their son, little Pedro Avion. And I honor the way you have coped with the struggle of having a child of your own. God has heard your prayers."

Jesus stood and said, "Kristin and John Luke, I am here to say that you are pregnant with twins, a girl and a boy."

At this great news, Kristin and John Luke hugged one another and then went to Jesus. The three of them hugged and cried.

Jesus continued, "The babies are both healthy and well. You are about six weeks pregnant. Just like in Scripture with Job, God provides a double portion of blessing because you honor Him. I love you both, and I am very happy to share this good news with you in person."

As Jesus finished speaking, they gathered around the table again and hugged tightly.

Kristin finally spoke and said through tears of joy, "We have been trying a long time, and we are so grateful to You, Jesus. The infertility treatments went on for years, and we gave up. Now You bring this great news. We love and appreciate You."

John Luke said with a broad smile, "Thank You for this amazing news, Jesus."

Jesus said with a smile, "I will take My leave now, and I suggest you call your doctor, and then your families, in that order." Then Jesus disappeared from their sight.

As Jesus suggested, Kristin called her doctor's office and told the receptionist she was pregnant. The receptionist located her doctor, who graciously took the call and asked Kristin to come to the office for an ultrasound that day.

Kristin and John Luke excitedly drove to the appointment. They saw two healthy babies on the ultrasound. John Luke asked the technician whether she could tell the babies' gender. The technician said she could not and explained that the doctor would arrive shortly to meet with them.

Dr. Marina Rodriguez arrived and confirmed that the babies appeared healthy and that Kristin was, just as Jesus had said, about six weeks pregnant. She asked whether Kristin had experienced any symptoms. Kristin shook her head.

"Then how did you know you were pregnant?" Dr. Rodriguez asked.

Kristin glanced at John Luke, who gave a small nod. "God told us this morning," she said simply. "We knew we had to call you."

Dr. Rodriguez smiled wryly. "Well, I am Catholic," she said, "and I have read about miracle pregnancies in the Bible." She looked back at the chart. "God is right. You are pregnant with twins. We should know the babies' genders in about eight weeks."

John Luke and Kristin smiled, the words settling over them like a blessing.

Dr. Rodriguez gave Kristin a pamphlet on twin pregnancy and explained that she would schedule more frequent appointments to monitor the babies' growth and Kristin's health. The couple left the office, drove home, and began calling their families.

When John Luke, and Kristin reached us and put the call on speakerphone, they shared the full story: Jesus arriving unannounced at breakfast and delivering the astonishing news Himself. We laughed and cried at once, overcome with joy. Kristin told us how precise Jesus had been: six weeks pregnant, twins, a girl and a boy. Joan was visibly moved, repeatedly saying, "Thank you, Jesus."

Fittingly, Kristin ended the call by saying she was suddenly very hungry for lunch.

They were happy, grateful, and began preparing for twins.

Chapter 31:

Jesus and the Rabbi

"Great and marvelous are your deeds, Lord God Almighty. Just and true are your ways, King of the nations. Who will not fear you, Lord, and bring glory to your name? For you alone are holy. All nations will come and worship before you, for your righteous acts have been revealed" (Revelation 15:3, 4).

This passage from Revelation is known as the Song of Moses and the Lamb, a universal call to recognize God's holiness and righteousness. It praises God's great and marvelous deeds, affirming His justice and truth. The song echoes the Old Testament prophecies and Jesus's words that all nations will come to worship God. In it, Jesus stands victorious over evil, embodying the ultimate triumph of divine justice.

Jesus will now lovingly reinforce that truth through both word and action among the Israelites, God's chosen people, culminating in a conversation with Chief Rabbi Yitzhak Cohen.

One morning, after breakfast, Jesus gave John Luke a familiar spiritual nudge as he worked in his home office. John Luke paused, said a prayer, wore the Mantle, and Jesus appeared in person.

"Good morning, John Luke. All seems to be going well with Kristin?"

John Luke answered, "Yes, Lord. She has a touch of morning sickness, but it passes quickly. The doctor says everything looks fine. We are so grateful to You for this wonderful news."

Jesus replied, "I am very happy for you both. I wanted to give you a little space before we complete our work in Israel, Egypt, and Palestine. Are you ready to take up the Mantle again this week?"

John Luke nodded. "Of course, Jesus. I will be sure my schedule is aligned with Kristin, but yes."

Jesus smiled and said, "You are a good husband, and you will make a great father. You are helping to carry on the work of creation and salvation history through your family, which will be a little church for God."

He continued, His voice steady. "Political intrigue is unfolding in Israel around Prime Minister Ariel Rabin. Members of his cabinet are urging him to respond to peace overtures from Egypt's Prime Minister Ibrahim Fawzi and to pursue a lasting accord with the Palestine National Council and its leader, Ahmad Abbas."

"Instead, the Prime Minister remains silent. His inaction toward Egypt and the PNC is obstructing the path to peace and inflaming tensions with Hamas within Palestine."

Jesus explained, "The Father's plan for peace calls for Israel and Egypt to agree on a lasting strategy for Palestine, one that honors the people, the land, and their faith. We must help the prime minister see that this path serves the greater good. If he does not, he may be removed and another, more willing leader will take his place. Many within his cabinet and party favor Shlomo Kariv as Prime Minister should a vote of no confidence be called against Ariel Rabin. Our work is to bring peace forward, with the right people at the right time."

John Luke said, "Thank You, Lord, for helping me see the larger picture. I had no idea there was such turmoil beneath the surface or how it connected to Your plan for our work."

Jesus replied, "Now that you understand, I would like us to begin work in Israel and Egypt this week. Please speak with Kristin and let me know whether this Thursday will work for you both."

John Luke said, "Of course, Jesus. I will speak with her and prepare for Thursday morning after breakfast."

Jesus answered, "That plan sounds perfect. We can meet in your office. We have some interesting work ahead of us."

With that, He embraced John Luke and disappeared.

In the weeks that followed, after Jesus had appeared and spoken to crowds in the town squares of Jerusalem, Cairo, and Gaza City, His message continued to ripple across social media, drawing millions of views worldwide. Some wondered whether the videos foretold the end of time. Others dismissed them as elaborate deepfakes, artifacts of the dark web.

Still, the message endured, unmistakable to those who had ears to hear. Many in the press wondered when and where Jesus might appear again.

Reporter Judith Schwartz contacted John Luke to request a follow-up remote interview. Jesus encouraged John Luke to agree. What followed was a front-page story about Jesus's appearances with John Ward. Ms. Schwartz asked John Ward whether he knew when Jesus would appear again. John Ward answered that people should accept Jesus's words at face value and that he had no idea when or whether Jesus would appear again.

In the interview, John Ward emphasized that people should watch the videos, read the stories, and appreciate how much Jesus loves every person as a child of God.

John Ward said, "The world thirsts for the Word of God, and we have evidence of His love in the rebuilding of the Jerusalem Temple."

While Ms. Schwartz wanted more insider information, she was satisfied that John Ward had told her what he knew at the time.

Yet Chief Rabbi Yitzhak Cohen heard from Jesus again. After Jesus appeared to Rabbi Cohen in a dream and told him about John Ward, the Rabbi began praying to Jesus in his nightly prayers. The Rabbi told only his wife about his original dream of Jesus and was uncomfortable sharing with fellow Rabbis on the council that he prayed to Jesus Christ.

In his prayers, Rabbi Cohen began to address Jesus by the title John Ward had used: the Word of God. The name settled easily on his tongue, natural and fitting for the Rabbi.

One night, he prayed again and said, “If You truly are the Word of God, and if You truly stand behind the rebuilding of our Temple, then I ask You, please appear to me once more in a dream. Allow me to speak with You. This Temple is a gift from heaven, and I wish to know You more.”

With those words, Rabbi Cohen fell asleep. Jesus answered his prayer.

Jesus appeared to Rabbi Cohen during a deep sleep, the phase of dreaming most likely to be remembered.

In the dream, Jesus appeared as He is described in the Book of Revelation, clothed in a radiant white robe with a golden sash and wearing luminous bronze sandals. His face matched what the Rabbi had long imagined: dark-skinned, with shoulder-length brown hair and a neatly trimmed beard.

The dream was no fleeting vision but a true dialogue, and the realization filled Rabbi Cohen with quiet joy. Jesus began the conversation with a greeting that was measured, respectful, and familiar.

“Rabbi Cohen,” He said, “I am honored that you prayed to Me as the Word of God. You may call Me Yeshua, if that is comfortable for you.”

Rabbi Cohen replied softly, “Thank You for answering my prayers, Yeshua. Since the dream first came to me, You have been in my thoughts each day and in my prayers each night.”

“Yes, Rabbi Cohen,” said Jesus. “I realize praying to Me is unusual for you. I know you are an honorable person and a good shepherd to God’s people. I am pleased to speak with you in this way. When you wake up tomorrow morning, you will remember this dream, and I encourage you to write down the information.”

The rabbi said, “I will do as You say, Yeshua, and thank You. Respectfully, I have questions if You will allow me.”

Jesus said, “Of course. You may ask Me anything.”

Rabbi Cohen asked, “Are You truly the Son of God, the Messiah whom Christian’s worship?”

Jesus answered, “Yes. I am the Messiah, sent by God as His only Son. I have existed with the Father and the Holy Spirit from all eternity. I came to save all who believe in God. My first disciples were Jewish believers who recognized Me as the Messiah. From their faith, they carried forward Jewish tradition, reshaped through My teachings, into what became the Christian churches.”

Rabbi Cohen said, “Thank You for telling me, Yeshua. May I ask how You rebuilt the Temple in a single night? And why did You rebuild it at all?”

Jesus answered, “I rebuilt the Temple by the power God has given Me. John Ward stood with Me as I spoke the Word, and the Temple came into being. That is why he calls Me the Word of God.

He is My witness to the world. I am the fulfillment of the Law and the Prophets. I spoke, and the Temple was restored.

"This final Third Temple was rebuilt to fulfill what the Lord declared through the prophet: *'My house shall be built'* (Zechariah 1:16–17). The Word of the Lord is living and active *(Hebrews 4:12).* I am here now, appearing again to God's people. My message has not changed. *I am the way, and the truth, and the life* (John 14:6)."

Rabbi Cohen hesitated, then asked, "Why then, Yeshua, did the leaders of our people deny You as Messiah?"

"I was not the Messiah the chief priests expected," Jesus answered. "I came not to be served, but to serve and to give My life as a ransom for God's children, in fulfillment of the Father's plan of salvation" (Matthew 20:28). "I told My disciples that the Son of Man would be arrested, scourged, and crucified, as foretold by the prophet Isaiah. I also told them that I would rise on the third day, as spoken through Hosea *(6:2).*"

"See the marks in My hands and feet. I am the Lamb of God, the final sacrifice of atonement, who takes away the sins of the world. This is why the Third Temple has no Holy of Holies. The blood of the Lamb now covers the whole world."

The rabbi said quietly, "Yeshua, this makes sense. I want to be a good shepherd. I believe in You."

Jesus smiled and said, "I know, Rabbi Cohen. My only commandment for you is to love God and His people. Are you willing to follow My commandment?"

Rabbi Cohen replied, "Yes, Yeshua. I love God, and I will share Your love with others."

Jesus said, "And I love you, Yitzhak, and you are now My disciple. We will speak again." Then the dream ended.

The next morning, Rabbi Cohen wrote down the details of the dream with perfect clarity. He then told his wife about the dream with great wonder.

The rabbi was now different because of this dream about Jesus, and his family and congregation noticed his new energy, happiness, and fulfillment.

Chapter 32:

The Mantle in Israel

"Then they gathered the kings together to the place that in Hebrew is called Armageddon" (Revelation 16:16).

Armageddon is historically and biblically identified as Mount of Megiddo, a hill in northern Israel. In the Book of Revelation, it marks the gathering place of humanity's powers, where resistance is chosen over repentance. The region surrounding Megiddo is both historically significant and strategically situated on a high plateau.

The struggle between good and evil is both spiritual and physical, and the Mantle's mission is to bring peace to the Middle East after decades of strife in Palestine. That work centers in Israel.

On Thursday of that week, as previously arranged, Jesus appeared to John Luke in person in his office.

"Good morning, John Luke. How are you and Kristin?"

John Luke replied, "Good morning, Jesus. I missed You. Kristin and I are doing well. She feels well overall but is tired later in the day. I am getting better at making dinners she can eat without indigestion."

Jesus smiled. "That is good to hear on both fronts. It is understandable, as Kristin is now caring for herself and two little ones. I know you will make great parents. Are you ready for some work with the Mantle?"

John Luke answered enthusiastically that he was.

Jesus said, "We must move the peace plan forward between Israel, Egypt, and Palestine. I ask you to call Rabbi Cohen in Jerusalem, as John Ward, of course. I will guide the conversation. Ask him to help persuade Prime Minister Ariel Rabin to pursue a lasting peace with Ahmad Abbas, with the support of Prime Minister Ibrahim Fawzi."

"The Palestine National Council does not trust Israel, and Prime Minister Fawzi can serve as a trusted mediator. The presence of Hamas in Gaza only deepens the distress."

Jesus then added, "Scripture shows the Father's design for Israel rests on a threefold bond, with the people, the land, and God. The Palestinian people long for the same. Despite Hamas's violence, we must help Prime Minister Rabin cultivate compassion for the Palestinians as they seek peace, freedom, and a homeland. We begin with Rabbi Cohen, a strong voice and a willing ally in advancing the Father's plan."

Jesus gave John Luke Rabbi Cohen's private number, and he called the Rabbi immediately. After exchanging pleasantries, Jesus guided John Luke's thoughts during the call.

John Luke said, "Rabbi, I call to ask a favor. Would you be willing to meet with me later today to discuss a peace plan for

Palestine? I realize the Sabbath starts at sundown. I may be in Jerusalem by 7:00 PM your time."

Rabbi Cohen responded, "John Ward, I am astounded that you know my private number and have such speedy travel capabilities. I am glad you called, and yes, I will meet you in my office in Jerusalem."

John Ward said he knew the place, and the call ended.

At precisely 6:55 PM Jerusalem time, John Ward stood in front of the Beit Yahav building on 80 Yirmiyahu Street in Jerusalem. A security guard brought John Ward to Rabbi Cohen's office on the fourth floor of the beautiful building at the western entrance of Jerusalem.

Rabbi Cohen greeted John Ward warmly in English and with great respect. "And how is the man who helped rebuild our great Temple these days?"

John Ward responded with a broad smile. "I am well, Rabbi. All is going well."

John Luke stopped himself from sharing any information about Kristin's pregnancy, maintaining his persona as John Ward.

As time was short, John Ward got to the point.

"Rabbi, God's plan for lasting peace between Israel, Egypt, and Palestine requires Prime Minister Rabin to negotiate a settlement for the land in Palestine. He appears hesitant to reach out to the leaders of Egypt and Palestine. God asks whether you would speak with the prime minister and encourage him to meet with the leaders of Palestine and Egypt and forge a lasting peace."

Rabbi Cohen sat back in his chair, not surprised by John Ward's request.

"John Ward, when you say that God asks, do you mean the Word of God, Jesus, is asking me?"

John Ward responded, "Yes, Rabbi. Yeshua, as the Word of God, is asking on behalf of the Father, *El Shaddai*. Jesus is carrying out the will of His Father in this plan for peace."

Rabbi Cohen answered, "Of course, I will do this work. I will ask the prime minister to meet with me after the last Shabbat service on Saturday."

John Ward replied, "Excellent, Rabbi, and thank you. I am sure Yeshua will be pleased."

Rabbi Cohen paused, then asked quietly, "John Ward, do you speak with Yeshua in person?"

This time, John Luke hesitated.

Jesus guided his reply.

"Yes, Rabbi. Jesus speaks to my mind and at times in person. He directs how I use The Mantle LLC in His work to better the world."

The rabbi nodded. "I thought so. You seem like the kind of person the Word of God would speak with."

John Ward said gently, "Rabbi, perhaps you might pray to Yeshua and ask Him to speak with you as well. He is always present."

Rabbi Cohen replied, "I pray to Him each night, and sometimes He appears to me in dreams. I was not surprised when you asked me to meet. I dreamed of Him this week. Would you keep this in confidence, between us?"

John Ward smiled and said, "Of course, Rabbi. Yeshua loves you very much, as His disciple."

The rabbi smiled broadly.

John Ward said, "Rabbi, I will not keep you, as the Sabbath is near. I will take my leave. Here is my card. Please let me know how your conversation goes with the prime minister when you are able."

Rabbi Cohen took the card and agreed to call John Ward.

John Ward then took his leave and returned to his home office. It was noon when John Luke arrived home.

Before John Luke removed the Mantle, Jesus appeared in person and said, "John Luke, you did well in your meeting with Rabbi Cohen. The prime minister must choose what is right for his people. My hope is that Rabbi Cohen will persuade him. If not, we will follow the Father's plan, with or without his cooperation."

John Luke replied, "I understand, Jesus. I will do what You ask. Thank You for using me in this important work."

Jesus embraced him in farewell, and John Luke went to be with Kristin.

At the Shabbat afternoon *Mincha* service, at four o'clock Jerusalem time, Rabbi Cohen delivered a moving sermon to a packed congregation in the Temple. He spoke of the love of God and the power of forgiveness, his words carrying a new depth and urgency.

Among those present were Prime Minister Ariel Rabin and Jerusalem's mayor, Shlomo Kariv.

Drawing from Scripture, Rabbi Cohen offered five examples of freely given mercy, each revealing the redemptive power of forgiveness and its enduring strength.

First, the rabbi spoke of Esau, who forgave Jacob for stealing his birthright *(Genesis 33).* Second, he recalled Joseph, who forgave his brothers for selling him into slavery *(Genesis 45).* Third, he described how God forgave Israel for its rebellion in the wilderness and still led the people into the Promised Land *(Numbers 14).*

Fourth, he spoke of King David, who received God's forgiveness after being confronted by the prophet Nathan for adultery and murder *(2 Samuel 12).* Finally, he reminded the congregation how God spared the city of Nineveh when its people repented of their sins *(Jonah 3).*

Rabbi Cohen then said, "I wish to share two further examples of how the Lord's forgiveness is extended to all people. When Jesus, whom our Christian friends call the Word of God, was crucified by Roman soldiers, He prayed in His final moments that *El Shaddai* would forgive them, for they did not know what they were doing. Even at death, He chose mercy."

He continued, "And in the *Qur'an*, which our Muslim brothers and sisters receive as sacred Word, it is written: 'Do not let those among you who are virtuous and affluent swear to withhold aid from their relatives, the needy, and those who have emigrated in the cause of Allah. Let them pardon and forgive. Do you not love that Allah should forgive you? And Allah is All-Forgiving, Most Merciful' *(Qur'an 24:22).*"

The rabbi spoke with renewed force. "My brothers and sisters, forgiveness and love stand at the heart of our faith and at the heart of the faith of our Christian and Muslim brothers and sisters as well. To forgive, to show mercy, and to extend peace, these are acts of reverence toward *El Shaddai*, the Lord of lords. When we forgive and cover the sins of others with love, we become most like our Lord in heaven."

"I leave you with this truth. There was never merely a time of miracles recorded in the holy Scriptures. There is a Lord of miracles. We have witnessed miracles in our own day, and we will see more still if we choose to share the love of *Elohim* through forgiveness."

After the service, Rabbi Cohen greeted members of the congregation as many made their way to the community room for refreshments. Mayor Kariv stepped forward, embraced Rabbi Cohen warmly, and said, "That sermon was one of your finest, truly unforgettable. Thank you."

Prime Minister Rabin lingered to the side with his security detail, waiting. Rabbi Cohen noticed and invited him to sit in the sanctuary, as the guards remained at a respectful distance.

Once seated, Prime Minister Rabin spoke quietly. "Rabbi, I sensed a deeper meaning in your message today. Was your sermon connected to our meeting?"

Rabbi Cohen replied, “In one sense, Ariel, yes. I heard that Egypt wishes to meet with you to pursue an accord with Palestine, and I encourage you to listen to their perspective. With all that is unfolding in the world, I believe the Lord is active in this moment and desires peace for His people. I ask you to show mercy and forgiveness toward the Palestinian people. Our nation longs for a peace that will endure.”

Prime Minister Rabin leaned back in his chair and drew a slow breath. After a long pause, he said, “I will consider it.”

The rabbi held his gaze. “Ariel, I believe God desires peace for Palestine, and that you are in a position to make it possible.”

The prime minister rose and departed the Temple with his security detail, without a word of farewell.

Rabbi Cohen remained behind and offered a prayer of thanksgiving. Yet even as he prayed, a troubling thought lingered: Ariel is struggling to believe. He feared what that struggle might mean for the prime minister’s future.

Over the next several days, Prime Minister Rabin weighed his conversation with the rabbi. He struggled with the choice because of his own experience and his deeply conservative beliefs.

At the cabinet meeting on Wednesday afternoon, the prime minister spoke plainly. “I know many of you wish for me to meet with Egypt to pursue a lasting peace accord with Palestine. Even Rabbi Cohen urged me to consider this path. Yet my experience tells me the Oslo Peace Accords remain a fair and sufficient guide.

I do not believe another round of talks or a new agreement is necessary."

He continued, "We have a cease-fire in place with Palestine, and at this time, I will take no further action. We must also account for Hamas's activities. I will inform Egypt that we will not meet, at least for now."

Most of the cabinet ministers were deeply discouraged by the prime minister's words. They felt the prime minister was living in the past and was an impediment to peace in modern times. The cabinet's dissonance was palpable.

Word of his decision leaked to the press. Some cabinet members and newspaper editorials openly called for his resignation. Prime Minister Rabin stood firm and refused to discuss the issue further.

That evening, after dinner, Jesus reached out to John Luke in his office. John Luke recognized the familiar stirring, said a prayer, and gently put on the Mantle.

Jesus appeared in person. "Good evening, John Luke. Thank you for responding to the call to meet."

His tone grew more serious. "We have a difficulty with Prime Minister Rabin. Ariel is a good man, yet his heart has hardened against renewed peace talks with Palestine and Egypt. Though he reflected on what Rabbi Cohen shared, he remains unwilling to change his position. Many within his cabinet are urging him to resign. He is no longer aligned with the Father's plan for lasting peace in the region, and millions of people long for that peace."

Jesus continued, "The Father has made a difficult decision. For a time of reflection, and God willing, conversion, Prime Minister Rabin is to be placed at Saint Luke's motel for forty days. I ask that you bring him there discreetly, to room number one. Pray for him, that his heart may be softened."

He added, "The staff at Saint Luke's is prepared for his arrival. A copy of the Tanakh has been placed on the desk in the room. The prime minister is in his office in Jerusalem even now, at this early hour. Please go to the Kiryat Ben Gurion Building and bring him to the motel."

John Luke paused momentarily and thought of when he had brought President Petrovitch to the motel. That placement was due to a war. This placement is due to disobedience. John Luke prayed silently for mercy, not punishment.

He finally responded, "Of course, Jesus. I understand how sensitive and difficult this is."

Jesus heard John Luke's prayer. "I know this work is difficult, John Luke. This time is for conversion, not punishment. We are following the Father's will. We know that God's ways are not always our ways. This placement will make sense in the end. And I am grateful for your faithfulness."

He nodded in agreement.

With that, Jesus disappeared. John Luke left at once for the Prime Minister's Office, heading to Building C of the complex, where Prime Minister Rabin was already at work.

Chapter 33:

Prime Minister Ariel Rabin

"After this I heard what sounded like the roar of a great multitude in heaven shouting: 'Hallelujah! Salvation and glory and power belong to our God, for true and just are His judgments'" (Revelation 19:1–2).

The nation of Israel and its leaders share a long history with God. Israel remains God's first chosen people. Yet its leaders have not always followed His will. In this moment, God wills peace for nearly six million Palestinians and for the people of Israel. The Father hopes that Prime Minister Ariel Rabin will experience a change of heart, a time of conversion, at the motel. God's ways are always true and just.

Using the Mantle, John Luke flew to Jerusalem and found Prime Minister Rabin seated at his desk, reading quietly. It was five o'clock in the morning, Jerusalem time. John Luke stood behind him, whispered a prayer, gently took his right arm, and carried him at the speed of light to Saint Luke's motel.

John Luke placed the prime minister in room one, before the desk where the Tanakh lay waiting. Then he departed. Ariel Rabin would remain there in solitude for forty days.

By Sunday night, the prime minister's family reported him missing. His security detail, along with the Israel National Police, launched an exhaustive search but found no trace of him. When word leaked to the press, commentators quickly drew comparisons to the recent disappearance of Russian President Ivan Petrovich.

The world was baffled that two of the most closely guarded leaders on Earth could vanish without explanation. Rumors spread. Some claimed Hamas was responsible, though no evidence supported it. Others suggested the prime minister was hiding, though no one could say to what end. Considering recent miracles, a few Israeli editorials dared to ask whether God Himself was behind the disappearance. Days passed, and there was still no word on the prime minister's whereabouts.

Ariel Benjamin Rabin was one of Israel's longest-serving and most conservative prime ministers. After earning an MBA at Brandeis University, he returned to Israel, served four years in the Israel Defense Forces, and later joined Mossad. During a decade with Mossad, Rabin participated in numerous operations in Palestine, developing a deep distrust of its leadership.

He later entered politics through the far-right Noam nationalist party within the religious Zionist movement and was elected to Israel's national parliament, called the Knesset. There, Rabin became known for asserting Israel's supremacy, advocating settlement expansion in the West Bank, and opposing Palestinian statehood.

Forming a coalition of centrist and right-wing members, he rose to the premiership. Aligned with conservative leaders in the United States and Europe, Rabin won three general elections and was serving his fourth term when he disappeared.

Over time, his closest allies and cabinet members encouraged him to soften his position toward a Palestinian state, as the people of Israel were tired of skirmishes with Hamas and economic issues stemming from the lack of an accord with the Arab world. Ariel Rabin's "hardness of heart," as Jesus said, impeded the greater good of the Middle East.

In the motel, Prime Minister Rabin was angry and dumbfounded. He had no idea where he was or why he was in this place. The prime minister never considered this act as the hand of God, as he rarely thought of God. Prayer is effective only with a glimmer of faith. The prime minister never once called out to God in prayer. He spent his days writing thoughts on paper and planning revenge on whoever placed him in the motel suite.

After a week without a prime minister, the Israeli cabinet appointed Jerusalem's mayor, Shlomo Kariv, as interim prime minister. On his first day in office, Kariv convened the cabinet and sought their counsel on pursuing a peace accord with Palestine, with Egypt's support. The cabinet voted unanimously to proceed.

Kariv immediately reached out to Egypt's prime minister, Ibrahim Fawzi, and to the leader of the Palestine National Council, Ahmad Abbas. The leaders moved swiftly, meeting the following day at the Administrative Capital Offices in Cairo.

Drawing upon the Oslo Accords and the Camp David framework, they formalized diplomatic relations, expanded trade agreements, clarified land boundaries, and committed to rebuilding neighborhoods destroyed by violence in the Gaza Strip. Israel and Palestine formally recognized one another as sovereign states.

Within days, Israel's parliament ratified the agreement, followed soon after by approval from the Palestine National Council. A lasting peace was finally secured. Across Israel, Egypt, and Palestine, the news was met with relief, hope, and cautious joy.

John Luke marveled at the speed of the Father's plan. Soon, another miracle would follow.

The morning after the accord was approved, Jerusalem awoke to it. The Jerusalem Pilgrim Road—the stepped street leading to the Temple Mount past the Western Wall—had transformed overnight. Its granite stones were now broad, smooth bricks of gleaming gold.

The first to see it was Rabbi Cohen, on his way to an early morning meeting at the Temple. News spread quickly. Within hours, images of the golden road filled international broadcasts and social media feeds.

The *Jerusalem Post* ran a front-page story, its headline drawn directly from Scripture: *"The great street of the city was of gold."* (Revelation 21:21). Quoted in the article, Rabbi Cohen said, "I believe this miracle is a sign that the Lord is pleased with us.

Scripture tells us, *'The Lord takes great delight in you... and will rejoice over you.'* (Zephaniah 3:17*)*. Elohim is rejoicing over His children. We worship a Lord of miracles."

When John Luke and Kristin saw the story, they sensed that Jesus had allowed Rabbi Cohen to be the first to witness the street of gold, a quiet gift for faithfulness and courage well shown.

The forty days Ariel Rabin spent at the motel passed quickly. When the time came, Jesus asked John Luke to return him to his home and family in Jerusalem. John Luke went to the room and brought him back.

Though his family rejoiced, the former prime minister was deeply shaken and angered that Shlomo Kariv had been elected prime minister in his absence by Israel's parliament. His attention did not rest on reunion or freedom, but on the loss of his position.

Ariel Rabin denounced the election as illegitimate. In the national press, he claimed he had been held against his will in an unknown location, suggesting that political rivals had engineered his removal to force approval of the peace accord with Palestine.

The coverage proved damaging. Rabin never held public office again.

By contrast, Prime Minister Shlomo Kariv thrived in leadership, with approval ratings reaching historic highs.

Israel achieved a lasting accord with Palestine, and political and trade relations with Egypt and other Arab nations steadily improved. Peace took root, and prosperity followed. Hamas was silenced. The work of the Mantle achieved its purpose.

Chapter 34:

Eden Restored

"I am the Alpha and the Omega, the Beginning and the End. To the thirsty I will give water without cost from the spring of the water of life. Those who are victorious will inherit this, and I will be their God, and they will be My children" (Revelation 21:6–7).

The phrase *water of life* first appears in the Gospel of Saint John, when Jesus speaks with the Samaritan woman at the well. Though unnamed, she is the first person to whom Jesus explicitly reveals Himself as the Messiah. He tells her, *"Whoever drinks the water I give them will never thirst. Indeed, the water I give them will become in them a spring of water welling up to eternal life"* (John 4:13–14).

The image appears three times in the closing chapters of the Book of Revelation, where the water of life is described as *"flowing from the throne of God and of the Lamb"* (Revelation 22:1).

Taken together, these passages reveal the water of life as God's gift of eternal life, first offered personally by Jesus and then fulfilled in Heaven, where divine presence and eternal communion are complete.

Number 12

Water is essential to life. In searching for life beyond Earth, scientists look first for water or ice. Where water exists, life follows.

Jesus lived in a land where water was scarce and precious. In that setting, Scripture points to something greater still: the water of life sustains the body but also leads to eternal life.

Science tells us that water exists in three states: vapor, liquid, and ice, and is formed from two parts hydrogen and one part oxygen. This simple formula, H_2O, produces a substance unlike almost any other found on Earth: complex, adaptable, and essential to life.

Unsurprisingly, Jesus compares eternal life to water. Both are indispensable, sustaining, and deeper than they first appear. The Mantle's work with John Luke reflects this truth, unfolding around water in two of the world's most critical regions: the Arctic and the Antarctic.

After their work in Israel, Egypt, and Palestine, Jesus met with John Luke in his home office to explain the next two missions of the Mantle.

"These missions," He said, "are aligned with the Book of Revelation, Eden restored."

Jesus continued, "Much of this work centers on water. The Father formed the Earth with two polar regions to regulate the climate and sustain life. The Arctic, with its glaciers and ice sheets, holds more than 20% of the world's fresh water. The Arctic Ocean, a vast saltwater basin, absorbs much of the sun's energy, helping prevent the planet from overheating and moderating temperatures across the globe."

"The Antarctic possesses similar and unique properties that stabilize the Earth's environment. Both poles are essential. Both now require our attention."

Antarctica is a vast ice sheet covering nearly one-fifth of Earth's surface. It helps regulate the planet's heat balance, reflects solar radiation, and, through its deep surrounding ocean, drives global water circulation.

Jesus said to John Luke, "Without healthy Arctic and Antarctic oceans, life on Earth would become unstable. Many species could not survive. Human-driven warming, caused largely by greenhouse gases like carbon dioxide, is melting critical Arctic regions and destabilizing the Antarctic ice sheet, disrupting the balance that the Father created."

Jesus then stated the mission plainly: to restore Eden to life as God intended, by healing these two regions through supernatural means. Human effort, though important, was not moving quickly enough.

John Luke felt a surge of excitement. "What should we do next, Lord, to help these places?"

Jesus replied, "If you are free now, let us go and see them together."

John Luke agreed without hesitation. He told Kristin of the plan, and with Jesus, he flew north to the Arctic Circle.

The Arctic Circle spans nearly 7.7 million square miles, about 4% of Earth's surface. The Arctic Ocean touches the lands of Canada, Greenland, Alaska, Iceland, Russia, Finland, Sweden, and Norway.

As they flew above the region, Jesus said, "As the Arctic warms so rapidly, many animals are forced from familiar habitats into uncertain territory, driven by rising seas, vanishing ice, and dwindling food sources."

Jesus said, "This grieves the Father to see creation disturbed in this way. It is not as He intended, and it brings distress to animals, to fish, and to humanity."

Flying low over Alaska, Jesus showed John Luke ice roads turned to gravel, fishing villages rebuilt farther inland as seas rose, icebergs thinning into water, and once-frozen tundra collapsing beneath its own thaw.

Troubled by what he saw, John Luke asked the question that pressed on his heart. "Jesus, can this be healed? Or are we too late?"

Jesus smiled gently. "Remember the question from Scripture: *'Is anything too hard for the Lord?'* (Genesis 18:14). Do not be afraid, John Luke. God can do all things. That is why we are here."

Jesus then said, "Let us go now to Antarctica."

They traveled more than 11,000 miles south, passing over Europe and Africa, and arrived in moments. Antarctica means *opposite of the Arctic*, a fitting name for a landmass of nearly 5.5 million square miles that forms an entire continent. It is high, dry, bitterly cold, and swept by relentless winds, its surface buried beneath ice. More than eighty percent of the world's fresh water is locked within its ice.

The land resembled a frozen desert, ringed by towering walls of ice and mountains carved by wind and time. The continent meets the Pacific, Indian, and Atlantic Oceans, binding the world's waters together.

After circling the region, Jesus guided them lower. Below, on a vast iceberg, thousands of emperor penguins huddled together, small lives enduring the extremes of creation.

Jesus said, "This continent has lost more than three trillion tons of ice, much of it in the west. Temperatures have risen more than five degrees in just twenty years. As the ice sheets melt, habitats for penguins, birds, and seals are disrupted, and ocean currents begin to shift. Warmer seas ripple outward, affecting fish and whales worldwide and fueling stronger storms, hurricanes, monsoons, and floods."

He paused, watching the penguins clustered against the wind.

Then he added, "The Mantle's mission to help heal the Earth's poles is critical, and it will take time. You have seen what must be done. Let us return to your office and plan the work."

They returned to John Luke's home office in seconds. Jesus appeared in person and said, "The Father's plan to heal the Earth's poles has two parts. The first is immediate and physical. The second is the sharing of knowledge."

He continued, "Just as the Mantle once guided atmospheric rivers over the Nubian Desert, it can now restore balance at the poles. Through the Mantle, you will help increase moisture over the Arctic and Antarctic, strengthening ice and stabilizing the climate. You will also work far above the atmosphere, beyond the exosphere, where harmful particles can be drawn upward and released harmlessly into space."

Jesus then explained that the oceans could be cooled at the poles by redirecting currents, drawing colder, deeper water upward to restore equilibrium in surface layers.

"This work will take time," He said, "and patience, to guide creation back toward its intended course."

John Luke answered without hesitation, "I am ready, Jesus. This work matters."

Jesus smiled. "How would you feel about taking a week away from your work to do this?" He paused. "If the Father created the world in seven days, we could begin healing it in the same span."

John Luke nodded. "That makes sense, Jesus. I will speak with Kristin and with my manager. I have plenty of vacation time."

Jesus's voice softened. "I also know this season matters deeply for you and Kristin, especially with the twins arriving soon. Understandably, concerns beyond the Mantle could weigh on your heart. Be sure to share all of this with Kristin."

John Luke answered without hesitation. "I will, Jesus. And I cannot imagine anything more important than helping create a better world for our children."

Jesus nodded, pleased.

Jesus said, “Once the physical work begins, the second part of our mission will be to share knowledge with world leaders, especially the science of climate change. This is not political theory or ideology. It is a scientific fact and faithful stewardship of the creation that the Father entrusted to humanity. Every person and nation bears responsibility for the care of the Earth.”

He continued, “Remember God’s covenant with Israel, which bound the people, the land, and faith in Him. The same pattern holds for all creation. God made humanity in His image and gave them the land for their good. In return, He asks faith in His ways that always lead to care. We will help the world understand why its habits must change so creation may remain healthy and whole.”

He said, “I understand, Jesus. I am ready to help.”

Jesus replied, “Well done, John Luke. You are a good and faithful servant. That is enough for now. Enjoy the rest of your day with Kristin and share this plan with her. And remember to tell your father as well.”

John Luke nodded. “I will. I promise.”

Jesus smiled, embraced him, and said they would meet again soon to begin the work. Then He was gone.

John Luke steadied himself and flew home with the Mantle.

Chapter 35:

Seven Days of Healing

"The angel said to me, 'These words are trustworthy and true. The Lord, the God who inspires the prophets, sent His angel to show His servants the things that must soon take place'" (Revelation 22:6).

The Book of Revelation reflects the Book of Genesis in profound ways. Genesis describes the creation of the world, while Revelation reveals the redemption and final restoration of that creation. The Hebrew word for revelation is *gala*, meaning to uncover or unveil. Through Scripture, God reveals His purpose for humanity and His intention to restore Eden.

Genesis, a name meaning *origin*, opens both the Hebrew and Christian Scriptures. Its first chapter tells of God creating the world in six days and resting on the seventh, delighting in His work. If the sacred story begins with creation, then believers are called not only to remember that account but also to care for what God made.

Scripture records that the Spirit of God first hovered over the waters (Genesis 1:2). Soon after, light separated from darkness, bringing order to the world.

God named the light day and the darkness night. In Hebrew, the word for day is *yom*, meaning the beginning of light. The word for sea or water is *yam*, differing from yom by only a single letter. Night is *lai'lah*, a word that signifies separation from the light. Land is called *erets,* the root of our word Earth.

From the beginning, creation is shaped by distinction, purpose, and care. Water and light, both essential to life, are ordered by God's word. Day is set apart from night, and sea from land.

God's creation was thoughtful and deliberate. From His example, we may infer that humanity must also act with purpose and care in how we steward water, land, and the world entrusted to us.

John Luke kept his promise and spoke at length with Kristin about the mission. Now three months pregnant, she was feeling well, her baby bump a quiet sign of new life. She agreed that providing their twins a healthy world to inherit matters most.

John Luke then called me and shared the details of Jesus' plan. Its depth and clarity struck me immediately, and I readily agreed on the importance of the work. John Luke arranged to take the following week off, and his manager approved without hesitation.

The Book of Revelation declares, *"I am the Root and the Offspring of David, and the bright Morning Star"* (Revelation 22:16). In Scripture, the morning star is a metaphor for the Messiah, a light given for humanity. That light is both word and action. The ways of Jesus are often unexpected and miraculous, and His Word carries insight drawn from an eternal, heavenly perspective.

The Mantle's final mission in this book, to help heal the Earth and restore creation toward its intended course, follows that same pattern of word and deed, shining like the bright Morning Star. Jesus planned to undertake this work with His disciple, John Luke, in seven days.

What follows is the account of those seven days.

Chapter 36:

Day One

On Monday morning of the mission week, John Luke prepared a healthy breakfast for Kristin and himself. He kissed her goodbye, kissed her baby bump, and went to his office. There, he said a prayer, wore the Mantle, and Jesus appeared in person.

"Good morning, John Luke," Jesus said. "Are you ready for day one of restoring Eden?"

John Luke smiled broadly. "I am, Jesus. I love this work."

"Good," Jesus replied. "We begin in Antarctica by healing the ozone layer."

Jesus continued, "The Earth's atmosphere has five layers. Closest to the ground is the troposphere, about seven miles high, where nearly all weather occurs. Above it lies the stratosphere, which holds the ozone layer that protects the planet from the sun's ultraviolet radiation.

"Above that is the mesosphere, where many meteors burn away. Higher still is the thermosphere where the International Space Station travels. Beyond it lies the exosphere, stretching hundreds of miles into space, where Earth's atmosphere fades, and solar winds carry particles away."

Then Jesus said, "We will begin in the troposphere above Antarctica and rise to the exosphere."

In seconds, they were there.

Then Jesus said, "We will go to the troposphere above Antarctica and move upward to the exosphere."

In seconds, they were there.

Jesus gestured. "Circle the Pacific. Fast. Draw up an atmospheric river and release it along the western coast. This region bears the greatest change."

John Luke swept into a wide counterclockwise arc, pulling a vast river of water from the ocean below. Above the roar, he called out, "Release River of water on the Antarctic Peninsula and West Antarctic Ice Sheet."

Ice pellets and liquid water spread across the land in a broad, steady cover.

Jesus spoke again. "Now to the opposite directions."

They split the sky, lifting the dry, frozen air of the troposphere. Winds rose, sustained and relentless, reaching hurricane force.

They climbed into the stratosphere, carrying water, wind, and snow that swept ozone-destroying chemicals away from the fragile layer. Still circling, they rose through the mesosphere and into the exosphere, each widening arc thinning the air around them.

At the edge of the atmosphere, Jesus said, "Tighten your pattern."

Nearly 440 miles above Earth, they steadied their flight.

Jesus's voice was calm. "Hold here. I am about to perform a miracle."

John Luke gazed into the deep black of space. Jesus breathed into the circling wind and water behind them, and the ozone-destroying particles were swept away, carried harmlessly into the void.

Below them, the breach sealed at once. The stratosphere over Antarctica was restored, and ultraviolet radiation returned to safe, natural levels.

For a moment, there was only silence.

John Luke understood that what had been wounded was made whole not by force, but by the breath of God that first stirred creation.

When the work was complete, Jesus said, "Now let us return to the troposphere, where we will shape the atmospheric rivers."

They descended, and Jesus spoke directly into John Luke's mind.

"I will form a river over the Atlantic. You will form one over the Pacific."

John Luke felt the weight of the invitation not as a burden, but as trust.

Guided by Jesus's will, he released his river along the western edge of the continent while Jesus released the other along the east. Snow and ice pellets fell in steady sheets, strengthening the ice shelves on both coasts and restoring strength to the frozen land.

When the task was complete, Jesus led John Luke down to the Ross Ice Shelf so they could witness the result.

Holding John Luke's hand, Jesus prayed, paraphrasing Saint Paul.

"Praise be to the God and Father, who has blessed us in the heavenly realms with every spiritual blessing" (Ephesians 1:3).

It was two in the afternoon.

Jesus said, "Our work for today is complete. The snow will continue for three more hours."

He embraced John Luke.

"Day one is finished, and the work is good. Fly home to Kristin."

John Luke smiled and returned to his home office as Jesus disappeared, surely to rejoice with the Father.

The restoration of Eden had begun.

Chapter 37:
Day Two

On Tuesday, the second day of the mission, Jesus met John Luke in his office shortly after breakfast. Together they flew once more to Antarctica, covering nearly 9,000 miles in seconds.

When they arrived, Jesus said, "Today our work lies beneath the ocean, at great depths. We will regulate the clockwise currents that circle the continent. I know this troubles you, given your fear of swimming. I give you My word, the Mantle will protect you from all harm below."

John Luke managed a small, uncertain smile. "I believe You, Jesus," he said. "I still marvel that the Mantle allows me to swim at all."

Jesus replied, "All will be well. Now we will draw cold water from the ocean's depths toward the surface. This will strengthen the ice shelves surrounding the continent."

He continued, "By guiding the currents of the Antarctic Ocean, we restore balance to oceans worldwide and help return Earth's weather to its natural flow."

John Luke listened in wonder. He knew, of course, that Jesus is God. Even so, he was amazed.

They moved along the ocean floor as if flying, first skirting the continent and then sweeping outward toward distant shores.

Beneath the waters near Argentina and the Falklands, past Africa and Madagascar, across to Australia and New Zealand, and back again toward South America, they worked in widening arcs.

Time seemed to stretch as they stirred deep, cold currents upward, strengthening the ice shelves that encircled the continent. Along the way, minke and humpback whales glided through the depths, silent witnesses to the healing underway.

At last, Jesus said, "Our work is complete. Let us surface at the Larsen Ice Shelf."

When they arrived, Jesus took John Luke's hand in prayer and lifted His eyes heavenward.

"Thanks be to God, who gives us the victory through His holy Name."

He embraced him. "Day two is finished, and the work is good."

John Luke smiled. "Thank You, Jesus. May I ask when I return to my office, where do You go?"

Jesus smiled. "Do you recall the Scripture, *'In My Father's house are many rooms'* (John 14:2)?"

"Yes," John Luke said. "You told us You go to prepare a place for us."

"I have My own room in Heaven," Jesus replied.

John Luke laughed softly. "I should have known."

Jesus smiled, lifted a hand in farewell, and disappeared.

The restoration of Eden continued.

Chapter 38:

Day Three

On Wednesday, the third day of the mission, Jesus met John Luke after breakfast.

"Today," He said, "we move to the Arctic Ocean."

John Luke grinned. "I'm ready."

The Arctic, named from the Greek *arktos,* meaning bear, spreads across land, water, and ice beneath the northern stars. Ancient and fragile, it now warms faster than the rest of the planet. Ice retreats, frozen ground shifts, and currents change, sending ripples through weather patterns worldwide. Jesus knew that without Divine intervention, the unraveling would continue.

"As in Antarctica," Jesus said, "we will draw water from the ocean over the land to cool the region and strengthen the ice. We will fly in tight circles. I will move clockwise. You will fly counterclockwise."

Two immense atmospheric rivers formed in their wake.

Jesus spoke into John Luke's mind. "Release yours over Greenland and the northern islands of Canada."

He guided John Luke again. This time, John Luke dropped the river over Sweden, Norway, Finland, and the far northern reaches of Russia.

He then guided John Luke again. This time, John Luke released the river over Sweden, Norway, Finland, and the far northern reaches of Russia.

They labored together for hours, shaping atmospheric rivers until cold waters blanketed the northernmost lands bordering the Arctic Ocean: Alaska, Canada, Russia, and the scattered islands of the Arctic Circle. Though they flew faster than the speed of sound, the work took an entire day, for the Arctic stretches across more than five million square miles.

At last, Jesus said, "Our work here is complete. Let us land on Victoria Island, near Cambridge Bay."

When they touched down, Jesus took John Luke's hand and looked upward through the falling snow.

"The heavens declare the glory of God; the skies proclaim the work of His hands" (Psalms 19:1).

Then He added, *"And God saw that it was good"* (Genesis 1:12).

Jesus embraced John Luke and thanked him for the day's work. John Luke returned home to Kristin, and Jesus went to His room in Heaven.

When John Luke arrived, the time was the same as when he left after breakfast. Grateful for the gift of time, he asked Kristin if she would like to shop for the babies' rooms.

Their plans were beginning to take shape. His former office would become the baby boy's nursery, and their home gym would become the baby girl's nursery. Kristin would move her workspace into a corner of their bedroom, while John Luke would relocate his office downstairs.

They spent the morning shopping, then lingered over lunch at their favorite Japanese noodle bar. Between bites, John Luke told her about the Mantle's work in the Arctic and Antarctic. Kristin listened in awe, especially when he described swimming in the deep ocean.

"The Mantle gives me confidence," he said with a smile. "I think it taught me how to swim."

"In Arctic water?" Kristin laughed.

"I leave the details of the mission to Jesus," he said. "It's not frozen, so it must be at least thirty-two degrees."

They drove home content.

After a moment, John Luke said, "We will need to choose names soon."

Kristin smiled. "I already have a list."

Of course you do, he thought, loving her even more.

Chapter 39:

Day Four

On Thursday, the fourth day of the mission, John Luke rose early and made breakfast. When Kristin joined him, she thanked him warmly for caring for her so tenderly. They ate together, talked about work, and cleaned the kitchen side by side.

Before leaving, John Luke hugged and kissed her, then went to his office. He said a prayer, gently wore the Mantle, and waited.

Jesus appeared in person, wearing His white robe, gold sash, and *bronze-plated swimming flippers!*

John Luke doubled over with laughter.

Jesus laughed with him. "Are you ready for a swim in the balmy Arctic Ocean?"

John Luke marveled once again at the God of the universe's sense of humor.

Together they flew nearly 3,700 miles to the Arctic Ocean at the speed of light.

The Arctic Ocean spans more than five million square miles, a shifting realm of ice and open water. Temperatures range from freezing to about forty degrees, and sea ice varies from inches to several feet thick. Eight nations border the region: Canada, the United States, Russia, Finland, Sweden, Norway, Iceland, and Denmark through Greenland.

Satellite imagery shows that Arctic sea ice has declined by nearly thirteen percent over the past decade, a rapid change with global consequences.

Jesus brought John Luke to the exact location of the North Magnetic Pole.

"The pole has drifted nearly ten degrees," He said, "away from Canada and toward Russia. Drift is natural, but not at this pace. Ice loss, stronger winds, and warming oceans have accelerated the change."

He continued, "Melting ice adds warmer fresh water to the sea, disrupting how currents sink and circulate. Combined with warmer winds, this has weakened the Gulf Stream to its lowest level in nearly five hundred years, destabilizing weather across North America and Europe and disturbing the ocean's food chain from the tropics to the Arctic."

"We must correct this course," Jesus said.

John Luke nodded. "I had no idea."

Jesus continued, "We will swim counterclockwise along the ocean floor, gently regulating the great conveyor that circulates water through this region."

Together they moved deep beneath the surface, swimming against the natural flow. Circling the Arctic at three rotations each hour, they blended fresh and salt water at a measured pace, easing temperatures and restoring equilibrium to the sea.

Jesus spoke into John Luke's mind. "We will repeat this action seven times. Then our work will be complete."

When they finished, Jesus brought them near Fairbanks, Alaska.

"Are you familiar with the Beaufort Gyre?" He asked.

John Luke shook his head. "Not really, Jesus. Would You explain it to me?"

"Of course," Jesus said gently. "The Beaufort Gyre is a system of winds and currents that helps maintain the Arctic's balance of fresh and salt water. Westerly winds from Canada and Alaska sustain it, but those winds have warmed significantly over the past fifty years."

John Luke nodded. "Thank You for explaining it so clearly."

Jesus smiled. "You are a trustworthy disciple, John Luke. My words take root in you."

He then explained that on Friday, they would work to cool the winds. For now, on the fourth day of restoring Eden, the task was finished. The slowed currents would allow the ice to rebuild naturally.

As always, Jesus took John Luke's hand and lifted His eyes in praise. *"Praise the Lord from the heavens... you highest heavens, and you waters above the skies"* (Psalm 148).

He embraced John Luke and said, "And God saw that it was good."

John Luke smiled and flew home to Kristin. Jesus disappeared as he departed.

Chapter 40:

Day Five

By Friday, the fifth day of the mission, John Luke stood in awe of the Father's plan and all that had been accomplished in four days. As usual, Jesus met him in his office after breakfast.

"Today is our final day of field work," Jesus said. "The miracles in creation are nearly complete. But as Eden is restored, God's people must understand their responsibility to care for the Earth. Tomorrow, we begin the second phase, calling world leaders to agree on concrete plans to protect this gift. That work will involve meetings, communication, and the media. We will use your alias, John Ward. How does that sound?"

John Luke grinned. "I'm in it to win it, Jesus."

Jesus laughed. "That's the Spirit."

Then He laughed again at His own joke.

Jesus continued, "Warmer westerly winds are driving ice melt and rising temperatures in both the Arctic and Antarctic. These winds move from west to east across the Earth's mid-latitudes."

"In the Northern Hemisphere, they stretch from the Tropic of Cancer to the Arctic Circle, passing through regions such as Mexico and Egypt. In the Southern Hemisphere, they run from the Tropic of Capricorn to the Antarctic Circle, crossing lands like Argentina and Australia."

“As the climate warms, these winds carry more heat and push farther north and south, accelerating damage in the polar regions.”

“These winds matter,” Jesus said, “because they influence the polar vortex in both hemispheres. The polar vortex is a vast ring of cold, low-pressure air around each pole that keeps cold air contained near the poles. When it weakens, weather patterns are disrupted worldwide.”

John Luke asked, “So our work today will help stabilize the polar vortex?”

“Precisely,” Jesus said.

“The vortex lies in the stratosphere, about 10 to 30 miles above Earth. When stable, as God intended, it forms a powerful ring of wind that holds cold air over the poles. When warmer westerlies disturb it, that cold spills into the jet stream, bringing extreme winter weather across the continents.”

John Luke nodded slowly. “That explains so much about the changing weather.”

“Yes,” Jesus replied. “A warming planet produces greater extremes, colder winters in some places and hotter summers in others. To stabilize the vortex, we must stabilize the westerly winds. Otherwise, the work we have done at the poles will erode over time. Everything in the Father’s creation is connected.”

He smiled. “Today, we stabilize the westerlies and with them the vortices at each pole. Are you ready to fly?”

John Luke grinned. “Let’s go.”

First, Jesus led John Luke south to the Tropic of Capricorn. As before, they drew vast atmospheric rivers from the South Pacific, lifted them into the upper stratosphere, and released them over South America, cooling Chile, Argentina, Paraguay, and Uruguay. Rain, ice, and snow steadied the winds, lowered temperatures, and renewed the land.

They repeated the work over Southern Africa and Australia. Jesus instructed, "We will do this three times, flying lower in the stratosphere and releasing smaller rivers, enough to cool and restore, but not enough to flood plains or rivers."

When the work was finished, Jesus said the temperatures had eased, and the land was drought-free.

Jesus then brought him into the polar vortex high in the stratosphere, nearly thirty miles above Antarctica. Centered over the South Pole, it spanned nearly five million square miles, its winds exceeding 100 miles per hour. Together, they entered the ring of cold air and circled it seven times, stabilizing the vortex and restoring balance.

Jesus then spoke into John Luke's mind. "Now we go north to the Tropic of Cancer above Mexico." Drawing atmospheric rivers from the Pacific, they released cooling waters over southern Mexico and into Central America, continuing across Colombia and Ecuador. The work was completed within the hour.

"Next," Jesus said, "Central Africa." They guided rivers of water from the stratosphere across the Republic of Congo,

Uganda, and Somalia, cooling the winds, nourishing the land, and restoring balance.

Then Jesus said, "Next, we go to southern India, Indonesia, and the Philippines. We will repeat the cycle three times, each pass lower and lighter, enough to refresh the land without flooding it." The work was finished within an hour.

He then added, "Now we turn to the Arctic polar vortex. This task is more difficult. The vortex is unstable, split in two, and stretched across nearly ten million square miles."

John Luke could only say, "Wow."

Jesus smiled, and they flew north. When they reached the Arctic, He paused, and at His command the scattered winds drew together, forming a single circling force.

"Fly within the vortex with Me," Jesus said. "We will move together until it becomes whole."

Side by side, they flew through the vast system. Within the hour, the vortex stabilized into a unified flow.

Then Jesus said, "Our work is complete. Let us touch down near Fairbanks, Alaska."

On the ground, Jesus took John Luke's hand. "Please pray with Me."

Jesus then quoted from the Book of Revelation: *"You are worthy, our Lord and God, to receive glory and honor and power, for you created all things, and by your will they were created and have their being"* (4:11).

Jesus looked at John Luke, and said softly, "The work is complete, and it is good. Eden is now restored to God's original design. It will remain so if nations choose to work together to address a warming world."

He smiled, deeply moved. "Thank You, Jesus, for including me."

Jesus said, "Thank you, John Luke, for helping Me. You remember that I sent the disciples out two by two. Faith is not meant to be carried alone. You are My disciple, and I am grateful for you."

John Luke felt the words of Jesus settle deeply. "I can't express how much this work means to me," he said. "Thank You for choosing me."

Jesus smiled. "You're welcome, my dear friend. Would you like to see My room in heaven before you return home?"

John Luke's eyes widened. "Now?"

"Yes," Jesus said gently. "Let's go."

Jesus took his hand, and they rose into a brilliant blue sky. Soon, the sky itself gave way to a field of living light, and they arrived in heaven.

Four radiant blue angels stood waiting. They bowed deeply as Jesus greeted them. *"Shalom and Berachah, chaverai."*

Turning to John Luke, Jesus said, "Hebrew is the language of heaven."

They passed the angels and came to a golden door. As Jesus approached, it opened.

"Please," He said. "Come in."

The room was elegant in its simplicity, filled with a quiet peace that seemed to breathe through the air itself, with four gold-toned walls and a glass ceiling above. A rich red-and-gold carpet lay across the floor, woven in an Arabic majlis style. A simple bed rested in the southern corner, and two upholstered cushions sat near the northern wall. The air was filled with the soft scent of incense.

"Please sit," Jesus said.

John Luke did and had to steady his breath. He was sitting in the room of the Savior of the world. John Luke felt it at once: the room fit the humble and gracious Jesus he knew and loved.

Sensing his awe, Jesus said gently, "You once asked where I go when our work is done. I wanted to welcome you here, just as you welcome Me into your home."

"Thank You, Jesus," John Luke said quietly. "I'm a bit nervous. May I have a glass of water, or is that too much to ask?"

Jesus smiled. "No trouble at all. Look at your right hand."

A glass of clear, sparkling water rested there, cool and steady.

Jesus then said, "Tomorrow, let us meet again at the same time in your office. We will begin the Father's work of teaching His people to care for creation. This part may prove more difficult than calming the polar winds."

John Luke smiled. "Still, nothing is too hard for the Lord."

"Well said," Jesus replied. "Good and faithful servant."

John Luke rose. "I won't trouble You any longer. I'm deeply grateful You welcomed me into Your home."

Jesus looked at him with love. "Someday, after your children, and their children, and their children after them, you will be with Me forever in My Father's house."

Jesus walked him to the door, and John Luke returned home to Kristin, his heart filled with a love deeper than anything he had known. He told her all that had happened.

Kristin listened, smiled softly, and said, "Jesus loves you very much."

Chapter 41:

Day Six

On the sixth day of Eden's healing, Jesus arrived promptly at John Luke's home office on Saturday morning, shortly after breakfast. He asked John Luke to sit, and together they discussed the work ahead, helping political leaders worldwide agree to reduce greenhouse gas emissions.

Jesus said, "International media are already reporting on the work of the past five days. Weather satellites show measurable improvement across the Tropics of Cancer and Capricorn, and at both poles. This attention will help sustain Eden's restoration."

Some commentators called it another act of God, echoing reports from Ukraine and Sudan.

Then Jesus turned the conversation deeper.

"Now we must speak of how Eden remains restored," He said. "Scripture tells us, *'God gave Solomon wisdom and very great insight, and a breadth of understanding as measureless as the sand on the seashore'"* (1 Kings 4:29).

Jesus continued, "Today, John Luke, the Father decrees that you will surpass Solomon in wisdom. For a time, this gift must be shared with the world under your alias, John Ward, to protect you and your family. If you are willing, I will open your mind to realms of science you have never studied and to depths of human behavior beyond what modern psychology can explain. Your insight will exceed that of great scientists and philosophers. This wisdom will bless you and your children for the good of civilization."

He paused, allowing the weight of His words to settle.

"Are you willing to receive this gift, known as the Mind of Christ?"

John Luke leaned back, stunned. After a long moment, he answered quietly, "Yes, Jesus. I receive this gift with awe and gratitude. Thank You for trusting me. But… why me?"

Jesus held his gaze.

"You know the Mantle carries great power because of My DNA," He said. "But the Father and I now give you the Mind of Christ apart from the Mantle, because We trust you. You have proven yourself to be a faithful disciple. In the deepest spiritual sense, you will grow more like Me each day."

Then His voice grew solemn.

"This gift is also a burden. Wisdom must always be used for the good of others, never for self. It demands humility, restraint, and love. We believe you will carry it rightly."

John Luke drew a steady breath. He bowed his head and said, "I am unworthy, yet let it be as You say, Lord."

And on that day, John Luke received the Mind of Christ.

Jesus said, "Thank you for saying yes. Now I will explain the Father's plan for sustaining Eden. When you speak to world leaders as John Ward, you will no longer need Me standing beside you to speak God's word. I will always be with you, but more than that, I will be in you. You will know which words to speak and which actions to take."

Jesus continued, "First, as Scripture declares, *'The Lord will open the heavens, the storehouse of His bounty'* (Deuteronomy 28:12). From this day forward, The Mantle LLC will have unlimited resources to carry out the Father's plan. In the past, My work sometimes relied on human wealth, even wealth gained unjustly. That is why I asked you to say, 'nearly unlimited resources.'"

He looked steadily at John Luke. "Now, The Mantle LLC will become the greatest philanthropic force on Earth, supplied directly from God's treasury. Wealth is not a human invention. All wealth, spiritual and material, comes from God. The care of Eden is too important to depend on human provision alone."

Then Jesus said firmly, "You may promise the world unlimited resources. The Father will provide."

Jesus continued, "You may already understand some of this, but let Me make it clear. The climate crisis has five root causes. You will explain these to political leaders and help guide them toward long-term, lasting change."

Jesus said. "Each cause requires a clear response. Together they form God's Five-Point Plan to maintain Eden. Each root cause is paired with a strategic response." Jesus paused, then said,

"These are the Five Points of God's plan to maintain Eden."

One: Humanity, the Land, and God

Jesus said, "The first cause is the growing strain on creation from how humanity now lives and works. This is not blame; it is simply the truth.

"People must be allowed to move freely and humanely to land that can sustain life without exhausting it. The Earth was given for all My Father's children.

"Work itself must change toward ways that protect the land while honoring human dignity.

"What has been lost will be restored. New forests will rise where deserts now spread, and life will return to places once stripped bare.

"Human intelligence, including tools such as artificial intelligence, must be turned toward healing, curing disease, reducing suffering, and sustaining the planet wisely."

Two: Energy and the Atmosphere

Jesus said, "The second cause is the warming of the Earth through carbon dioxide and other greenhouse gases that trap heat in the air.

"Humanity must expand clean energy, drawing more fully from the sun and the wind I set in motion at creation.

"The oceans will provide fresh water through affordable desalination.

"Greenhouse gases will no longer be wasted or feared but captured and reused for good. Even the moisture of the air will be gathered and stored, bringing water to dry lands."

Three: Responsible Use of Resources

Jesus said, “The third cause is how humanity extracts and uses fossil fuels.

“Plastics and other harmful chemicals that poison land and sea must be eliminated.

“Humanity must learn to use fossil resources wisely, removing harmful byproducts so that economies may endure without poisoning creation.”

Four: Healing Agriculture and Forests

Jesus said, “The fourth cause is how humanity grows its food.

“Harmful agricultural chemicals must be replaced. Forests must no longer be destroyed.

“Farmers, shepherds, and foresters will be given tools and better knowledge, so their work sustains life rather than exhausts it.

“Humanity will also learn to rely more on plants for nourishment, easing pressure on animals and the land.”

Five: Stabilizing Earth’s Great Systems

Jesus said, “The fifth cause is imbalance in the great systems of the Earth.

“The polar vortices must remain stable.

“The winds and ocean currents that govern the planet’s climate must remain in harmony.

“Cool regions must remain cool, and warmer regions must be sustained with water and natural relief.”

Jesus continued, “You remember how I told you that God’s covenant with Israel, the first of the chosen people, was always about the people, the land, and God. This design is now for all humanity. Soon, the world will understand how deeply creation is connected, how what wounds the Earth also wounds its people."

He added, "This truth will become common knowledge. Your family will help carry it forward, and God will open hearts and minds to receive the words spoken through John Ward."

To John Luke's amazement, his mind now held the breadth of the plan. Ideas unfolded, new methods, new inventions, new paths toward healing creation.

Jesus said nothing more. He looked at John Luke with deep delight, watching wisdom take root.

And Jesus was pleased.

Chapter 42:

Day Seven

Jesus told John Luke that the time had come to bring the Father's plan into the light of the world. A press conference would mark the turning point. When Jesus asked if he was ready for this next phase, John Luke answered without hesitation. He was eager, willing, and steadfast.

"I ask you to call the President of the United States, Rosalyn Jones," Jesus said. "Ask her to meet with you and hear the plan. She is a godly woman. If she wishes to stand with you at the press conference, she is welcome. If not, the Father's work will still go forward. The plan is already in motion."

Jesus then gave John Luke a private number to reach the president's assistant at the White House. With a quiet nod of confidence, He added with a gentle smile, "There is no time like the present."

He dialed the number from The Mantle LLC's secure phone. The president's assistant answered, and John Luke introduced himself as John Ward, asking whether President Jones might be available. Moments later, the line shifted.

Not surprisingly, the president took the call.

Rosalyn Jones was fifty years old, a married woman of color with three children and a former governor of Tennessee. She holds an undergraduate degree in physics from the University of Tennessee and earned both her master's and doctoral degrees from Vanderbilt University. Dr. Jones was the first woman of color and the first Ph.D. to be elected President of the United States.

She had won the presidency a year earlier on a platform that promised environmental restoration alongside economic strength.

Her running mate and vice president, Marvin Stevens, was a respected attorney, former member of the Federal Reserve Board of Governors, and longtime senator from California. At sixty-two, married with four children, he brought gravitas and legal clarity to the administration.

Jesus knew they could become strong allies in the Father's plan if they were willing to listen.

President Jones greeted him warmly. "John Ward," she said with a trace of amusement, "why am I not surprised you have my assistant's private number?"

John Ward laughed softly. "God has His ways. Mrs. President, I'm calling to ask whether you would be willing to meet with me about a plan from The Mantle LLC, one designed to maintain the environment while strengthening the economy."

Two details immediately pleased President Jones. First, he addressed her as Mrs. President, the title she preferred. Second, he spoke of maintaining the environment, a phrase that aligned with the satellite data she had reviewed from NASA, which showed recent, unexplained improvements in global weather patterns.

"I would be delighted to meet with you," she replied. "And again, why am I not surprised that you seem fully aware of these positive changes? I have a sneaking suspicion you may be connected to the weather itself."

John Luke smiled, charmed by the gentle teasing carried in her warm Southern cadence.

"Yes, Mrs. President," he said, choosing his words carefully, "to be transparent, the Mantle has been at work helping to restore normalcy to global weather patterns."

The president did not hesitate. "I want to hear this plan as soon as possible. I happen to be available tomorrow, Sunday. I usually stay in Washington for church and family time. Could you come for brunch at the White House around 11:30?"

"I would be honored, Mrs. President," John Luke replied.

The call ended. John Luke turned to Jesus, a broad, almost disbelieving smile spreading across his face. "I can't believe I'm having brunch with the president!"

Jesus smiled. "She will invite the Vice President as well. He will be especially interested in The Mantle LLC's investment role. You may tell them we are prepared to invest up to $1 trillion worldwide in God's Five-point plan."

John Luke stared at Him, momentarily speechless. "A trillion dollars, Jesus?"

Jesus smiled and said, *"Have I not kept this in reserve and sealed it in my vaults?"* (Deuteronomy 32:34). "The Father has riches stored for His people. I will ensure the funds appear in The Mantle LLC's Swiss National Bank account for this work."

John Luke laughed in disbelief. "I guess I'll never say more money than God again. God is… well, loaded."

Jesus laughed with him. "That was a good one, John Luke."

Then Jesus asked John Luke to call me and begin drafting the plan for the president, refining the details of God's Five-point strategy. John Luke called and asked whether I would meet with him and Jesus to help shape the plan. I answered without hesitation.

Moments later, John Luke arrived by the Mantle and took me to the meeting. When I entered, Jesus rose from His chair and embraced me warmly.

"I'm so glad to see you, John Mark," He said. "We have work to do, and I know you will add wisdom and clarity to God's plan to maintain Eden."

I smiled, overwhelmed and grateful. "Jesus, I'm so happy to see You and honored to help."

John Luke pulled out a flip chart and a box of markers. For the next two hours, we brainstormed and mapped out the Father's plan for the president and, ultimately, for the world.

Jesus guided the discussion, ensuring we addressed all Five Points. He offered ideas that were both astonishing and elegantly simple: new ways to capture solar and wind energy, low-cost methods to desalinate seawater, and revolutionary approaches to locating and using oil, gas, and coal with minimal environmental impact. As He spoke, Jesus sketched the concepts on the paper Himself.

It was astonishing to watch the Son of God holding a marker and drawing on a flip chart.

We also explored the financial and economic implications of each point, considering how markets might adapt and how prosperity could grow without exploitation. Together, we discussed humane, voluntary pathways for migration that allow people to move with dignity to regions better able to sustain life and opportunity.

I noticed that John Luke now spoke with an almost encyclopedic grasp of the world's sparsely populated regions, places capable of sustaining far more life than they currently did. He began writing rapidly, outlining how artificial intelligence could be used to develop the technologies and inventions needed for each point, translating Jesus's guidance into practical design.

We discussed ways to make farmland more sustainable and to reforest areas stripped bare by overharvesting. Jesus asked John Luke to note the use of robotics for planting, weeding, and harvesting crops. We also explored how plants could better serve humanity as primary food sources and as sustainable materials for clothing and manufacturing.

Jesus was pleased with our collaboration and the completed plan. His wisdom shaped every detail. His insight made all the difference.

Kristin, now clearly glowing with new life within her, heard our voices and came upstairs to the office. She stopped short, astonished and delighted to find Jesus, John Luke, and me working side by side.

Jesus rose, embraced her warmly, and said, "Kristin, you look radiant. I am so glad to see you."

Kristin beamed with delight and stayed with us, pulling a chair closer to the table. After listening for a few moments, she began offering thoughtful insights, refining the Father's plan and shaping ideas for the press release with clarity and grace.

Jesus looked at her with evident warmth. "You see the heart of this work, Kristin," He said. "Truth must be spoken clearly if it is to be heard."

Kristin smiled, a little humbled. "People need to know this isn't fear-driven," she said. "They need to hear hope, that caring for creation strengthens families, economies, and futures."

Jesus nodded. "Exactly. Wisdom spoken with hope opens hearts."

When brainstorming concluded, I volunteered to draft a concise document outlining the five points at a high level. John Luke said he would develop the financial models, economic projections, and investment returns and organize them into spreadsheets. He would purchase a 3D printer to bring ideas into physical form.

I watched my son as he worked, marveling at the speed and precision of his thinking. Something in him had shifted, quietly and unmistakably, for the better. At the time, I did not yet know that the Lord had entrusted him with the Mind of Christ.

We completed our work. John Luke, in the role of John Ward, was ready to meet the President of the United States for brunch. Jesus hugged each of us goodbye, and we returned to our daily routines with a song in our hearts, *"speaking to one another with psalms, hymns, and songs from the Spirit"* (Ephesians 5:19).

After Sunday morning church, the four of us lingered over coffee in the meeting space. John Luke shared more details about his upcoming White House visit. Kristin sat beside him, radiant with pride. She looked wonderful, five months pregnant now, feeling strong and gaining weight just as she should for twins.

As we walked to our cars, John Luke turned to Joan. "Mom and Dad, we were wondering, when the twins are born, would you be willing to come to our house as needed and help watch the babies while we're in meetings? Mom, we know you have your real estate work."

I nearly reached out to grab Joan's feet; certain she was about to float ten feet off the ground.

"Of course!" she gushed. "We would be delighted to care for the babies anytime."

That conversation all but completed Joan's life. We headed home smiling, making sure John Luke would arrive on time for brunch, his life, and ours, quietly changing before our eyes.

On that seventh day, the work of healing had given way to the work of wisdom.

Chapter 43: John Ward at the White House

"And I heard a loud voice from the throne saying, "Look! God's dwelling place is now among the people, and he will dwell with them. They will be his people, and God himself will be with them and be their God" (Revelation 21:3).

The Book of Revelation speaks of a new heaven and a new Earth, the moment when God restores humanity and creation through His Son, Jesus. Through Christ, God will dwell with His people forever. The old order passes away, and the Lamb upon the throne makes all things new.

In its own way, the work of Jesus and John Luke to heal Eden echoed this promise. For the first time since the healing of Eden began, the work of heaven would now step into the public light of the world.

John Luke went to his office, said a prayer, and wore the Mantle. Carrying a portfolio with the Father's written plan, he flew to Pennsylvania Avenue and landed a block from the White House at precisely 11:25 AM.

He walked toward the familiar black wrought-iron gates and spoke briefly with the guard who was expecting him.

John Ward was escorted to the Entrance Hall of the White House, where President Jones and Vice President Stevens surprisingly greeted him in person. Kristin had chosen his wardrobe carefully: an exquisite, blue-checked three-piece suit, a light-blue shirt, and a red-and-white paisley tie.

President Jones greeted him warmly, shook his hand, and introduced him to the vice president. With her familiar Southern lilt, she smiled and said, “John Ward, don’t you look sharp. That is a fine suit and tie. Are you running for political office? We certainly do not need the competition.”

The vice president laughed heartily as he shook John Ward’s hand. Together, they walked to the Family Dining Room on the State Floor, where coffee and juice were served alongside eggs Benedict, fresh fruit, and generous bowls of Southern grits.

John Ward sampled the grits and smiled. “I have never had these before. They are remarkable.”

President Jones laughed. “They are an acquired taste for most Northerners.”

John Ward was quietly impressed when President Jones invited the Secret Service agents to brunch. Although they politely declined the meal, all three accepted coffee. He also noticed that Vice President Stevens naturally deferred to the president, respectful and entirely genuine. They made a strong team.

After some pleasantries, President Jones said, "John, would you mind if we talked business while we eat?"

"Not at all," John Ward replied. "I am grateful for your time. May I give you both hard copies of my presentation? I do not want to interrupt the enjoyment of such excellent food."

President Jones smiled. "Please do, and I will do my best not to spill coffee on your work."

"No worries, Mrs. President," John Ward said with a smile. "I brought backup copies."

John Ward spoke plainly to both the president and the vice president. "This document is titled God's Five-Point Plan to Maintain Eden. The reference comes from the *Book of Revelation*, which speaks of restoring the world to its original design, the Garden of Eden. As you know, The Mantle LLC is a non-profit, independent philanthropic organization dedicated to carrying out the will of God on Earth."

He continued, "As we discussed on the phone, Mrs. President, the Mantle was involved in recent efforts to stabilize global weather patterns. These points form a worldwide strategy to sustain that healing, grounded in a biblical vision of partnership between God, humanity, and the land."

John Ward paused. "This plan is greater than any one nation. God invites all people into partnership with Him and with creation itself. Humanity, the Earth, and all living creatures are interconnected, and God calls us to care for what He has made."

He looked from the president to the vice president. "We are sharing this plan with you first because we believe you can be strong allies in this work. To that end, The Mantle LLC is prepared to commit up to $1 trillion to make this vision a reality."

At that, Vice President Stevens politely interrupted. "Forgive me, John. Did you say a trillion dollars? Does the Mantle LLC have resources at that level?"

John Ward smiled calmly. "Yes. We are prepared to commit that amount to this effort. You may verify the funds in our account as needed."

President Jones nodded. "Do not worry; we will. You certainly have my attention, John. Please, tell us more."

John Ward continued,

First: Humanity and the Land

"We acknowledge that population growth and human activity place increasing strain on the planet. Our response is humane and voluntary, rethinking where and how people live and work so the Earth can sustain humanity."

Second: Energy and Emissions

"We will significantly reduce greenhouse gases through expanded solar and wind energy and cost-effective desalination."

Third: Pollution and Plastics

"We will remove plastics from the oceans and eliminate 'forever chemicals,' replacing them with environmentally safe alternatives."

Fourth: Agriculture and Forests

"We will reform agricultural chemicals and reforest the planet at scale."

Fifth: Planetary Balance

"We will stabilize the polar vortices of the Arctic and Antarctic, restoring balance to the global climate."

He paused briefly. "Many of these methods are not yet public. I assure you, however, that we possess the means and the technology to carry out this plan. We believe our work thus far demonstrates its credibility."

President Jones nodded and set down her coffee. "How do you intend to publish and communicate this plan," she asked, "and how would you like us to support The Mantle LLC?"

John Ward replied, "We plan to hold a press conference as soon as feasible. With your support, we would be honored to host it here at the White House. We will present the plan publicly and distribute copies of the document, along with additional details about the technology behind each of the Five Points."

He paused deliberately, giving the president and vice president space to absorb what he shared.

"After the press conference," he continued, "we would seek the opportunity to address the United Nations and form a global pact, one committed to people, the planet, and profit. Central to that pact would be a humane, coordinated approach to immigration and refugee care. Our plans and innovations would be shared immediately, with safeguards to ensure they serve the common good."

John Ward's voice remained steady. "Everything we do is meant to honor people, respect the Earth, and strengthen the global economy. This effort must rise above political divisions and rest on scientific truths. If we fail to act, Eden cannot be sustained. In time, we risk slipping backward, perhaps beyond recovery."

President Jones exchanged a glance with Vice President Stevens. "I do not know about you, Marvin," she said, "but this may be the most intriguing meeting of my presidency."

She turned back to John Ward. "Supporting this plan is a leap of faith without seeing your inventions firsthand. Reading proposals on paper is one thing, but witnessing science in action is another. Still, your work in Ukraine, Sudan, and Iraq speaks for itself. You have kept your word, every time."

She folded her hands thoughtfully. "I need time to review this with my team. May I call you in a few days?"

John Ward said he completely understood the need to review with her team.

Vice President Stevens nodded thoughtfully. "I appreciate your understanding of the economic implications of this plan. Taking time to absorb this information is prudent. We will need more detail as well."

John Ward replied with measured courtesy. "Of course. Please know that our organization is moving forward with this plan for the good of the world. We will gladly provide any information you request before the press conference. Nothing that serves the people of God or honors the planet will be withheld."

He paused, then added gently, "That said, we deeply value your support and endorsement. I am grateful for your time and for this conversation."

President Jones smiled and said, "John Ward, I am glad you are a philanthropist and not a politician; you would be a formidable opponent."

John Ward laughed easily. "You never have to worry about my opposition. Our only aim is to serve God."

The meeting concluded shortly thereafter. Security escorted John Ward from the White House, and once he was a block away, he disappeared with the Mantle.

Jesus spoke gently to the mind of John Luke. "You were an excellent secret agent of God today, John Luke. Hopefully, they will agree to the press conference, and the Father's work will continue. Well done, good and faithful servant."

Moments later, John Luke arrived home. He whispered a prayer of thanksgiving, removed the Mantle, and found Kristin waiting for him.

He told her about the meeting, then added with a grin, "How is it we have never had Southern grits?"

Kristin laughed. "You just had brunch with the leaders of the free world, and you are thinking about the food."

Chapter 44:

God's Plan Unfolds

"He who was seated on the throne said, "I am making everything new!" Then he said, "Write this down, for these words are trustworthy and true" (Revelation 21:5).

John of Patmos, the author of the Book of Revelation, beheld the Lamb upon the Throne and was given a vision of a new heaven and a new Earth. He was commanded to write what he saw and heard, for the words were trustworthy and true. In his time, John Luke stood in a similar place, recording, shaping, and sharing God's plan for the healing of the Earth.

Through the power of Jesus and with the Mind of Christ, John Luke excelled in his work at the university, advanced God's Five-Point Plan, and faithfully embraced his calling as a husband, with twins on the way.

On Wednesday morning of that week, The Mantle LLC phone rang. The president's assistant was on the line, asking Mr. John Ward to hold for President Rosalyn Jones.

President Jones said, "Good morning, John. Please know you're on speaker with Vice President Stevens, Secretary of the Interior Juanita Ruiz, and our Communications Director, Stephanie Duchesne. Is this a good time to talk?"

"Good morning, Mrs. President, and to everyone on the line," John Ward replied. "Any time is good to speak with you."

President Jones laughed softly. "Oh, John Ward, you are charming. We want to discuss your Five Point Plan and the press conference. I've asked the vice president to begin."

Vice President Stevens said to John Ward, "Good morning, John. Thank you for taking our call. Do you have additional cost and benefit analysis estimates on aspects of the plan?"

John Ward responded, "Good morning, sir. I have spreadsheets containing return-on-investment (ROI) estimates for each of the Five Points of God's plan. I will email the documents to your office."

Secretary Ruiz asked, "Do you have estimates for voluntary immigration by country and proposed regions for relocation?"

"Yes, Mrs. Secretary," John Ward replied. "As the proposed process is voluntary, we prepared a draft framework for your office and for the United Nations to review. The draft includes preliminary estimates and mapped proposals for underpopulated regions in the United States and other industrial nations that can responsibly absorb population growth. I'll email the documents to your office."

Communications Director Duchesne asked, "John, do you have preliminary details for the press conference, and would you grant an interview to *The Washington Post*?"

John Ward responded, "Yes, Director Duchesne. I prepared a draft press release, a proposed conference agenda, and a list of national and international media contacts. I would be happy to interview with the Post. I'd also like a follow-up interview with *The Jerusalem Post*, as I have a working relationship with reporter Judith Schwartz. I'll send all the materials to your office shortly."

President Jones asked, "John, are you able to share details now about some of your proposed technologies, specifically the schematics for solar energy systems and water desalination?"

"Yes, Mrs. President," John Ward replied. "We developed several prototypes using artificial intelligence and 3D printing technologies. I would be glad to share the schematics with your office. Some of these designs have already been field-tested, while others are still in development."

After a brief pause, the president said, "Once we receive and review the materials and determine that they are both scientifically sound and fiscally responsible, we will schedule a press conference here at the White House for next Monday afternoon at two o'clock. Would that work for you?"

"Absolutely," John Ward replied. "That works!"

President Jones said, "That covers our questions. Do you have any for us?"

"Yes, Mrs. President," John Ward said. "If you find the information sound and the technology feasible, will you formally endorse the plan and assist us with a follow-up meeting at the United Nations?"

"Yes," President Jones answered without hesitation. "That is our intention."

"Thank you, Mrs. President," John Ward said.

The call ended, and God's Five-Point Plan moved forward, quietly, decisively, and with purpose.

The next morning, John Luke gathered the documents requested by the White House and sent them via encrypted email, following the president's assistant's instructions. Once that task was complete, he set up his new 3D printer and began creating prototypes of the inventions inspired by Jesus.

He worked with gratitude, aware that the wisdom God had entrusted to him now operated on a new level. Mathematics, engineering, physics, and biology came easily to him. He spent nearly twelve hours daily balancing his university responsibilities with the work of the Father's plan, yet still made time for Kristin as they worked from home.

As the day wound down, John Luke smiled to himself. Having the Mind of Christ, he reflected, was remarkably useful!

On Friday morning, John Luke received an encrypted email from the White House stating the information had been reviewed and found to be fiscally and scientifically sound. The press conference was scheduled at the White House for Monday at 2:00 PM Eastern.

That weekend, John Luke dedicated all his time to Kristin. They worked in the children's rooms, went grocery shopping, ate together, did yard work, and watched movies. Life was both peaceful and exciting.

That Sunday after church, over coffee in the meeting space, John Luke shared more details with Kristin, Joan, and me about his conversation with Jesus and the gift of God's wisdom. He spoke of how his mind now formed connections effortlessly, solving problems in math, physics, and human systems he once would never have imagined possible. When he spoke with the president's team, he sensed their needs before they voiced them. He felt deeper empathy, an instinctive understanding of each person's perspective.

Then he added quietly, "I feel more present now, more grateful for every moment of every day."

Joan and I sat spellbound. I couldn't help but think back to all the money we spent on tutors when John Luke was in high school. My parental pride soared beyond measure.

My child has the Mind of Christ.

Jesus had chosen well indeed.

Chapter 45:

The Press Conference

"He said to me, "It is done. I am the Alpha and the Omega, the Beginning and the End. To the thirsty I will give water without cost from the spring of the water of life. Those who are victorious will inherit all this, and I will be their God, and they will be my children" (Revelation 21:6–7).

When Jesus died on the cross, His final words were, "It is finished." His mission to ransom humanity from sin and death was complete. Yet His work did not end there. Three days later, He rose from the grave, revealing the power of resurrection.

In the Book of Revelation, the Lamb of God declares that the work of restoration is complete. The Alpha and the Omega bring creation to fulfillment.

In this story, Jesus stands as both the beginning and the end of every good work to heal the Earth, now working through His disciple, John Luke.

On Monday morning, John Luke rose early, made breakfast, and shared the meal with Kristin before settling into his home office until noon. They ate lunch together, and afterward Kristin helped him choose his outfit for the press conference: a dark blue suit, a light blue shirt, and a dark blue-and-olive striped tie, finished with a matching pocket square.

"These colors will look great on camera and live stream," she said with a smile. "You look smashing."

John Luke smiled, gathered his materials, and prepared to leave. He carried a portfolio with the press release and a large brown attaché case containing extra copies of his remarks, his laptop, and a 3D scale model of Jesus's seawater desalination design. By 1:30 PM, he was ready. He kissed Kristin goodbye, said a prayer, wore the Mantle, and flew to the White House.

A security guard was waiting and escorted him directly to the James S. Brady Press Briefing Room. Forty-nine reporters filled the seats, with another twenty standing along the back wall. The conference would be broadcast live across the nation and around the world.

Communications Director Stephanie Duchesne stepped to the podium, welcomed the press, and outlined the purpose of the briefing. She then introduced President Rosalyn Jones, who spoke of her campaign promise, shared with Vice President Stevens, to advance environmental sustainability, strengthen the economy, and create jobs. The President concluded by introducing John Ward and formally endorsing the plan he was about to present to the world.

President Jones said, "Our partnership with The Mantle LLC will help usher in a new economy, one that protects the environment while expanding opportunity. Together, we will make the ideal of people, planet, and profit a global reality."

John Ward stepped to the podium. He opened with a clear, confident introduction to God's Five-Point Plan for Maintaining Eden, using his laptop. For the next twenty minutes, he guided the room through a high-level, yet detailed presentation of each point projected onto the large screen, one that held the full attention of reporters, officials, and viewers around the world.

"This presentation," John Ward said, "offers a high-level view of the plan, the principles, benefits, and economic impact. Satellite evidence of regions displays healing through our recent work."

He concluded by lifting a small but striking object into view, a working 3D prototype of a seawater desalination device using ion concentration polarization (ICP). The ICP was proof, solid, visible, and undeniable of the innovations The Mantle LLC was ready to place in the world's hands.

He placed the prototype on a table in front of the cameras, then turned to the front row and handed a glass of seawater to *The Jerusalem Post* reporter, Judith Schwartz. As lenses tightened on her, she raised the glass, tasted it, and nodded. "Salt water," she confirmed.

John Ward took the glass back, poured the seawater into the prototype, and waited. Within seconds, he poured the processed water back into the same glass and returned it to her.

Ms. Schwartz lifted it to her nose, took a sip, then smiled broadly. "This water is wonderful."

The room, including President Jones, burst into applause. As it settled, John Ward added, "For the sake of transparency, this device was originally developed by research scientists at MIT. We built upon their remarkable work, refining the design to be smaller, faster, and far less expensive. This technology is not theoretical. It is available for use now."

John Ward closed simply and clearly. "This is one example of the Five Point Plan: water, the foundation of all life." He added, "The Mantle LLC will commit $1 trillion to help make God's Five-Point Plan a global reality."

This time, the applause rose into cheers.

President Jones stepped back to the podium beside John Ward and announced, "John Ward and I will present this plan to the United Nations this Friday. He will bring additional working prototypes designed to address climate change while creating new, meaningful jobs worldwide. We are proposing a global partnership to move this plan forward."

John Ward and the President stepped back as Communications Director Duchesne took questions. President Jones invited Vice President Stevens to join them. John Ward answered with precision, then deferred seamlessly to the President or Vice President at the right moments. The exchange was measured, confident, and unified.

Later that day, the Communications Office reported that the television audience had exceeded 85 million viewers, making it the most-watched presidential press conference in history. Within the week, polls showed President Jones's approval rating had climbed above 88%, the highest recorded in more than 60 years.

Meanwhile, clips from the press conference surged across social media, surpassing one billion views even before the presentation at the United Nations. Global stock markets responded with the largest five-day gain on record.

The work of restoring Eden had now entered the public eye.

Chapter 46:

The Bride of the Lamb

"And he carried me away in the Spirit to a mountain great and high, and showed me the Holy City, Jerusalem, coming down out of heaven from God. It shone with the glory of God, and its brilliance was like that of a very precious jewel, like a jasper, clear as crystal" (Revelation 21:10–11).

John of Patmos saw the Holy City, Jerusalem, descending from heaven, restored by God as a symbol of redeemed humanity renewed in His image and radiant with His glory. In this vision, humanity becomes the bride of the Lamb, joined to Him as a faithful partner.

So, it is with God's Five-Point Plan to restore and sustain Eden. Humanity is again invited into partnership with the Creator, entrusted with caring for creation as God intended.

Now the plan was ready to be revealed to the world.

On Friday, the same week as the White House press conference, John Luke prepared for the United Nations General Assembly in New York City. His presentation and prototypes were finished. Kristin, attentive as ever, chose his wardrobe to echo the UN flag: a pale blue pin-striped suit, a slightly darker blue shirt, and a blue-and-white striped tie. She even made a pocket square bearing the UN emblem.

John Luke studied his reflection and joked, "You know the saying, if you can't be good, at least look good."

Kristin smiled. "You look marvelous, and you are great."

As always, Kristin was his strongest advocate.

John Luke went to his office and lifted his arms heavenward as he said the Lord's Prayer. He then placed the Mantle gently over his head, took a briefcase in one hand and a display case in the other, and flew to New York.

He joined President Jones at 8:15 AM, ahead of the 9:00 AM presentation before the United Nations General Assembly.

Secretary-General Mateo Gomez of Argentina greeted the President warmly, and she introduced him to John Ward. John Ward responded in fluent Spanish, addressing him with the proper title, *Su Excelencia*, to Señor Gomez's visible delight.

President Jones leaned toward John Ward and said quietly, "You amaze me. You know protocol, and you speak Spanish like a native."

John Ward smiled and replied, "I know just enough of both to get by."

The President added with a grin, "And a nice touch with the colors of the UN flag. That didn't escape me."

John Ward smiled broadly and resisted the urge to say that Kristin had chosen the outfit.

Señor Gomez then announced that all 193 member nations were present in the General Assembly Hall and that the address would be broadcast live and recorded for history.

As the presiding officer, President Jones spoke first.

"As members of the United Nations," she began, "our administration is here today to present a plan that reinforces the United States' long-term commitment to its environmental goals. This address reflects our resolve to confront climate change in ways that are both economically viable and environmentally sustainable."

She concluded by thanking the General Assembly for its partnership and support, then introduced John Ward of The Mantle LLC, a global philanthropic organization.

"You may recognize The Mantle," the President added, "for its work in Ukraine and Sudan, where it helped foster lasting peace, and for its critical support to Iraq following the devastating Earthquake."

The General Assembly responded with sustained applause.

President Jones then declared, "Our administration fully endorses and supports The Mantle LLC, and the plan John Ward will present to us today."

John Ward stepped to the podium and received warm applause. He paused, then greeted the Assembly in the six official languages of the United Nations: Mandarin, French, Russian, Arabic, Spanish, and English. The unexpected gesture drew appreciative smiles across the chamber and another round of applause. Returning to English, John Ward began his address.

"The Mantle LLC is a nonprofit, independent organization devoted to carrying out the will of God on Earth for the good of humanity. Our fidelity is simple and unwavering: to love God, to love people, and to love creation."

He then activated his presentation, and the large screens throughout the GA 200 chamber illuminated, mirroring the White House briefing, as he clearly and confidently outlined God's Five-Point Plan to Maintain Eden.

After the introductory slides, he presented a clear alignment between God's Five-Point Plan and the United Nations' Seventeen Sustainable Development Goals, supported by concise graphics and practical detail.

John Ward then announced that The Mantle LLC would commit $1 trillion to bring the plan to life. The General Assembly responded with sustained applause at the magnitude of the pledge.

He continued, "A vital part of this plan calls for the United Nations to consider a global pact, one that ensures the humane, voluntary care of immigrants and refugees. Copies of the proposed framework will be distributed to every member nation following this conference."

Then he displayed five working prototypes, each aligned with a goal. He provided an overview of the features and benefits of each invention. As each prototype was displayed, the members of the General Assembly became increasingly engrossed in the presentation.

In response to the growing population, human activity, and new ways to sustain life, John Ward showed a video of an AI- and 3D-printer-generated rainforest in the Gobi Desert.

John Ward said, “The plants, trees, and water you are seeing in this video, an entire one-acre rainforest, are real. They are grown from natural genetic material, enhanced through responsible cloning, and integrated with emerging metamaterial technology.

“These materials are engineered composite structures designed with precise electromagnetic properties. When blended with living systems, they accelerate growth in ways that appear almost supernatural yet remain fully natural.

“The rainforest is protected beneath a transparent, porous dome of hydrogel, which I will explain shortly. In my final demonstration, I will show this technology operating in real time.”

The Assembly leaned forward, visibly captivated, and responded with warm, sustained applause.

Next, addressing the removal and recycling of carbon dioxide and other greenhouse gases, John Ward placed a miniature working prototype on the table before him, with the audience seeing it magnified on camera.

The device resembled a small tree: a wind turbine made of metamaterials. As it rotated, John Ward explained, the structure captured harmful atmospheric chemicals, including chlorofluorocarbons (CFCs), and converted them into pure water through a chemical process.

The simplicity of the design, paired with its profound implications, drew audible murmurs of amazement from the Assembly.

John Ward explained, "Tree-shaped wind turbines already exist to generate electricity. This device goes further. It generates electricity and produces water while purifying the air. Its silent leaves generate power by drawing in water vapor and harmful chemicals from the atmosphere.

"Through a combination of hydrogel and an electronic conversion process, those chemicals are transformed into pure water, which is automatically stored in underground cisterns. Hydrogel is a water-absorbing polymer that is safe for human consumption and uniquely suited for this application.

"Now imagine a small forest of these turbine trees, providing clean electricity and fresh water at minimal cost, even in desert regions."

The room grew noticeably attentive, especially among delegates from several African nations.

Regarding the removal of plastics from the ocean, John Ward presented another prototype, a miniature robotic submarine powered by liquid fluoride thorium and made from recycled metal and plastic.

John Ward explained, "These submarines are modeled after baleen whales. Like keratin-based baleen plates, they gently filter even microscopic plastic particles. The captured material is stored onboard and later converted into recycled polyester yarn for low-cost, lightweight clothing."

He continued, "Next, imagine a fleet of these vessels, nature-inspired and autonomous, slowly circling the most polluted regions of our oceans, such as the South Pacific. Powered by safe, clean, long-life nuclear energy, they could operate for centuries, continuously cleansing the seas while transforming waste into usable resources.

"Guided by satellite and able to dock at any seaport, these ships turn pollution into provision."

Delegates from South Pacific nations, including Malaysia, New Zealand, and Australia, broke into sustained applause.

Addressing the use of agricultural chemicals in farming, John Ward played a video of a low-cost farming robot that converts any soil into rich, organic humus based on the biological principles by which Earthworms improve soil fertility.

John Ward said, "This technology fuses artificial intelligence with biology. These next-generation agricultural robots, built with advanced metamaterials, are nearly indestructible. They are low-cost, solar-powered, simple to operate, and guided by precision lasers.

"They can till soil, plant seeds and saplings, remove weeds, prune crops, harvest produce, and irrigate fields, running for years with minimal maintenance."

He explained, "The technology exists now. It will create jobs, restore dignity to farm labor, and lower the cost of food worldwide."

Delegations from agricultural nations, Canada, the United States, and Eastern Europe, responded with sustained applause.

Regarding ways to stabilize the planet's overall climate through natural cooling and heating methods, John Ward waited until last to display their most amazing invention, a Silver Maple tree, synthetically designed with AI and a 3D printer.

John Ward excitedly said, "We call this invention the *Tree of Life!*" (Genesis 2:9). John Ward asked the Assembly to please grant him exactly thirty seconds as he worked on his laptop.

In thirty seconds, the system produced a 4-foot tree, its root system visible through a glass container before the Assembly and television cameras. Another command, and within thirty more seconds, the tree grew an additional four feet in real time. Gasps rippled through the hall, followed by sustained applause.

John Ward said calmly, "In our rainforest prototype, this system designs the optimal tree height, width, and structure for any environment. These trees are engineered to trap carbon dioxide, provide shade, and endure drought, heat, and cold."

He gestured to the model. "For New York City, I selected a Silver Maple. The tree is grown from natural materials blended with metamaterials, creating a living structure that adapts to its surroundings, matures naturally, and can later be harvested as a low-cost building material. It will last more than a century and withstand the harshest climates on Earth."

He paused, then added, "These trees can be mass-produced and planted worldwide, reversing deforestation at scale."

John Ward concluded, "This system could produce Mahogany trees for the Amazon, Baobab trees for Africa, Joshua trees in Israel, Mangrove trees in Egypt, Conifers for Siberia, fruit trees for the United States, and Jacaranda trees for Argentina. The Tree of Life can grow any tree, any place, any time, for less than an American dollar."

The General Assembly rose to its feet in thunderous applause and cheered at the conclusion of his presentation. President Jones joined John Ward at the podium, drawing more applause.

When the noise died down, President Jones said, "My friends, let us implement this plan now!" The Assembly roared in approval.

John Ward paused to look at the General Assembly and smiled broadly when he saw Jesus, disguised as an audience member, sitting next to the Israeli Ambassador. Jesus was dressed in beautiful traditional Middle Eastern clothing, including a blue-and-white *tallit* and *kippah*. John Luke thought, I knew He was with me, as he waved at Jesus, and Jesus waved back with a smile.

After the General Assembly meeting, John Ward explained to President Jones that he used labs at a private university to design and produce the prototypes. He said the information on the prototypes, and specifically the AI language program, is open source and that he would gladly share it with her administration and the world.

President Jones said, "You just changed civilization for the better forever, and you crushed this presentation! My administration is ready to start working with you immediately. I cannot thank you enough."

John Ward smiled and said, *Ad majórem Dei glóriam.*

President Jones smiled. "For the greater glory of God. I know that one, as I studied Latin at Vanderbilt."

John Luke, still as John Ward, walked out of the United Nations building to find Jesus standing on the sidewalk. He laughed out loud and said, "Lord, I knew You were here. I felt Your presence. Look at you. Your clothing is beautiful."

Jesus laughed and said, "Oh, this old thing? I found it in the back of the closet." Jesus laughed at His own joke as they walked together on the sidewalk.

Jesus said, "John Luke, I would not miss your presentation. I am so proud of you. I am also grateful for your humility in using the alias of John Ward and crediting God for your creativity."

John Luke said, "Jesus, I remembered the details of our brainstorming session. My mind is focused, and my memory is photographic. I am so grateful that You blessed me with Your wisdom."

Jesus said, "At the beginning of our journey with the Mantle, I told you that you would do greater works than Me. And you have. My ministry unfolded in a small region around the Sea of Galilee.

You united the world. Aligning the Father's Five Points with the UN's goals was inspiring. You are a masterful teacher."

They walked across the street to a sidewalk along the East River.

Jesus continued, "John Luke, our work with the Mantle is nearing completion. As John Ward, you will continue to advance the Father's Five-Point Plan. I ask that you oversee the implementation and the distribution of funds in coordination with President Jones and the UN Secretary-General. They are trustworthy, and our efforts will hold.

"As John Luke, I want you to continue using the Mantle for travel and other needs that arise in your work. Yet know this: We trust you completely to carry out this mission as you see fit."

John Luke, humbled and grateful, told Jesus how much he loved and appreciated Him.

Jesus replied, "I love you and your family very much. Pray and call upon Me as needed, and I will be with you." They embraced on the sidewalk by the river, and Jesus departed.

John Luke discreetly donned the Mantle and returned to his home office, where he shared the day's events with Kristin, Joan, and me.

As he finished speaking, this passage came to mind: "*All this is for your benefit, so that the grace that is reaching more and more people may cause thanksgiving to overflow to the glory of God"* (2 Corinthians 4:15).

The work of restoring Eden continued on a grand scale.

Chapter 47:

The Most Important Work

"The angel who talked with me had a measuring rod of gold to measure the city, its gates, and its walls" (Revelation 21:15).

John of Patmos walked with an angel who showed him the great Holy City, a new home for believers, measured with a golden rod and perfectly square.

As John Luke worked with Jesus, he kept this image close. He wanted his life to be just as ordered, his home a steady and secure place for Kristin and their growing family. For all the work God had placed before him, John Luke knew that nothing mattered more than the life he had at home.

About a week after the presentation at the United Nations Assembly, John Luke and I met for lunch at a nearby café. We spoke of Jesus, the Mantle, the Book of Revelation, God's Five-Point Plan, his work with President Jones and UN Secretary-General Gomez, his alias John Ward, his role at MIT, and the quiet joys and responsibilities of fatherhood.

"Dad, when I last met with Jesus, He said our work was nearly finished. But then He said I could continue using the Mantle, and that He would still be with me. I wanted to ask what He meant, but the moment passed. What do you think He was saying?"

I considered his question. "I've learned to take Jesus at His word. Clarity often comes later, when we return to Him with the question. Have you thought about asking Him again?"

John Luke nodded. "I have. I just wanted to talk with you first."

I smiled. "That makes sense. Jesus gave you great wisdom. It's natural to want understanding, not just obedience."

He leaned back and said, "Do you think something big is going to happen next? I reread Revelation: a new Heaven and Earth. Eden restored. Once the work is done, does everything end?"

"I don't think so," I said. "Jesus told us there would be a thousand years of peace after Satan was bound. Only the Father knows the end time. If something drastic were imminent, I don't believe God would be using you to restore the Earth. Perhaps this is what a new heaven and new Earth look like, creation healed and humanity learning to live rightly within it."

John Luke nodded, thoughtful.

After lunch, we lingered over coffee. Then he said, "I need to be careful. Balancing my work as John Ward, The Mantle LLC, and my responsibilities at the university, it's a lot. There are ethical lines to watch."

"You'll know where they are," I said. "Jesus chose you for who you are. Wisdom doesn't erase responsibility, it sharpens it."

He smiled, half in awe. "A trillion dollars for research. It's overwhelming."

"So is fatherhood," I said.

That made him laugh. Then he grew serious. "Dad, the twins arrive in three months. Kristin's doing great. But I'm nervous. I've never even changed a diaper."

"Changing diapers is the easy part," I said. "The most important work a father ever does is being present and showing up with love. Giving time, encouragement, and example. And loving their mother well. When children see that, they understand love before they ever learn its definition."

His eyes misted. "You and Mom did that for me. And now for Kristin."

"We'll always be here for you," I said, my voice softening. "That's what family is, presence, given freely."

John Luke reached for the check. "This one's mine. You're on a retirement income."

I laughed. "Someone has to work in this family."

He stood and said, "I'm going to ask Jesus to meet with me this weekend."

"I think that's a good idea," I said.

Driving home, I reflected on our conversation. For a moment, I wondered whether John Luke might be the final bearer of the Mantle, and what role it would have in a world marked by peace. Then I reminded myself of a truth I had learned long ago: we do not need to fear the past, because Jesus forgives it. We need not fear the future because God is already there. And in the present, Jesus is always with us.

The Mantle gave our family the greatest gift, not power, but a relationship.

Then I smiled and thought, when are those two finally going to name those twins?

That afternoon, I sat down to write more of the history of the Mantle and the remarkable days behind us. Writing, I realized, was still my work. In retirement, it gave me purpose and joy.

When Joan came home, dinner was ready. I earned a few husband points for both the meal and the clean kitchen.

I must admit, this retirement thing is pretty good.

Chapter 48:

Jesus and John Luke Meet

"I did not see a temple in the city, because the Lord God Almighty and the Lamb are its temple. The city does not need the sun or the moon to shine on it, for the glory of God gives it light, and the Lamb is its lamp" (Revelation 21:22–23).

Imagine a world without the sun to light the day or the moon to shine at night. The prophecy of Revelation describes astonishing visions of that coming world. The glory of God will provide the light and power humanity needs in the age to come.

Until that day comes, humanity is called to care for the world God has given. John Luke continued his work with the Mantle. Now he wished to meet with Jesus again, to ask questions and consider the mission's next steps.

The next morning, Saturday, after breakfast with Kristin, John Luke went to his home office, said a prayer, wore the Mantle, and waited.

Jesus appeared in person with a broad smile.

"How is My secret agent of peace today?" He asked.

John Luke smiled. "You know Kristin loves it when You call me that. Thank You for appearing in person. I had lunch with my dad yesterday, and I have a few questions, if You don't mind."

Jesus said, "Of course. I always enjoy our time together. Our time by the East River was brief. You have some questions about your work with the Mantle."

John Luke said quietly, "Yes, Jesus. May I ask what You meant when You said our work is nearly finished? Does it mean something momentous will happen once the Father's Five-Point Plan is fully set in motion?"

Jesus smiled gently. "Ah. You wonder about the end times."

"Yes," John Luke said. "Is this work ushering in the end of time, as the Book of Revelation foretells?"

Jesus answered with calm assurance. "Those are natural questions, especially with the twins on the way and so much responsibility before you. Your father spoke wisely when he told you not to fear the future. The Father already holds it."

He continued, "As for the Mantle, your work is far from over. You still have much to do at the university, and as John Ward, helping to carry this plan forward with President Jones and Secretary-General Gomez. You will use the Mantle for some time. We trust you completely, to oversee the work, to discern wisely, and to guide it toward a good and faithful end."

Relief washed over John Luke. "Thank You, Jesus," he said softly. "I was carrying more anxiety than I realized."

Jesus nodded, His voice warm. "And now you need not carry it alone."

Jesus added, “Remember, the Book of Revelation reveals the work, and the work unfolds in harmony with the prophecy. Yet, as I have told you before, only the Father knows the end.”

He continued, “The work you are doing with the Mantle is essential to safeguard God’s people, to restore the Earth, and to sustain a new heaven and a new Earth, one marked by peace, dignity, and mutual respect.”

Jesus then quoted Scripture: *“Creation itself will be liberated from its bondage to decay and brought into the freedom and glory of the children of God”* (Romans 8:21).

“This work,” He said gently, “is a release from bondage. When it is complete, I will follow the Father’s will, and so will you. Do not trouble yourself about a successor to the Mantle. That concern belongs to God. Instead of worrying about what comes next, let your imagination run free with all the good research, discoveries, and healing that will flow from your work.”

John Luke smiled broadly. “My dad told me You would help me understand,” he said. “Thank You, Jesus.”

Jesus continued, “You have the wisdom to know what to do and when to do it, both in your work at the university and in your role as John Ward with The Mantle LLC. You will be John Luke among scholars and researchers, and John Ward when you engage governments, partners, and the stewardship of resources. You will not face ethical compromise or conflicts of interest. None will be required of you.”

"With the Mantle, you are free to be present where you are needed. You may be yourself in a university meeting and, at the same moment, stand as John Ward before President Jones. The work will not fracture you. It will be ordered. Nothing will derail the plan. The Father's will be done."

A deep relief washed over John Luke. "Jesus," he said softly, "You always know what to say. I feel so much better."

Jesus smiled. "Trust yourself, John Luke. You will choose well."

Then, with a spark of humor in His eyes, He added, "And speaking of choices, when are you two going to name those babies?"

Jesus laughed, clearly pleased with Himself.

John Luke smiled and said, "Soon, Jesus, I promise!"

Jesus's tone then became serious. "John Luke, you will learn some great news about the twins from your doctor. I will not keep you waiting. Please let the doctor explain the news to you and Kristin in more detail. The babies, even though one is a girl and the other is a boy, are identical."

"Your doctor will speculate these babies are fraternal twins, but after they are born, a DNA test may show the children are identical. This instance is a rare genetic occurrence and makes these children very special. They will share a rare bond as identical sister and brother."

John Luke said, "Wow, Jesus! This news is fantastic!"

Jesus responded, "Please share the news with Kristin, and let the doctor explain the science to you. John Luke, this gift is one more way the Father is blessing you for your good work and fidelity. You are a special person, and a most dear friend."

John Luke hugged Jesus tightly and thanked Him for the news.

Jesus said, "I know you have many important meetings ahead, at the university and in the work of The Mantle. Use the Mantle to accomplish what lies before you. I will be with you every step."

They said their goodbyes, and John Luke went to find Kristin, eager to share the joy still echoing in his heart.

When he told her about the twins, Kristin smiled softly. "These babies will be the best of friends all their lives. God is so very good to us."

John Luke laughed. "My dad and Jesus were teasing me about choosing names. Have you given any more thought to your list?"

Kristin raised an eyebrow playfully. "Well, if God is asking, we'd better decide."

She stepped into her office and returned with a printed page. Holding it out, she said, "I'm down to two choices for each baby. I love all the combinations. What do you think?"

John Luke looked at the list. For the boy, the first line read **John Stephen,** and the second **Joshua Michael**. For the girl, he saw **Emma Grace** on the first line and **Jane Rose** on the second.

He paused and considered the names.

"I think I'd like to pass on using John for the boy," he said. "If you're comfortable with J names for both, I'm drawn to Joshua and Jane. No one in either family has those names, and they sound right together. What do you think of Joshua Michael and Jane Rose?"

Kristin smiled. "Jesus will certainly approve of Joshua; it's His name in English. And while I've never known anyone named Jane, Jane Rose feels strong and elegant. I love that it carries your mom's middle name."

John Luke nodded. "Let's pray on it a little longer, but I think we're close."

Kristin laughed softly. "I love your new and improved mind, John Luke."

They laughed together, light and hopeful, already sounding like parents.

Chapter 49: The Mind of Christ

"Nothing impure will ever enter it, nor will anyone who does what is shameful or deceitful, but only those whose names are written in the Lamb's book of life" (Revelation 21:27).

The Second Coming of the Lamb of God will be marked by a purity the world has not known since the beginning of Genesis, before the fall. No sin or shame will enter the gates of the Holy City. Humanity, restored and made whole, will be spotless before God.

One remarkable fruit of John Luke receiving the Mind of Christ was the quiet transformation of his inner life. His thoughts were increasingly free from malice or impurity, his judgments charitable, and his actions marked by kindness and integrity. He remained fully human, yet closer to his best self. Like Jesus, he began to see others with grace, offering love rather than suspicion.

Other aspects of life improved as well. John Luke learned to manage his time with new clarity. He realized that multitasking was largely a myth and began giving himself fully to one task at a time. With demanding meetings ahead, both at the university and within the President's administration, he moved through his responsibilities with calm precision. Being in two places at once was an extraordinary gift, but the greater gift was peace.

The week ahead unfolded with remarkable exactness. On Monday in Cambridge, John Luke met with his team to align his schedule, plan parental leave for the twins, and clarify his family's relationship with John Ward and The Mantle LLC. Later, he conferred with the Vice President of Academic Affairs to coordinate research partnerships with the federal government.

Tuesday took him to Washington as John Ward, where he met with the head of the General Services Administration to finalize contracts and philanthropic donations.

On Wednesday, he returned to the university and joined international researchers working on seawater desalination.

On Thursday, he met remotely with United Nations representatives as John Ward to shape a humane framework for immigration and refugees.

And on Friday, he was in New York again as John Ward, with Secretary-General Gomez and delegates from the United States, Brazil, Bolivia, Colombia, and Peru to address deforestation in the Amazon, before closing the week with a remote meeting to share turbine technology capable of generating electricity, capturing water, and cleansing the air.

He ended the week with a final remote meeting with the largest metamaterials manufacturer to secure the resources needed for prototype installations.

The following week, John Luke was arranging for the prototypes to be tested in the field with researchers from his university, the US government, and the United Nations.

Studying the calendar on his laptop, John Luke said softly to Kristin, “Sometimes I wonder how I ever arrived at this place in my life, and how I could do this without the Mind of Christ.”

Kristin smiled and answered without hesitation. “That’s exactly why Jesus entrusted you with His wisdom. He knows you can carry this work and carry it well.” She was, as always, his true partner in life.

Over the next sixty days, John Luke turned vision into action. Prototypes reflecting the Father’s Five Points, aligned with the United Nations’ environmental goals, were implemented worldwide, from Asia and Africa to Europe, the Americas, Australia, Oceania, and even Antarctica. The Arctic, though not a continent, was also included, spanning North America and Europe. Eden was no longer an idea. It was taking root.

All prototype installations were approved by the United States government and the United Nations Educational, Scientific, and Cultural Organization (UNESCO) and required permission from local governments. Some of the prototypes he implemented on his own using the power of the Mantle. Most of the fieldwork was done in a group effort, as John Luke flew commercially to various sites with different teams.

Firstly, John Luke used the Mantle, with Jesus by his side, to install more than 1,000 wind turbines around the Antarctic Circle.

The turbines were variable-geometry-oval-trajectory (VGOT) devices that generated electricity for use by scientific communities in Antarctica; another purpose was to help regulate the Southern Polar Vortex.

Jesus showed John Luke where to place each turbine and how to angle them for maximum influence on the vortex. Together, they installed the prototypes, saving time, conserving resources, and ensuring the work was done precisely as intended.

John Luke knew he would explain the details to the researchers later. For now, what mattered was finishing the work in this remote place, guided by Jesus and carried out in trust.

Secondly, John Luke flew with a team of researchers from multiple universities, funded by The Mantle LLC, to the Amazon rainforest in South America. There, they planted a forest of more than 500 metamaterial-blended mahogany trees in a deforested area in Brazil. The area was designated for scientific research and secured using satellite technology, with permission from the Brazilian government, to prevent illegal deforestation.

Thirdly, John Luke, working as John Ward, met with Chinese and Mongolian officials to attempt an audacious experiment: creating a rainforest in the southern Gobi Desert.

Guided by the mind of Christ and supported by artificial intelligence and 3D technology, the team cultivated a thriving 100-acre forest, sustained by water drawn from Lake Bosten. A vast, porous synthetic dome of modified hydrogel shielded the land, replicating the Amazon's atmospheric balance. Beneath it, native species flourished: fruit trees, maples, and other life took root through the Mantle's "tree of life" technology, transforming the desert into abundance.

This project was completed in two weeks because John Luke quietly finished some assignments while the research team was asleep. The research team was stunned by the project's swift and successful completion, as the Chinese government assumed responsibility for the area's security.

Meanwhile, John Luke was motivated to complete the work due to the twins' imminent arrival. The project was a success, and John Luke moved on to the Middle East with desalination equipment.

The fourth prototype was installed in the Middle East, which is part of both Africa and Asia. MIT researchers and John Luke led the desalination equipment team. They had permission to install prototype equipment in several countries, including Iraq, Kuwait, Saudi Arabia, and the state of Palestine.

They established bases of operation and drew water from the Red Sea and the Persian Gulf. Both are hypersaline environments, mixtures of fresh and salt water, well-suited for the prototype.

Within days, the systems provided potable water to regions that had long struggled to supply fresh water for households and agriculture. The work received widespread attention, particularly from the Iraqi government, which expressed deep gratitude to The Mantle LLC for its support during reconstruction following the earthquake. Coverage was positive and extensive.

Every prototype performed exactly as promised, and the researchers were celebrated as heroes. John Luke was quietly satisfied. As John Ward, he provided the technology to participating nations at no cost, securing commitments for wider deployment once testing concluded.

The proposals were submitted to the United Nations, and God's Five-Point Plan continued to move steadily toward fulfillment.

Chapter 50: People Protect What They Love

And God said, "Let the water teem with living creatures, and let birds fly above the Earth across the vault of the sky." So, God created the great creatures of the sea and every living thing with which the water teems and that moves about in it, according to their kinds, and every winged bird according to its kind. And God saw that it was good (Genesis 1:20–22).

The famed French oceanographer Jacques Cousteau once observed, "People protect what they love, they love what they understand, and they understand what they are taught."

His words capture the spirit of God's Five-Point Plan for the Restoration of Eden and of The Mantle LLC's mission in partnership with the United Nations. They also reflect God's desire for humanity to share responsibility for the care of creation.

On day thirty of the sixty-day trial, John Luke, acting as John Ward, flew with a research team to Perth and boarded the Royal Australian Navy carrier, HMAS Stirling. From there, they sailed into the remote waters off Tasmania and the Kimberley region, areas among the most plastic-polluted seas on Earth.

There, they deployed three baleen whale–inspired submarines, engineered to filter even the smallest plastic particles from the ocean.

The crew of the Stirling unloaded the small submarines into the ocean, and John Ward programmed them to travel around several islands, along the shoreline, and to the bottom of the ocean to gather small particles that had infiltrated the ocean's ecosystem for the next few days.

These small plastic pieces, called microplastics, are less than five millimeters long and harm the ocean and aquatic life. Ocean life and birds mistake these tiny particles for food.

On Friday at noon, the subs were returned to the aircraft carrier's deck, loaded with a full cargo of plastics, bundled in crates for use in manufacturing lightweight, inexpensive clothing.

John Ward arranged for the shipment of crates of plastic to an environmentally responsible clothing manufacturing facility in Christchurch, New Zealand. The facility, funded by The Mantle LLC, would convert plastic into clothing and shoes, creating jobs in the area.

The experiment was a success, and the submarines were returned to the ocean, programmed to patrol additional areas of the Indian Ocean and to dock in Perth when their cargo holds were full. The plastic would again be shipped to manufacturers in New Zealand. The fifth prototype experiment was complete.

For the sixth prototype experiment, John Ward and a team of international researchers flew to the farm country in Bilka, Ukraine. Ukraine is considered the breadbasket of Europe and is a large producer of wheat, corn, barley, and sunflower oil.

The purpose of their work was to implement low-cost farming robots that could convert soil into rich, organic humus, leveraging the biological principles by which Earthworms improve soil fertility. These programmable, laser-guided robots are useful throughout the crop life cycle.

They till the soil, plant seeds, remove weeds, water the fields, and harvest crops without using any fertilizers. John Ward chose a nearly one-hundred-acre barren field and programmed the robots to prepare it and then plant hundreds of sunflowers. After tilling and planting were complete, the robots watered the crops.

With this experiment complete, they moved to a barley field and successfully weeded it without damaging the growing crops. Finally, they moved to a cornfield and harvested the crop neatly into trailing grain bins. With a day's work behind them, John Ward spent the next day teaching farmers to use the robots and software, with free laptops provided.

A technician would remain on site to support the project through the end of the harvest season. The Mantle LLC provided the funds necessary for the project's success.

For the seventh prototype, John Luke, as John Ward, and a team of international researchers, went to the Arctic to replicate the project completed in the Antarctic. With approval from multiple government agencies, the team installed thousands of metamaterial-based wind turbines that resemble trees.

In addition to generating electricity and recycling CO_2 and other greenhouse gases from the atmosphere, John Luke strategically placed the turbines to help maintain a stable polar vortex over the Arctic Circle. In each region, work soon began to deliver electricity to the participating countries' power grids.

Huge cisterns and irrigation systems were also under construction to provide fresh water to the region. As work progressed across multiple sites, John Ward discreetly used the Mantle to fly into the polar vortex and observe the strength and direction of the airflow. His observations aligned with the satellite data. The turbine placement was accurate.

With the inspection complete, John Ward left the teams to finish their work on the electrical grid and irrigation systems, then quietly returned home using the Mantle.

While John Luke worked in the field as John Ward, the Mantle allowed him to continue his university duties with equal dedication, fully present wherever he was called to serve. What once seemed impossible now felt ordered and purposeful.

The work was advancing. The plan was unfolding. John Luke moved forward in peace, grateful, steady, and ready for what would come next.

Chapter 51:

The Healing of the Nations

"The leaves of the tree are for the healing of the nations" (Revelation 22:2).

The final chapter of the Book of Revelation presents a powerful image of God's restored creation. Flowing from the throne of God is the river of the water of life, and beside it stands the tree of life, bearing fruit each month for the healing of the nations. In this vision, humanity is renewed, creation is restored, and the blessings of God bring life and healing to the whole Earth.

The phrase *living water* appears more than 700 times in Scripture. It is a rich metaphor for God's blessing, often pointing to wisdom, salvation, and eternal life.

In the Gospel of John, during His conversation with the Samaritan woman at the well, Jesus uses the image in a way that echoes the vision of Revelation: *"Indeed, the water I give them will become in them a spring of water welling up to eternal life"* (John 4:14). Living water flows from the Word of God and brings abundant life to those who receive it.

The land of Israel has long been shaped by its rivers and valleys. The Jordan River begins in the mountainous region where modern Israel, Syria, and Lebanon meet. From there, it flows south through the Sea of Galilee and continues to the Dead Sea, sustaining life along its banks.

Just outside the walls of Jerusalem lies the Kidron Valley, which separates the Temple Mount from the Mount of Olives. Jesus often walked these paths during His ministry and was baptized by John the Baptist in the waters of the Jordan. In the vision of Revelation, the river of life symbolizes the restoration of Eden itself, when God renews the Earth and brings healing to the nations.

As the Father's plan for the restoration of Eden was coming to a successful conclusion, a series of wonderful events took place at home and in the world, including along the Jordan River. These events appeared to parallel the words of the final chapter of Revelation, as Jesus told John Luke.

A week after John Luke completed the sixty days with the prototypes, Kristin's water broke, around 1:00 AM on May ninth. John Luke rose quickly, gathered Kristin's hospital bag, and called their obstetrician, Dr. Leia Brennan.

Dr. Brennan previously told Kristin and John Luke that the babies would be delivered by a Cesarean method, or C-section surgical delivery. She told John Luke to meet her at the hospital.

Their drive to the hospital was less than fifteen minutes. John Luke called both sets of grandparents. Joan and I excitedly got dressed and went to the hospital. Kristin's parents had a one-hour drive and arrived at the hospital around 3:00 AM.

On the drive to the hospital, Kristin's contractions became stronger. They arrived to find a surgical team waiting for them. As a nurse prepared Kristin for surgery, Kristin told the team she felt the babies were coming now.

Dr. Brennan examined Kristin, and the babies were being delivered quickly and naturally. Dr. Brennan called out for her assistant to help her as she abandoned the C-section plans and told Kristin to push.

John Luke thought the assistant looked familiar, even behind the mask. He held Kristin's hand, and within a minute, baby Jane Rose was born at 1:33 A.M.

Less than thirty seconds later, Kristin felt the urge to push again, and Joshua Michael was born at the very same minute as his sister.

The odds of a woman giving birth to twins are less than three percent of all pregnancies. The probability of twins being born naturally is even rarer, estimated at less than 0.04 percent. The likelihood of twins being born in the same minute is even smaller.

Even the nurses paused for a moment, aware that something rare and wonderful had just happened.

These miracle babies set a new standard and sparked many conversations about the future, with Jane proudly claiming the role of the family's oldest child, much to Joshua's future chagrin.

John Luke was able to cut the umbilical cords of both children, and Kristin joyfully held both babies, one in each arm, Jane on her right and Joshua on her left. Interestingly, Jane became right-handed, and Joshua became left-handed.

In a few minutes, Dr. Brennan examined the babies and pronounced them healthy, happy, and hungry. Jane Rose weighed 5.1 pounds, and Joshua Michael weighed 5.3 pounds. After everything was in order, Joan and I were allowed into the room to see our grandchildren. We were both overcome with emotion, and Joan set a world record for using the word "beautiful" in a sentence.

As things settled down, John Luke and I walked to the cafeteria in search of coffee. Somehow, the shop was still open at 2:30 AM. A man in hospital scrubs stood with his back to us, pouring fresh cups as though he had been expecting us.

When he turned around, we saw Jesus. For a moment, the quiet cafeteria felt brighter.

John Luke and I burst out laughing.

"You didn't think I would miss the birth of these babies, did you?" Jesus said with a smile. "Especially after you showed such good taste in naming the boy Joshua."

He told John Luke that He had been in the room when the babies were born and congratulated him on the empathy and care he showed Kristin.

John Luke grinned. "You were Dr. Brennan's assistant in the surgical center! I knew I sensed Your presence. Nothing gets past You, Jesus."

Jesus smiled. "Well, I am known as *the Great Physician*." (Luke 5:31). "I thought you'd both feel better knowing I was nearby." He handed us cups of coffee on a tray and said, "My work here is done. Now go back to your wives and share My love with them. I'll see you soon."

With that, He disappeared.

I said with glee, "John Luke, how many parents can say Jesus helped deliver their babies!" We both had a hearty laugh as we walked to the room. I thought, *Jesus, You are so good to us.*

Upon returning to the room, John Luke told Kristin and Joan about seeing Jesus.

Kristin smiled and said, "You know, I thought the assistant looked familiar. And John Luke, did you sense the peace in that room? It was perfect. I barely felt the pain."

We looked at one another and smiled.

Joan added, "How wonderful that the babies were born on May 9th." Kristin's birthday is May 10, and John Luke was born on May 11.

We stayed another two hours before Kristin's parents arrived to join the celebration. Two days later, the little family returned home.

As planned, John Luke began the university's thirty-day paid family leave, while Kristin took ninety days of paid leave from her company. John Luke handled the nighttime feedings so Kristin could get uninterrupted rest. Joan and I stayed overnight two days each week, so John Luke could also catch up on sleep.

For Joan, this arrangement was a dream; she adored her grandchildren. Of course, I did as well.

The babies ate and slept well, and the rhythms of life with twins soon fell into place. Everyone felt deeply grateful.

Thirty days passed quickly for John Luke. He was able to work from home for another two months until Kristin's leave time ended. Kristin and John Luke asked Joan to care for the babies two days a week as they planned their work schedules in Boston and remote meetings upon their return to work. Joan eagerly agreed. I joined Joan on those days, so I would not miss the fun.

When John Luke returned to his routine, he quickly caught up at the university and confirmed that the prototype projects were operating smoothly.

With the work of God's plan now complete, President Jones called The Mantle LLC and asked to speak with John Ward.

"John Ward," she said, "I know you prefer to stay out of the spotlight and do not seek recognition for your work. Nevertheless, I have decided to award you and The Mantle LLC the Presidential Medal of Freedom, the highest civilian honor in the United States. You will receive an official invitation soon. The ceremony will take place on Thursday, July 7th, at 2:00 PM in the East Room of the White House. As you are the sole recipient, I trust you won't leave me standing at the podium by myself."

John Ward laughed. "Mrs. President, I would never stand you up. I'm deeply honored to accept the award, though it isn't necessary. Still, I'm grateful for the recognition."

President Jones replied, "Good answer, John. The work you and your organization have done to protect the environment worldwide is extraordinary. This award is the least we can do to show our appreciation."

"I look forward to seeing you," John Ward said. "I'll respond to the invitation right away."

After the call ended, John Luke quietly went downstairs so he wouldn't wake the babies from their naps and shared the news with Kristin. She was overjoyed.

"I'm so proud of you," she said, then laughed. "I was wrong, being married to you is even better than Matt Damon."

John Luke grinned.

The next morning, John Luke sensed that Jesus wished to meet with him. He went to his office, gently put on the Mantle, and Jesus appeared in person.

"Well," Jesus said with a smile, "the Presidential Medal of Freedom is a very big deal. Congratulations."

"Thank You, Jesus," he replied. "But all of this belongs to the Mantle and the glory of God. I'll gladly receive it as John Ward."

Jesus said, "I have an idea. You, Kristin, and your parents should attend the ceremony as audience members. With the Mantle, you can be in two places at once, John Ward on the podium and John Luke with your family."

John Luke hesitated. "You don't think that kind of use of the Mantle is… frivolous?"

"Not at all," Jesus said. "Recognition helps our work and brings attention to The Mantle LLC. The press coverage will advance the Father's Five-Point Plan. I want your family to share in the moment."

John Luke smiled. "Then we will. Thank you for the idea, Jesus."

Jesus continued, "I also have more good news. Your university will soon contact you. The research conducted with The Mantle LLC has brought great benefit, and they wish to recognize your work."

He paused. "The provost will call with news of a substantial bonus. The Father desires to bless you and your family not as payment, but as provision. You carried out this work without seeking reward. As Scripture says, *'Surely the righteous are rewarded'*" (Psalm 58:11).

John Luke was stunned. "Jesus, we never even discussed compensation. I don't know what to say."

Jesus smiled. "The gift comes through the university. And remember, '*it pleases the Father to give you the kingdom*'" (Luke 12:32). Receive it with gratitude and humility. "John Luke nodded. "Thank You, Jesus. Please tell the Father how grateful we are."

When John Luke later shared the news with Kristin, Joan, and me, we were astonished and deeply thankful. An unexpected gift born not of ambition but of service reminded us again of God's generosity and care.

I thought of this passage from Deuteronomy: *"The Lord will open to you His good treasury"* (28:12). John Luke resolved to make a large gift to charity and steward the rest wisely for the future.

On July 7th, John Luke used the Mantle to bring the four of us to the White House as his alias, John Ward, to receive the Presidential Medal of Freedom.

Incredibly, we sat in the audience while, through the Mantle, John Luke appeared simultaneously as John Ward on the podium.

President Jones said, "The Presidential Medal of Freedom is the Nation's highest civilian honor, presented to individuals who make exemplary contributions to the prosperity, values, or security of the United States, to world peace, or to other significant endeavors. John Ward, chair of The Mantle LLC, is most worthy of this recognition for his contributions to world peace and prosperity."

She placed the medal around his neck, and we beamed with pride.

After the ceremony and photographs, John Luke leaned toward Kristin and whispered with a smile, "I'm grateful for the award, but even more grateful I didn't have to give a speech."

Chapter 52:

The Jordan River

"Then the angel showed me the river of the water of life, as clear as crystal, flowing from the throne of God and of the Lamb" (Revelation 22:1).

In the closing vision of Revelation, a river of living water flows from the throne of God, bringing life wherever it runs. For generations, believers have seen in this image a promise of renewal and restoration. In Israel, the historic Jordan River has long symbolized that hope.

For John Luke, the Jordan was more than a river of history; it was a living reminder of God's promise to restore creation.

Later that summer, John Luke received an unexpected call from Prime Minister Kariv of Israel. Acting as John Ward, he answered in fluent Hebrew, much to the Prime Minister's delight.

John Ward said, "*Shalom l'cha, Rosh HaMemshala.*" "Peace to you, Prime Minister."

Prime Minister Kariv replied, *"Aleichem shalom.*" "Unto you peace."

Then he continued in English.

"John, your work bringing clean water to many nations caused me to think about the Jordan River. The river is environmentally fragile, and its water flow has decreased significantly over the years. I want to ask a favor. Our government has plans to improve Jordan, but progress is slow. Would you study the river and recommend improvements to our current plans?"

John Ward replied, "I think so, Mr. Prime Minister. Please tell me more."

The Prime Minister smiled on the phone. "John, please call me Shlomo. If you agree, we will coordinate support with Jordan, Syria, Lebanon, and Palestine. I have already spoken with Prime Minister Fawzi and Mr. Abbas, and both support the effort. They understand the river's importance to our country and the region. Prime Minister Fawzi has also offered financial support. Israel and Egypt are prepared to help fund the improvements."

John Luke paused, thinking of the prophecy in Revelation about the river of life flowing through a restored world. He sensed that this call and the opportunity it presented were no coincidence.

"Shlomo," John Ward said at last, "The Mantle LLC would be honored to assist with this project. The Jordan River is deeply significant to your people and to the entire region. We would gladly help restore its health."

After the call ended, Prime Minister Kariv began coordinating with his advisors and neighboring governments, including Egypt and the Palestinian Authority, to prepare for the work ahead.

Next, John Luke said a prayer and wore the Mantle. Jesus spoke to his mind immediately. Jesus congratulated John Luke for his communication with Prime Minister Kariv. He told John Luke that the project was important and that the Lord would bless it.

John Luke said, "I was concerned, Jesus, because we did not discuss this project before I committed to it."

Jesus said, "You have My wisdom, and you made a good choice."

Those words were all John Luke needed to hear. He thanked Jesus for His blessing and began organizing a team of highly skilled hydrologists and researchers able to work on this project with Israel.

Within a week, a large team of experts received approval to set a base at the foot of Mount Hermon, on the border of Syria and Lebanon. Under the alias of John Ward, he met with the assembled team in the Holy Land. In the first week, he explained the research goals and the plan to recommend improvements to Jordan's environmental health.

The first phase of the work was to assess the Israeli government's current work. The second phase would be recommendations for the current work. The final phase would be to implement the recommendations and measure success.

John Ward gave them a ninety-day schedule to conduct the study, make recommendations, and begin implementation. He told the team that the Israeli and Egyptian governments would fund the work and that all ideas were welcome to support the river's long-term health. The team was excited to perform this work and felt the timeline was aggressive but achievable.

The Jordan River was now part of Eden's restoration. John Luke was gratified to perform this work.

With assistance from the water authority, the team, led by John Ward, recommended a plan to implement a wastewater treatment plant along the Jordan, utilize desalination techniques to convert salt water into fresh water before it flows into the river, remove impurities from the Sea of Galilee, and release more fresh water gradually from the Sea into the Jordan.

Secondly, the team recommended a recyclable irrigation system to bring water to farmers along the river. Thirdly, the team recommended plans to improve farming and soil conditions along the river, including the use of robotic and Tree of Life technologies.

Finally, the team increased pumping and desalination of water from the Mediterranean Sea into the Sea of Galilee to increase the watershed's water volume.

While the Israeli and Egyptian governments approved the implementation plan, Jesus told John Luke about one additional resource.

Far beneath the sands of Egypt, He explained, lay a vast body of living water, fresh, ancient, and untouched. Fed by distant sources near Lake Victoria, it moved slowly through the deep foundations of the continent.

Hidden nearly 6,000 feet below the surface, the water rested in a cavernous chamber shaped by God long before humanity learned to measure the Earth. The underground lake renewed itself continually, a quiet reservoir beneath a thirsty land.

"Human hands cannot reach it," Jesus said. "No drill, no pump, no science yet devised can draw it up. But nothing is impossible with God."

Jesus explained that they would descend together into the depths and call the water upward, not by force, but by command. The water would rise like a living river of air and mist, carried unseen through the night. It would be released into the Nile, the Jordan, and the Sea of Galilee, restoring balance to all three and blessing the lands they sustained. The work would be done quietly, without spectacle, while the world slept.

Together they descended beneath Egypt, through stone, through darkness, through layers of time itself. At last, they entered a vast chamber like a cathedral of the Earth, where the freshwater lake lay still and luminous, its surface reflecting a pale inner light.

Jesus raised His hand.

At His word, the waters stirred.

The lake began to rise, not spilling or surging, but lifting as though the Earth itself exhaled. The water thinned into vapor and stream, forming a great atmospheric river that shimmered with life. John Luke felt its power and steadiness as he and Jesus guided it upward through rock and soil, through hidden channels known only to God.

They emerged beneath the night sky.

Silently, the river divided at the direction of Jesus. One stream flowed into the Nile, swelling it with fresh water. Another traced an unseen path into the Jordan, where the river deepened and quickened along its ancient course. The third descended gently into the Sea of Galilee, restoring clarity and balance to its waters.

By dawn, the miracle had already taken root.

When technicians and researchers arrived at their stations, they were stunned. Instruments confirmed what their eyes could scarcely believe. The Jordan flowed with renewed strength. Reports poured in from Egypt and from the Sea of Galilee: freshwater levels had risen, salinity had eased, and ecosystems had revived overnight.

No storm had been recorded. No seismic event explained the change.

And yet the waters had come.

Within hours, the story spread across the world. Satellite images confirmed the transformation. Scientists searched for causes. Nations watched in wonder as rivers of life flowed again through lands sacred to millions.

The teams soon completed their work, and the governments of Israel, Egypt, and Palestine celebrated the results.

Reflecting on the miracle, John Luke remembered the words of Psalm 29:3: "*The voice of the LORD is over the waters; the God of glory thunders.*"

Then Jesus spoke quietly to him.

"The restoration of Eden is complete."

Chapter 53:

The Rabbi's Dream

"The throne of God and of the Lamb will be in the city, and His servants will serve Him" (Revelation 22:3).

Jesus continued to appear in dreams to Yitzhak Cohen, the Rav Ir, drawn by his sincere, nightly prayers. Knowing him to be a faithful servant of the Father, Jesus answered those prayers with dreams that were vivid and luminous. Often, He guided Rav Ir to passages of Scripture, shaping sermons for the rabbi's ever-growing congregation at the Jerusalem Temple.

Each morning, Rav Ir carefully recorded the dreams in a private journal, sharing them only with his wife.

Despite all that had taken place during the rebuilding of the Holy Temple, the rabbi hesitated. He believed his congregation would find it improper, even troubling, to pray to Jesus, and he wondered whether the dreams were simply the stirrings of an overactive mind.

Yet the Scriptures were filled with patriarchs and prophets who had received God's guidance through dreams.

And these dreams were unlike any he had ever known.

Jesus appeared clothed in a gleaming white robe, a gold sash at His waist, bronze sandals upon His feet. He spoke directly to the rabbi, answered his questions, and addressed matters of great weight: Jewish, Christian, and Muslim relations; the healing of ancient wounds; and the responsibility of spiritual leaders in an age of peace.

In one recent dream, Jesus encouraged Rabbi Cohen to invite Christian and Muslim leaders to the Temple for an interfaith service and conference. His voice was gentle, yet resolute.

"This gathering will be a great blessing," Jesus said. "I will be present to support you. But the decision is yours, Yitzhak."

The dream lingered long after the rabbi awoke. Its clarity and the authority of Jesus's words left him unable to dismiss it. He shared the dream with his wife, who listened quietly before taking his hand.

"You must do this," she said. "Faith is sometimes shown by courage."

And so, the rabbi resolved to act.

The rabbi proposed an interfaith service to the leaders of his congregation. After the discussion, they agreed the plan had merit. When he asked whether he should present the idea to the full congregation during Shabbat services, the council again encouraged him to do so.

That Shabbat, the rabbi closed his sermon with a quiet confession.

"I have an idea that will not release me," he said. "I have shared it with my wife and with our council, and they believe it has merit.

I want to host a worldwide interfaith gathering here at the Temple, bringing together Jewish, Christian, and Muslim leaders."

For a moment, the sanctuary was still. Then the congregation erupted in applause.

Buoyed by this affirmation, the rabbi called his friend, John Ward, to discuss expanding the idea into a larger interfaith service and conference in Jerusalem. From their past conversations, the rabbi knew that John Ward often spoke with Jesus. He hoped the call would confirm that this vision was truly from God.

John Luke did not know that Jesus continued to speak to the rabbi in dreams.

When the call came through, John Luke felt a surge of joy. Seeing the Jerusalem number on The Mantle LLC phone, he answered at once.

"*Rav Ir*, *shalom aleichem!*" he said warmly. "How wonderful to hear from you."

The rabbi smiled at the sound of his voice.

"John Ward, *shalom aleichem!* You recognized my number. That is very kind of you."

Mindful of the time difference, Rav Ir asked politely, "Is this a good time for you to talk?"

John Ward replied in English, "Yes, Rabbi, it's noon here. Any time is a good time to speak with you."

Rabbi Cohen, as always struck by the graciousness of his young friend, spoke thoughtfully.

"I have an idea I would like to share. I am considering hosting an interfaith service here at the Holy Temple. Our congregation believes it could be deeply meaningful. I would invite key leaders from Judaism, Christianity, and Islam to spend a long weekend together to encourage genuine dialogue and fellowship.

"I am calling to ask whether you think this plan has merit and whether you would be willing to participate. You made a profound impression the last time you were here."

John Ward was both honored and surprised.

"I would be deeply honored to attend and to participate in any way you see fit," he said without hesitation. "May I also ask whether The Mantle LLC might help sponsor the event financially?"

Rav Ir paused. "I had not considered that," he admitted. "Yes, we would be grateful for such support. I do not wish to burden our finance committee, and I believe this gesture would be most welcome."

"It would be an honor to support such an important gathering," John Ward replied. "Have any details been decided?"

"Not yet," Rav Ir said with a gentle smile. "We are still in the talking phase. But perhaps you may have some ideas?"

John Ward replied, "Next April, Passover, Easter, and Ramadan will coincide for the first time in decades. Hosting an interfaith gathering during these three holy seasons could speak powerfully to the world about unity and peace. What do you think?"

Rav Ir paused, then said thoughtfully, "I had forgotten that alignment. If the leaders were willing to travel during such sacred days, the timing could indeed be profoundly meaningful. You are an idea person, John Ward."

John Ward smiled. "Perhaps this gathering could even mark the beginning of a new Pentecost in Jerusalem."

Rav Ir's eyes brightened. "Ah, yes, Pentecost. In our tradition, the feast is *Shavuot*, a time of thanksgiving for the first fruits of the wheat harvest and a remembrance of the Law given to Moses on Mount Sinai. For Christians, it marks the birth of the Church."

John Ward thanked the Rabbi for receiving the idea so warmly. Then he added gently, "Rav Ir, I want to step out in faith for a moment. I sense you may wish to say something more. Would you like to share it with me?"

Rabbi Cohen smiled faintly. "You seem able to read hearts as well as minds, my young friend. Though we do not yet know each other well, everything I have seen in you is good and noble. May I ask for your confidence in what I am about to say?"

John Ward replied, "I am well practiced in keeping confidence. You may trust me completely."

Rabbi Cohen hesitated, then spoke quietly. "Since the miracle of the Holy Temple's rebuilding, I have prayed to Jesus each night. I share this with you because I know how close you are to Him. He has been with me, guiding me through dreams that feel like living conversations. I ask questions, and He answers with clarity. He appears in a white robe, with a gold sash and bronze sandals.

He even gives me Scripture and ideas for my sermons. Have you ever heard of such a thing?"

John Luke paused and prayed silently, asking Jesus for guidance.

The response came at once, steady and certain. You may trust him.

John Ward then said, "Yes, Rabbi. I speak with Jesus often about the work of The Mantle LLC, and He gives me direction as well. The image of Jesus you see in your dreams comes from the Christian Book of Revelation."

Rabbi Cohen exhaled, his voice soft with relief. "Thank you for telling me, John. I knew I was not imagining these things. I know Jesus is real. You have stood at the center of many supernatural events. You understand what it means to follow His word. You once told us that He is the Word of God. I want to follow that Word."

John Ward answered gently, "Yes, Rav Ir. His word is holy, and His intentions are always pure. I believe it is important that you follow what He has placed on your heart."

"I will," the rabbi said. After a moment, he added, "John Ward, would you be willing to come to Jerusalem and speak with our council of elders to help guide this work?"

"Of course," John Ward replied. "Tell me when, and I will be there." The unexpected and personal conversation ended with plans set. They would meet the following week at the Temple in Jerusalem.

Chapter 54:

John Ward in Jerusalem

"They will see His face, and His name will be on their foreheads" (Revelation 22:4).

In the Book of Revelation, the Holy City represents the people of God, those who belong to Him and bear His name. Believers are set apart, in this world and the next, marked not only by a sign but by a calling. In their own way, John Luke and his family had been set apart by the miracle of the Mantle, a gift they carried with humility and gratitude.

In Jerusalem, Rabbi Cohen's dream of an interfaith gathering among God's people was beginning to take shape. The Mantle LLC had emerged as a principal sponsor of this work of peace.

Under his alias of John Ward, and using the Mantle for transportation, John Luke arrived in Jerusalem on a Monday evening to meet with a committee of elders from the Holy Temple. The lights of the Old City glowed beneath the evening sky as he approached the Temple precincts.

John Ward gathered with the committee members. Together they began planning a major gathering of Jewish, Christian, and Muslim leaders, an event scheduled to take place in seven months.

Their first task was to articulate a mission statement. After thoughtful discussion, they agreed upon a single guiding purpose:

"The mission of this interfaith service is to foster understanding, peace, and love among Jewish, Christian, and Muslim leaders."

From there, the committee turned to practical matters, selecting speakers, coordinating worship services and conferences, arranging hotels and meals, and managing communications, registration, and security for the 3-day event.

When the discussion turned to cost, John Ward spoke.

"With respect to funding," he said, "I would like to offer that The Mantle LLC underwrite this entire event. The conference should be free for all participants, including travel and lodging for our religious leaders. This gathering aligns fully with our mission."

The elders exchanged glances, stunned by the scope of the offer. Gratitude quickly followed astonishment. The Mantle LLC account, still drawing from what Jesus called God's storehouse, had ample resources. With humility and thanks, the elders accepted John Ward's generosity.

In addition to hosting the gathering at the Holy Temple, the Chancellor of the Hebrew University of Jerusalem, Dr. Adam Gorr, a member of the council of elders, offered the university's facilities and resources to support the event. His proposal was received with enthusiasm, further anchoring the conference within Jerusalem's academic and spiritual life.

The discussion then turned to speakers. John Ward said:

"While I speak from an outsider's perspective, I would encourage the committee to remain faithful to Rav Ir's original vision. We may invite as many senior leaders of the world's three major faith traditions as possible to help bolster the event."

The rabbi smiled warmly toward John Ward.

The committee agreed and the resulting invitation list read like a "who's who" of global religious leadership: Pope Paul VII of the Roman Catholic Church; the Archbishop of Canterbury, Justin Welby; Ecumenical Patriarch Bartholomew of Constantinople; the Grand Imam of Egypt, Ahmed Mohamed; Iraq's Ayatollah Ali al Sistani; and Jewish, Christian, and Muslim leaders representing every region of the world.

The meeting concluded with a shared commitment. The committee would vet and invite every major Jewish, Christian, and Islamic leader of the twenty-first century. Invitations would be distributed immediately, and no peaceful religious leader would be excluded. The next meeting was scheduled for September.

What had begun as a dream given to Rabbi Cohen was steadily becoming reality.

That September meeting exceeded expectations. Invitations were formally sent, and early commitments soon followed from prominent religious leaders. Many acknowledged that the conference would fall during sacred holy days, yet agreed that the opportunity to gather in peace outweighed any inconvenience.

Representation from every major branch of Judaism, Christianity, and Islam was secured.

Near the close of the meeting, a brief discussion arose about extending invitations to other world religions, including Buddhism and Hinduism. Rav Ir listened respectfully before offering his counsel. The room grew quiet as the elders waited for Rabbi Cohen to respond.

"While our differences are real," he said, "the Jewish, Christian, and Muslim peoples share a common heritage under Father Abraham. This gathering is intentionally timed to coincide with Ramadan, Passover, and Easter. Let us remain faithful to that purpose."

As always, the elders deferred to Rav Ir's wisdom. The committee reaffirmed its original mission and continued its work. Responsibilities were assigned, timelines established, and the next meeting scheduled for October.

Chapter 55: The Little Church

"They will not need the light of a lamp or the light of the sun, for the Lord God will give them light. And they will reign forever" (Revelation 22:5).

Jesus often reminded John Luke that a Christian home is a little church. Christ is the light of the world, and His light now shone gently within the small home John Luke and Kristin shared with their children.

The family was thriving. At four months old, the twins were healthy, curious, and deeply bonded. Jane and Joshua slept, ate, and played on the same rhythm, rarely apart. Jane was already more vocal, experimenting with sounds and early words, while Joshua was focused on movement, sitting upright and determinedly trying to crawl.

Both were endlessly fascinated by Zoey the cat and Doctor Dog, who endured their attention with patient dignity.

Joan and I continued to stay with them two days each week, helping John Luke and Kristin balance work and family life. Joan's real estate business was flourishing and provided a welcome part-time income. I remained busy writing the history of the Mantle, work that kept me both grounded and grateful.

In truth, life felt whole. I often reflected that the greatest accomplishments of my life were, first, my marriage to Joan; second, raising John Luke; and third, earning my doctorate. Becoming "grandad" had now settled comfortably into third place, where it belonged, and where it brought daily joy.

While John Luke's work with the Mantle had grown less frequent, he continued to meet with Jesus to discuss preparations for the interfaith service planned for April in Jerusalem. Jesus was pleased that Rabbi Cohen had acted on the dream and that John Luke helped guide the vision into reality. The seminar mattered deeply to Jesus, and He listened with visible joy as John Luke shared updates and progress.

At the October committee meeting in Jerusalem, Rabbi Cohen announced that most major religious leaders had agreed to attend. The elders received the news with pride and gratitude, encouraged by the unity forming around their Rabbi's leadership.

Planning quickly moved into practical stages. Hotel rooms were reserved, and the Hebrew University of Jerusalem committed conference space for the gatherings. Some speakers would be housed in the university's well-appointed guest quarters. John Ward also made a substantial donation to the Holy Temple's account to cover expenses incurred to date.

By the close of the meeting, the committee recognized that preparations were ahead of schedule. There was a quiet confidence in the room, a shared sense that the work unfolding before them was both timely and blessed.

The November meeting was scheduled a week early to accommodate John Ward's Thanksgiving holiday. In the meantime, committee members continued working independently on their assigned tasks.

At six months old, the twins entered a new phase. Teething began, solid foods were introduced, and their engagement with one another and with the four of us increased daily. They listened, mostly, to bedtime stories and, to everyone's delight, began sleeping through the night. John Luke and Kristin were now enjoying a glorious and consistent eight hours of sleep.

One of my regular duties was taking the twins out for walks in their elegant double stroller. It cost more than my first car, was far safer, and featured matching sunroofs that allowed me to keep an eye on both children. During our walks, I played classical music softly on my phone, loud enough for the babies to hear and gentle enough not to disturb their naps.

I had learned that classical music often calms infants and supports healthy development. Whether by science or grace, it seemed to soothe them, and I made it part of our routine whenever we walked and the weather allowed.

By the time of the November committee meeting, all long-term action items for the interfaith conference had been completed. The focus shifted to detailed planning, mapping the seminar agenda, coordinating meals to meet diverse dietary requirements, scheduling speakers and prayer services, organizing group sessions, and designing the closing interfaith gathering.

With preparations well ahead of schedule, the committee, along with John Ward, agreed to cancel the December meeting. Any remaining details would be finalized in January and February.

A final budget was calculated, and John Ward insisted that The Mantle LLC cover all remaining major expenses, leaving the Temple treasury responsible only for incidental costs as the event approached. Rabbi Cohen and the committee expressed deep gratitude for the generosity.

John Ward, as always, deflected the praise, giving glory to God as the true source of The Mantle LLC's provision. Rabbi Cohen noted his sincerity and faithfulness aloud, to the quiet approval of the elders.

"You are truly one of the most faithful and generous human beings I have ever known," Rabbi Cohen said.

Then, with a twinkle in his eye, he added, "Are you certain your ancestors were not Jewish?"

Laughter filled the room. John Ward laughed along, delighted by the rabbi's rare joke.

At home, December brought special joy as the family prepared for the twins' first Christmas. Jane and Joshua were now crawling and pulling themselves to stand, and both homes had been thoroughly baby-proofed. Jane's first word was "Momma," and Joshua took his first tentative steps. Christmas trees stood in both houses, their lower branches left bare and undecorated.

The twins spent two days each week at our home, giving John Luke, and Kristin time to focus on their work. Joan turned our guest bedroom into a cozy nursery, and the arrangement suited everyone.

Christmas Eve was spent at John Luke and Kristin's home. On Christmas Day, after church, we gathered at Kristin's parents' home for a feast that rivaled any fine restaurant. Kristin's father cooked with remarkable skill, and her mother baked until she ran out of flour.

Kristin had sewn matching outfits for the twins, Mr. and Mrs. Claus, on Christmas Eve, and cheerful elves on Christmas Day. The babies looked adorable and were far more interested in ribbons and wrapping paper than the gifts themselves.

On the third Monday of January, John Luke, again acting as John Ward, returned to Jerusalem for a meeting of the Temple elders. The committee finalized the speakers, agenda, accommodations, and arrangements to address the diverse dietary needs of attendees at the April interfaith seminar.

With the budget and attendance lists nearly complete, the elders scheduled a final planning meeting for February. The group left encouraged and grateful, confident that the work was ready and that the gathering ahead would be both meaningful and historic.

At home, the twins were nearly nine months old and now joined the family for dinner, perched proudly in their highchairs at the dining room table. They slept well, ate well, and crawled with determination. Jane remained more verbal, experimenting with sounds and words, while Joshua was more physical, always in motion and always exploring.

In February, John Luke, appearing as John Ward, attended a meeting of the Temple elders in Jerusalem to review preparations for the upcoming seminar. More than 2,000 invitations were sent, and the event was being widely promoted through social media and religious networks.

Registration quickly surpassed 1,000 religious leaders from around the world, with more than half coming from the Middle East and the United States. The committee began to worry about lodging and budget if attendance continued to grow.

John Ward addressed the concern calmly.

"We agreed from the beginning that no peaceful person would be turned away. God is a God of abundance, and He will provide. The Mantle LLC has budgeted for up to 2,000 participants. Jerusalem has eighty-eight hotels with more than 11,000 rooms. Let us continue securing accommodations as needed and pray that all 2,000 seats are filled."

"Well said," Rabbi Cohen replied. "Let us pray that all 2,000 will be with us."

Reassured, the elders returned to their work.

At home, February also brought Valentine's Day. John Luke and Kristin celebrated with the twins, Joan, and me. We all wore red, and the babies appeared in handmade outfits Kristin had designed, Jane as the right half of a heart and Joshua as the left.

Joan and I were moved to tears when we saw them. It was a celebration of love, family, life, and God.

In March, John Luke attended the final planning meeting for the interfaith conference. Over the previous thirty days, another 750 leaders had registered. More than 1,000 participants were now confirmed from the United States and the Middle East alone.

In response to the growing interest, the committee added three additional speakers: Houston-based evangelist Joel Osteen; Lebanese American Sunni Muslim scholar and author Hisham Kabbani; and Eric Yoffie, President Emeritus of the Union for Reform Judaism in North America.

The agenda was adjusted, hotel rooms secured, and travel arrangements finalized.

The committee was ready.

Rabbi Cohen closed the meeting with prayer, offering the words of the prophet Jeremiah:

"For I know the plans I have for you, says the Lord, plans for peace and not for evil, to give you a future and a hope" (Jeremiah 29:11).

Chapter 56:

Final Stages

"The angel said to me, 'These words are trustworthy and true. The Lord, the God who inspires the prophets, sent His angel to show His servants the things that must soon take place'" (Revelation 22:6).

The Word of God is trustworthy and true. Jesus declared that He is the way, the truth, and the life. Now, Rabbi Cohen's dream of Jesus was nearing fulfillment, and The Mantle LLC's support of the interfaith conference stood as another sign of God's faithfulness. Servants of God from across the world would soon gather in Jerusalem.

One week before the seminar, Rabbi Cohen called a final planning meeting. Registration surpassed 2,000 attendees. Methodically, he reviewed the remaining details: catering, hotel accommodations, guest speakers, seminar titles and schedules, media arrangements, audio and recording technology, prayer services, and the closing interfaith gathering. The convergence of Passover, Easter, and Ramadan would occur over the weekend of April 19–21.

"John Ward," he said, "the committee of elders and I have a request. We would like you to join me in opening the seminar on

Friday evening. It seems fitting to honor you and The Mantle LLC in this way. Will you accept?"

"I would be honored, Rav Ir," John Ward replied.

The rabbi smiled.

John Ward added, "I plan to arrive on Thursday, April 18, to assist with final preparations. Two friends will accompany me—Dr. John Luke Hopkins and his father, Dr. John Mark Hopkins, will attend as my guests."

"Splendid," Rabbi Cohen said. "I look forward to meeting them."

On the morning of April 18, I met John Luke at his home. Joan and Kristin remained behind to care for the babies. We went to John Luke's office, where he prayed quietly and donned the Mantle. In an instant, we traveled to Jerusalem at the speed of light. Accounting for the seven-hour time difference, we arrived at 8:00 AM.

"I asked Jesus that we arrive at this hour," John Luke said with a smile. God, after all, governs time.

Rabbi Cohen welcomed us warmly at the Temple, where the committee of elders had already gathered.

John Luke explained, "John Ward will arrive shortly. We wanted to greet you first and offer help with any last-minute needs."

"All is well here," Rabbi Cohen replied. "But would you accompany Dr. Adam Gorr to the Hebrew University of

Jerusalem? He could use assistance overseeing the setup of several conference spaces."

"Of course," John Luke said. "Anything you need."

We joined Dr. Gorr on the short drive to the university. He was fascinated to learn that we were both academics and impressed by John Luke's work at MIT. Upon arrival, he gave us a brief tour. The campus architecture was striking, and the Ariovitch Auditorium was a spacious, light-filled hall ideally suited for the seminars.

John Luke answered, "Of course. Anything you need."

We helped arrange chairs and tables while Dr. Gorr positioned podiums and tested presentation systems. During our work, John Luke quietly mentioned that he was using the Mantle to be in two places at once. While we assisted at the university, John Ward had already arrived at the Temple to greet the elders. I could only chuckle at the extraordinary reach of the Mantle's power.

Once preparations were complete, we returned to the Temple with a grateful chancellor.

Back at the Holy Temple, Rabbi Cohen gathered the committee for prayer. Using the Siddur, the traditional Jewish prayer book, he concluded with the priestly blessing from Numbers 6:24–27:

"The Lord bless you and keep you; the Lord make His face shine on you and be gracious to you; the Lord turn His face toward you and give you peace."

Then he said, "So they will put My name on the Israelites, and I will bless them." The people responded, "Amen."

Everything was ready.

Across Jerusalem, lights glowed late into the night as delegations continued to arrive. The Mantle LLC covered all travel and lodging costs, with total contributions exceeding $15 million. Rabbi Cohen was deeply moved by John Ward's generosity and thanked him repeatedly. Guests arrived through Jerusalem International Airport and proceeded to their hotels throughout the city.

Approximately one hundred participants, including John Luke and me, stayed at the Hebrew University Faculty Club and Guest House on the Edmond J. Safra Campus. The accommodations were elegant and welcoming, and many guests, particularly academics, rabbis, and imams, were pleasantly surprised by the setting's beauty.

That night, we rested well.

Rabbi Cohen's dream had become a reality.

Chapter 57:

A New Pentecost

"Look, I am coming soon! My reward is with me, and I will give to each person according to what they have done. I am the Alpha and the Omega, the First and the Last, the Beginning and the End" (Revelation 22:12-13).

For Christians, Jesus is the beginning and the end of earthly and eternal life. The prophecy of Revelation speaks not only of the end of time, but also of the beginning of new life. God has a plan for the world, and His plan is for good.

As Rabbi Cohen often explained, Jewish and Christian communities observe the Feast of Pentecost in related yet distinct ways. For Jewish believers, the feast celebrates the harvest and commemorates the giving of the Law to Moses. For Christians, Pentecost marks the gift of the Holy Spirit and the birth of the Church, an event deeply rooted in the Jewish tradition of honoring God's Word.

At the time of the interfaith gathering, the sacred calendars of the three Abrahamic faiths had aligned in remarkable harmony. Jewish families were celebrating Passover, Christians were observing Easter, and Muslim believers had begun the holy month of Ramadan, a time of fasting that would culminate in Eid al-Fitr.

The interfaith seminar began the following morning in the Holy Temple. All 2,000 attendees gathered comfortably within the temple courts.

Grand Mufti of Jerusalem Kamil al-Husseini opened the service by inviting the assembly to join in the Jewish declaration of faith, the Shema. Grand Imam of Egypt, Ahmed Mohamed, then led the congregation in the Muslim morning prayer of Fajr.

Finally, Archbishop of Canterbury Justin Welby concluded the service with a brief morning prayer from the Book of Common Prayer.

After the prayers, Rabbi Cohen warmly welcomed the guests and thanked them for attending despite the sacred observances of Passover, Easter, and Ramadan.

Then he turned toward the front row.

"Mr. Ward," he said with a smile, "would you please join me at the podium?"

Rabbi Cohen began, "I would like you to meet the primary sponsor of this important gathering, Mr. John Ward of The Mantle LLC."

Warm applause filled the sanctuary as John Ward acknowledged the crowd with a quiet smile and a nod of gratitude.

Rabbi Cohen, with a broad smile, said, "While I never like to talk about money from the bimah…" (Hebrew for the temple podium). The rabbi paused, allowing a ripple of laughter to pass through the congregation.

"This event is possible through the generosity of John Ward and The Mantle LLC organization. Your travel and accommodations are paid for by a donation of fifteen million dollars from John."

The sanctuary erupted in applause, some voices rising in spontaneous cheers of gratitude.

Rabbi Cohen waited, then added, "John Ward is one of the most gracious, humble, and charitable individuals I have ever known. Please join me in welcoming him."

The applause returned, louder and longer this time.

John Luke stepped forward, speaking as John Ward.

"Rabbi Cohen, thank you for your gracious introduction, and thank you all for this extraordinary welcome.

"The mission of The Mantle LLC is simple: to serve God and to seek peace in our world. We have gathered here to honor the one God we share and to learn more deeply from one another's faiths and traditions. This interfaith gathering was born from Rabbi Cohen's vision. We are here because of his faith in God, and in us as believers and peacemakers.

"My prayer is that we leave this place more united, more understanding, and more loving toward one another. I believe this gathering will be life-changing and, God willing, world-changing.

"I close with words we all cherish: *Shalom. Al-Salam. Peace.* And as Jesus taught, *'Peace I leave with you; my peace I give to you.'*"

For a moment, the Temple was silent. As he stepped back from the podium, the interfaith choir rose and led the assembly in a unified English rendition of Let There Be Peace on Earth, written by Jill Jackson-Miller and Sy Miller.

As John Luke sang with the congregation, he noticed a familiar figure seated in the last row.

Jesus.

He was dressed in traditional Israeli attire, a white-and-blue *kippah*, a matching *tallit*, and *tefillin*.

John Luke broke into a broad smile and met His gaze. They shared a quiet, knowing look.

Then John Luke nodded toward me in my third-row seat and mouthed softly, "Jesus is here."

I mouthed back, "Of course."

The first day of the interfaith seminar unfolded beautifully. Seminars were held throughout the Holy Temple complex, marked by thoughtful dialogue and genuine engagement. The day concluded with a prayer service led by Lebanese American Sunni Muslim scholar Hisham Kabbani, assisted by Rabbi Cohen and Bishop Heinrich of the German Evangelical Church. The temple cantor coordinated the music with great care, drawing the congregation into shared worship.

Jesus also attended the closing prayer service, once again seated unobtrusively in the back row. Participants were invited to share feedback through a mobile app, and the responses were overwhelmingly positive. Members of the elders' committee answered questions and engaged thoughtfully with comments as they came in.

Around 8:00 PM that evening, attendees began returning to their hotels. John Luke and I rode in a shuttle van with about twenty other participants. When we arrived at the Hebrew University lobby, we were pleasantly surprised to see Jesus waiting for us, still dressed in His traditional attire.

"I am attending most of the events, especially the prayer services," He said warmly. "I want to support you and the committee. Everything is going splendidly. I will see you both tomorrow. And remember, I am always with you."

We hugged Him goodnight. Seeing Jesus, even briefly, was a great blessing. The first day had been long and deeply good.

Day two was held at the Hebrew University on the Rehovot campus, in the Ariovitch Auditorium. The setting was beautiful, and all two thousand participants were comfortably seated for morning prayer. This time, the service was led jointly by Rabbi Yoffie, President Emeritus of the Union for Reform Judaism in North America; Greek Orthodox Patriarch Theodore II of Alexandria; and Imam Choudhary of India.

Imam Choudhary delivered a stirring address on the necessity of interfaith unity and the call to understanding and acceptance among the three great faiths.

The second day continued smoothly, with a full schedule of engaging seminars across the campus. One seminar, led by American Christian evangelist Franklin Graham on teaching interfaith understanding and fostering dialogue among religious leaders, drew particularly strong praise and was the highest-rated session of the day.

The evening concluded with a closing prayer service in the auditorium, led by Reverend Graham, with support from Dr. Firdaus, former president of Mauritius and a biodiversity scientist, and Dr. Gorr of the Hebrew University.

The interfaith choir performed several moving hymns representing all three traditions, including a contemporary Christian song composed especially for the event to promote dialogue and unity. The congregation received it warmly, responding with sustained applause as the service concluded.

As promised, Jesus attended once again, seated in His customary place in the last row, dressed in traditional attire. John Luke noticed Him singing the hymns with quiet joy. After the service, Jesus joined John Luke, and me for the walk back to our rooms.

Along the way, Jesus spoke approvingly of Dr. Firdaus and encouraged us to attend her seminar the following day. "She weaves science, politics, and faith together in a way that is thoughtful and non-threatening," He said. "Her presence here is significant to the work of the Mantle."

We agreed and thanked Him for His guidance and for being with us. After a warm embrace and quiet goodnights, Jesus disappeared. We returned to our rooms, once again humbled and amazed by His wisdom.

Day three arrived quickly. John Luke and I both hoped and prayed that the gathering had achieved what Jesus and Rabbi Cohen envisioned. We rode the shuttle back to the Holy Temple, joined the community for morning prayer, shared breakfast, and then attended the first seminar of the day, led by Dr. Firdaus.

She did not disappoint us. Speaking from her experience as the first female president of the Republic of Mauritius, Dr. Firdaus addressed the audience with grace and authority.

"As people of faith and science," she said, "we must listen to the science of climate change while honoring God's creation. Highly industrialized nations must partner with countries around the Indian Ocean to promote commerce, end poverty, and respect the culture and religion of all peoples."

The audience listened intently, captivated by her poise, intellect, and clarity of vision.

The remainder of the day unfolded smoothly with lunch, additional seminars, and then dinner. After the evening break, participants gathered once more in the Holy Temple for the closing interfaith prayer service, unaware that a profound surprise awaited them.

The service began at sundown, 7:00 PM on Easter Sunday, and was led by Pope Paul VII, assisted by the Grand Mufti of Jerusalem, Kamil al-Husseini, and Rabbi Cohen. The celebration was broadcast live across social media platforms and recorded for global viewing.

In honor of Passover, Easter, and Ramadan, the service wove together the sacred rites of all three traditions. The Grand Mufti led the ablution ritual. Pope Paul VII lit the Easter Candle from a fire of dried palm branches. Rabbi Cohen offered prayers drawn from the Passover liturgy.

Sacred readings followed from the Hebrew *Tanakh*, the Christian *New Testament*, and the Muslim *Qur'an*. American evangelist Joel Osteen then delivered a reflective teaching centered on Abraham and the shared belief in one true God.

Speaking with warmth and gentle humor, he conveyed his message to the congregation with great depth.

When Pastor Osteen concluded, the interfaith choir rose and led the assembly in an original hymn written for the occasion, "One Faith, One Lord, One Love."

When the hymn ended, a deep and peaceful silence settled over the Holy Temple.

Jesus sat in the back row of the congregation wearing a white robe, a gold sash around His waist, and bronze sandals.

The silence broke as He rose and began walking slowly down the center aisle. With each step, His bronze sandals glowed softly. His robe radiated a brilliant white light, and the gentle fragrance of incense filled the sanctuary.

Awe fell upon the congregation.

As recognition spread, a hushed murmur rippled through the crowd.

Jesus reached the *bema* and turned to face the people. Then He spoke.

"My dear people, my name is Yeshua of Nazareth. I am also called the Word of God. Rabbi Cohen's dream of a united interfaith service is fulfilled today as we gather to worship the one true God in love."

"God the Father is the creator of the world. His Word is present in the Holy Scriptures of His people, found in the Tanakh, the Bible, and the Qur'an. God's love for His people is everlasting. His forgiveness of sin is boundless. His plan for your lives is a glorious future."

"This gathering is a glimpse of eternity of **Vilon** in Hebrew, **Heaven** in English, and **Jannah** in Arabic."

Jesus paused. The Temple was utterly silent.

"I once told my followers that *'in my Father's house there are many mansions'* (John 14:2). A place is prepared for each of you in eternity. Your destiny is secure. Yet this service is not only about eternity, but also about now."

"God is present in the world. Today you worship together as descendants of Father Abraham and as believers in the one true God."

Jesus continued.

"The great prophet Muhammad said, 'Four things support the world: the learning of the wise, the justice of the great, the prayers of the good, and the valor of the brave.'

"You are chosen as leaders of God's people. You are called to be wise, just, prayerful, and brave, and you are."

"As leaders, you are now called to return to your congregations and carry the message of the prophet Zephaniah (3:17):

'*The Lord your God is in your midst, a mighty one who will save; he will rejoice over you with gladness; he will quiet you by his love; he will exult over you with loud singing.*'"

Jesus lifted His hands.

"Learn with one another and from one another. Do not be afraid. God hears every whispered prayer. Care for your people with tenderness. Pray without ceasing. Let your charity be quiet and sincere. Guard the earth entrusted to you. Live boldly in this moment, and with hope that reaches far beyond it."

"I am with you always."

As Jesus spoke these final words, the flame of the Easter candle suddenly leaped upward, dividing into radiant tongues of fire. They drifted gently through the sanctuary, settling like living light upon each person. A warm glow crowned their heads, and in that instant, Jesus vanished from their sight.

The congregation rose as one. Applause surged through the Temple like a wave, voices lifting in praise through the melodies of many traditions. Rabbi Cohen pressed a trembling hand to his mouth as tears of joy streamed down his face.

What unfolded before them was a new Pentecost in Jerusalem.

Epilogue:

Word of God

"Father, I want those you have given me to be with me where I am, and to see my glory, the glory you have given me because you loved me before the creation of the world" (John 17:24).

In the days that followed the interfaith service, participants returned to their homes across the world. Recordings of the gathering spread rapidly through television broadcasts and social media, reaching millions within hours. The testimony of respected and beloved religious leaders carried unusual weight, and with it came a renewed outpouring of the Holy Spirit.

International news outlets covered the event extensively. Headlines appeared across continents: *Jesus Lives, The Second Coming Is Here,* and my personal favorite from *The Jerusalem Post, Word of God, Speak!*

Jewish, Christian, and Muslim communities found themselves newly united, not in uniform belief, but in shared reverence. Rabbi Cohen began preaching sermons that wove together Hebrew Scripture, Christian teaching, and reflections drawn from the Qur'an. Across traditions, many began to refer to Jesus simply as the Word of God, a name that has resonated deeply for centuries of faith.

Churches, mosques, and temples are filled with worshipers. A spirit of peace settled over nations in a way unseen in living memory. The interfaith seminar became a catalyst for understanding, replacing suspicion with dialogue and fear with humility.

Tolerance and coexistence grew not as political slogans, but as lived realities. Nations renewed their commitment to care for the Earth and to honor creation as a sacred trust.

For now, the work of the Mantle of Jesus was complete.

Yet the story was not finished.

Across the world, people continued to speak of what had happened in Jerusalem. Some called it a miracle. Others called it a turning point in history. For many, it became a reminder that God had not abandoned His people and that His Word still moved among them.

Eden flourished once more, not as a distant memory, but as a living promise.

And the Word of God continued to speak.

Author's Reflection

Stories have always helped people imagine what the world could become when faith, courage, and love guide human action. *Number 12* was written in that spirit.

This book is a work of fiction, yet its themes are drawn from the real hopes shared by people of faith across generations. The Scriptures of Judaism, Christianity, and Islam speak of a world shaped by justice, mercy, and reverence for God. The story of the Mantle of Jesus explores what might happen if people truly embraced these values and chose peace over fear.

The interfaith gathering in Jerusalem imagined in these pages reflects a simple idea: that sincere believers from different traditions can meet not as rivals, but as neighbors who share a common reverence for the Creator. Throughout history, moments of cooperation between faiths have brought healing and renewal. I hope that readers will see in this story a reminder that such cooperation is still possible.

The characters in this book wrestle with the same questions many of us face today. How do we live faithfully in a complicated world? How do we honor our own traditions while respecting the beliefs of others? And how do we hold on to hope when the world often seems divided?

In the story, the answer begins with humility before God and compassion toward one another.

The figure of Jesus stands at the center of this narrative because, for Christians, He represents the Word of God made visible in human life. Yet the message that echoes through the book is broader and timeless: that God's love is greater than human conflict, and that peace becomes possible when people choose mercy over judgment and understanding over fear.

While the events of *Number 12* belong to the realm of imagination, the longing behind them is very real. Every generation is given opportunities to build bridges, heal wounds, and care for the world entrusted to us.

Perhaps that is the deeper message of this story.

The work of peace is never finished.

This work continues wherever people pray, forgive, learn from one another, and act with courage and kindness.

May we all take part in this work.

Thank you for walking this journey with John Luke and his family.

Coming Soon:

The Twins

Book Three of the Mantle Trilogy

The world had changed.

After the miraculous events in Jerusalem, a spirit of peace spread across nations. Religious leaders returned to their communities with renewed hope, and many began to believe that humanity had entered a new chapter in its history.

For John Luke Hopkins and his family, life had also changed in quieter ways.

At home, the laughter of children filled the house. Jane and Joshua, the twins born during the extraordinary journey of the Mantle, were growing quickly. Even as infants, they shared a bond that surprised everyone who met them. Their curiosity about the world seemed endless, and their parents often wondered what role God might have prepared for them in the years ahead.

The Mantle of Jesus rested safely, its work seemingly complete.

But history rarely stands still.

Across the world, new questions were beginning to emerge. Some people celebrated the peace that had taken root among nations. Others questioned the meaning of the miracles that had taken place. And in quiet places, far from the spotlight of Jerusalem, forces once thought defeated were beginning to stir again.

The future of the world would soon rest not only in the hands of leaders and scholars but also in the hearts of a new generation.

Jane and Joshua Hopkins were only just beginning their story.

And the Word of God was not finished speaking.

www.ingramcontent.com/pod-product-compliance
Lightning Source LLC
LaVergne TN
LVHW010631110826
845149LV00014B/2829

* 9 7 8 1 9 6 9 6 4 9 8 2 0 *